KNOWLEDGE MANAGEMENT IN DIGITAL LIBRARIES

KNOWLEDGE MANAGEMENT IN DIGITAL LIBRARIES

Dinesh Kumar, Arjun

Knowledge Management in Digital Libraries

ISBN: 978-81-7835-918-2

Published in 2012 in India by
Kalpaz Publications
C-30, Satyawati Nagar,
Delhi-110052
E-mail: kalpaz@hotmail.com
Phone : 9212729499

Lasser Type Setting : Quick Media, Delhi
Printed at : Chawla Offset Printers, Delhi

Dedicated to
My Loving Family
My Strength against all odds

Contents

	Preface	11
	List of Contributors	13
1.	Knowledge Management in Library in Modern Society *Kulwinder Kumar*	19
2.	Knowledge Management Practices and Electronic Resources *Sabita Manjari Biswal*	33
3.	Application of Knowledge Management in Modern Libraries *Dr. Kanchan Kamila*	43
4.	Knowledge Management: Opportunities and Challenges *Mr. Sambhaji G. Patil, Dr. Shamkant Deshmukh*	59
5.	Knowledge Management: The New Challenges for Libraries in Digital Era *Surbhi Saini*	77
6.	Knowledge Management of Libraries in Digital Environment Era *Mahipal Sharma, Daizy*	89
7.	E-Resources in Library Management: An Overview *Rachana*	105
8.	Total Quality Management in Libraries *Manju Devi*	115
9.	Knowledge Management for Modern Public Library in Digital Era *Dinesh Kumar, Arjun*	123

10. Knowledge Management Use in Library in Modern Era 141
Vinay Shanker Mahajan, Mohd. Asif, Mustafa Khan, Syed Misham Abbas Abidy and Vipin Kumar

11. Tools for Knowledge Management in Academic Libraries 149
Divya Sharma

12. Knowledge Management: Value Added Functioning 159
Noushia Parveen

13. Knowledge Management Issue, Concept and Challenges for LIS Professionals: In Modern Information Technology Age 169
Sunil Tyagi

14. Knowledge Management of Libraries in digital Environment Era 191
Lata Patil

15. Role of Total Quality Management as a knowledge Facilitator 203
Harmanpreet Singh, Harpreet Kaur Rana

16. Knowledge: Impact and Implication for Libraries and Information Centers 221
Navita Sharma

17. Application of Information Technology in Libraries in Delhi: A Study 233
Chiranji Lal

18. The Application of Web 2.0 Model to the Library Services 247
Bharat Kumar M. Chaudhari

19. Use of Hybrid Library in the Information Era 259
Ramvveer Sagar, Dr. Satya Parkash

20. Online Book Portal 269
Akansha Bhargava

21. Indian Agricultural Doctoral Dissertations Repository Krishiprabha Database 291
Anoop Kumar Bajpayi

22. Use of SMS and E-Mail in Current Awareness Services : A Practical Approach 305
Fayaz Ahmad Loan

23. Data Curation in Digital Library: A Reference to Invenio Digital Library 313
Naresh Kumar

24. Digital Libraries and Services in India 321
Dr. Shamkant Deshmukh, Mr. Kuldeep Pawar

25. Impact of IT in Modern Libraries of India: A Study 333
Anjali Sharma

Index 343

Preface

The main thrust of the book is on the academic and research libraries across the globe are striving hard to harness technology for achieving scholarly knowledge management, which is fast proliferating, distributed and scattered.

We fee that the book will be of value to the students of Library and information Science at the Graduation and Post graduation level in various universities, colleges and institutes.

In the preparation of the book, we had the advantage of the feedback of the Knowledge Management in digital libraries.

We wish to acknowledge the help rendered by a large number of colleagues and professional.

We fervently hope that this book will continue to grow from strength to strength as it travels to different host countries in Asia, and will continue to provide a stimulating and enriching platform for innovative ideas, to enable us to design and develop digital libraries that will transcend cultures, races, beliefs and religions to create world citizens who are knowledgeable, tolerant, and understanding, in order to create a world that is harmonious and peaceful for everyone for a long time to come.

We hope this manageable volume book would serve to dispel awe towards digital library from the minds of library science students and provide a concise and up-to-date information source for prescribes who wish to remain informed of the current concepts and developments concerning knowledge management.

We sincere thanks are due to my colleagues for their valuable comments and suggestions.

Dinesh Kumar, Arjun

Preface

The main thrust of the book is on the academic and research fraternities across the globe are striving hard to harness technology for achieving scholarly knowledge management, which is fast proliferating, disintegrated and scattered.

We feel that the book will be of value to the students of library and information science at the Graduation and Post graduation level in various universities, colleges and institutes.

In the preparation of the book, we had the advantage of the feedback of the Knowledge Management in Digital libraries.

We wish to acknowledge the help rendered by a large number of colleagues and professionals.

We fervently hope that this book will continue to grow from strength to strength until travels to different host countries in Asia, and will continue to provide a stimulating and enriching platform for innovative ideas, to encourage us to design and develop digital libraries that help to transcend cultures, race, beliefs and religions to create world citizens who are knowledgeable, tolerant, and understanding, in order to create a world that is harmonious and peaceful for everyone for a long time to come.

We hope that the present volume book would serve to mandate a move towards digital libraries from the arena of information science students and provide a complete and up-to-date information source for practitioners who wish to remain informed of the current concepts and developments underlining knowledge management.

Special thanks are due to my colleagues for their valuable comments and suggestions.

Dinesh Kumar Arjun

List of Contributors

1. **Kulwinder Kumar**
Department of Pharmaceutical Sciences and Drug Research, Punjabi University Patiala, Punjab, bansalco16@gmail.com

2. **Sabita Manjari Biswal**
Roland Institute of Pharmaceutical Sciences, Brahmapur-760010 (Odisha), India.
E-mail: sbsmbiswal@gmail.com

3. **Dr. Kanchan Kamila**
Librarian, Uttar Banga Krishi Viswavidyalaya
Pundibari, Cooch Behar - 736165
drkanchankamila002@gmail.com

4. **Mr. Sambhaji G. Patil**
Researcher Student/N.M.U. Jalgaon, Maharashtra
Librarian/MET's Institute of Engineering
Bhujbal Knowledge City, Adgaon, Nashik-3, Maharashtra
Email id: - sambhajipatil07@gmail.com

Dr. Shamkant Deshmukh
Librarian/Researcher Guide
Arts, Commerce and Science Nutan Maratha College, Jalgaon, Maharashtra.
Email id: - deshmukhshamkant@gmail.com

5. **Surbhi Saini**
Research Scholar, Research and Teaching Assistant (RTA), Dept. of Lib. & Inf. Sci. School of Social Sciences (SOSS), IGNOU, Maidhan Garhi, New Delhi-68
E.mail: innovation.surbhi@gmail.com

6. **Mahipal Sharma**
Asstt. Librarian
Aggarwal College, Ballabgarh
E-mail:Sharma_m81@rediffmail.com
Daizy
Librarian
Dasmesh girls college of education
Vpo - Badal, TehMalout, Distt - Muktsar
Punjab
E.mail: daizy.aggarwal@gmail.com

7. **Rachana**
Asst. Librarian, IAMR, Institute, Ghaziabad UP.

8. **Manju Devi**
Research Scholar, Singhania University, Rajasthan
E-Mail- manjudahiya2007@ rediffmail.com

9. **Dinesh Kumar**
Associate Editor (International Journal of Library Science), Library-incharge and Professional Assistant, Department of Pharmaceutical Science and Drug Research and Department of Biotechnology, Punjabi University Patiala, Punjab
E-Mail:- dineshpta@gmail.com
Arjun
Associate Editor (International Journal of Library Science) and System Administrator (Automation Program), Rajiv Gandhi National University of Law Punjab, Patiala, arjunpta@gmail.com

10. **Vinay Shanker Mahajan**
Librarian, Kendriya Vidyalaya, Godhra (GJ), Email: vsmahajan85@gmail.com
Mohd. Asif
Librarian, Indus Business Academy (IBA) Greater Noida, Email: akhan@ibagreaternoida.org
Mustafa Khan
Asstt. Librarian, Indus Business Academy (IBA), Greater Noida, Email: meesam@ibagreaternoida.org

Syed Misham Abbas Abidy and Vipin Kumar
Research Scholar, Bundelkhand University Jhansi, Jhansi (U.P.), Email: vkumar@ibagreaternoida.org,

11. **Divya Sharma**
Librarian
Utkarsh Business School, Bareilly (U.P)
E Mail: divya.sharma39@gmail.com

12. **Noushia Parveen**
Lecturer,
Dept of Library and Information Science
CSJM University, Kanpur.
noushia.khan@gmail.com

13. **Sunil Tyagi**
Library and Information Centre
Indian Pharmacopoeia Commission
Ministry of Health and Family Welfare
Government of India
Sector-23, Rajnagar
Ghaziabad-UP
Suniltyagi1979@gmail.com

14. **Lata Patil**
Manager – Knowledge Management Essar Group
E-mail: lsoniap@gmail.com

15. **Harmanpreet Singh**
H.O.D
Knowledge Centre, DAVIET Jalandhar
e-mail: spikersandhu@gmail.com
Harpreet Kaur Rana
Librarian (Sr. Scale)
Rayat Institute of Engg. and IT, Railmajra
e-mail: harpreet_rn@yahoo.co.in

16. **Navita Sharma**
Librarian
Rayat Bahra Institute of Management,
Mohali Campus, Punjab India.
navitavatshisht@gmail.com

17. Chiranjilal
Library in-charge,
Amity Law School, Affiliated to GGS IP University
Dwarka, New Delhi LIBRARY
library@als.amity.edu
chamoli2002@yahoo.co.in

18. Bharat Kumar M. Chaudhari
School of Petroleum Management
Pandit Deendayal Petroleum University,
Gandhinagar
E-Mail: Bharat.chaudhari@spm.pdpu.ac.in,
openbharat@gmail.com

19. Ramvveer Sagar
Deputy Librarian
Manav Rachna College of Engg. Delhi Surajkund Road,
Sec.43 Faridabad
sagar_ramveer@rediffmail.com,
sagar_ramveer@yahoo.co.in
Dr. Satya Parkash
Librarian
Accman Institute of Management Greater Noida,
satyaprakash_73@yahoo.co.in

20. Akansha Bhargava
(asst. prof)
Biff & Bright College of Technical Education
Jaipur
akansha.bg@gmail.com

21. Anoop Kumar Bajpayi
Librarian,
Medanta-The Medicity Hospital, Gurgaon, Haryana .
anoopmlib@gmail.com

22. Fayaz Ahmad Loan
Documentation Officer
Centre of Central Asian Studies,
University of Kashmir, Srinagar (J&K), India
E-mail: fayazlib@yahoo.co.in

23. Naresh Kumar
Assistant Librarian,
Spice Foundation, New Delhi
Research Scholar, DLIS, University of Delhi
E-mail: nareshiiim.kumar@gmail.com

24. Dr. Shamkant Deshmukh
Research guide
Manav Bharti University
Solan
Himachal Pradesh (India)
e-mail - shamkantdeshmukh@yahoo.co.in
deshmukhshamkant@gmail.com
Mr. Kuldeep Pawar
Research Scholar
Manav Bharti University,
Solan
Himachal Pradesh (india)
E-mail-mr.kuldeep_pawar@rediffmail.com

25. Anjali Sharma
Librarian,
Trinity Institute of Professional Studies,
Sector-9, Dwarka,
New Delhi-11007

1

Knowledge Management in Library in Modern Society

— *Kulwinder Kumar*

ABSTRACT

Knowledge is the main source for social development in the modern electronic age. And the requirement of society for the latest information and Knowledge are increasing day by day. So in the present Knowledge-based society the library is a big treasure house of human Knowledge. Library now-a-days plays an important role in the development of modern Knowledge-based society.

Keywords: *Knowledge/Knowledge Management/ Knowledge based Modern society/ Tacit, Explicit and Culture Knowledge.*

INTRODUCTION

Knowledge plays an important role in the modern society of organisation. The term Knowledge Management was first introduced in the keynote address to a European Management Conferences held in 1986.

The term 'Knowledge Management' was used to be simply the transfer of Knowledge from one person to another whereby the result enabled the recipient to advantage from the collected wisdom of the more experienced members of organisation or group. Knowledge management, a new discipline that promotes an integral approach to identify, capture retrieved share and evaluate an enterprise's Knowledge assets is the driver of productivity and growth of any organisation. It is a strategy of systematic and constructive management of vital Knowledge and its associated processes of creating, gathering, organising, diffusion, usage and exploitation.

The most important aim of Knowledge management is to provide the right Knowledge at the right time to right persons. For the development and success of the society, Knowledge management is very essential as it not only helps in discovering the resources, but also helps in evolving new techniques, rules and models. In the Present Information Age, the increasing demand of new technology has been forced to take advantages of present advanced information communication technology for providing Public library services in digital form. It is, therefore essential to give new shapes to library services by automating the Public libraries in the modern society. According to the present modern society, Library is modernised by making use of barcode, radio frequency identification, digital library, Internet, databases, subscribing electronic books and journals. Knowledge Management in Public libraries should be focused on effective research and development of Knowledge, creation of Knowledge bases, exchange and sharing of Knowledge between library staff users, trainers, researchers etc. In modern society or electronic age, library should play an essential role in speeding up explicit processing of the implicit Knowledge while realising the importance of its sharing. So with the wide array of solutions available today, how come Knowledge management efforts still fail so often? Although many reasons have been postulated, few are as important as making sure that you understand how Knowledge is used and created in your organisation, and making sure that you have a balanced Knowledge system portfolio that not only captures, stores, and disseminates your corporate Knowledge, but also allows opportunity for the creation of Knowledge. Why do current Knowledge Management systems find it so hard to achieve solid Return-On-Investment (ROI)? At the same time, it is extremely unreasonable to believe that so many Knowledge Management success stories revolve around the unplanned, unofficial applications of technology by informal Communities of Practice? In order to take a fully balanced approach to building a comprehensive and successful Knowledge Management system, you have to take several factors into account. What is the Knowledge that you're trying to collect? What form is it in? What are the resons you are trying for and particularly for whom?

WHAT IS KNOWLEDGE?

Knowledge is the full utilisation of information and data, coupled with the potentiality of people's skills, competencies, ideas, intuitions, commitments and motivations. In the present economy, Knowledge is people, money, leverage, learning, flexibility, power, and competitive advantage. Knowledge is more relevant to sustained business than capital, labour or land. Nevertheless, it remains the most neglected one. It is more than justified true belief and is essential for action, performance and adoption. Knowledge provides the ability to resolve unseathed situations. Some considers Knowledge to be present in ideas, judgments, talents, root causes, relationships, perspectives and concepts. Knowledge is stored in the individual brain or encoded in organisational processes, documents, products, services, facilities and systems.

Knowledge is the basis for, and the driver of, our society. Knowledge is the result of learning which provides the only sustainable competitive advantage. Knowledge is the next paradigm shift in computing, following data processing, during 1945-1965 and information management 1966-1995. Knowledge is action, focused innovation, pooled expertise, special relationships and alliances. Knowledge is value-added behaviour and activities. For Knowledge to be of value it must be focused, current, tested and shared.

TYPES OF KNOWLEDGE

Knowledge is of various types as given below:

- Genetic Knowledge
- Tacit Knowledge

- Explicit Knowledge
- Cultural Knowledge

Genetic Knowledge

Genetic Knowledge is Knowledge we have at birth. We inherit these ideas (genes) from our parents. This type of Knowledge has been referred to as that which is 'deep within', innate, inborn or instinctive. Freud referred to such Knowledge as the Id. A 'gifted' child is born with certain genetic ideas significantly different from other children. Genetic Knowledge is present before experience. Cultural Knowledge, the subject of the next chapter, is acquired after birth, by experience.

All organisms have genetic Knowledge. When the seed of a plant or a tree (an embryo) grows, it acts on its environment in a particular way. It inherits a set of genetic ideas on what to do in life. The tree knows what to do. Part of this knowing includes being able to interact with any changes of environment, not only on a day-to-day basis, but also second by second, depending on environmental cues as well as its genetic goals. For example, a tree will not open its leaf pores fully on a hot day and so suffer from loss of water. The tree has a leaf pore opening and closing belief system (with the belief system being various inherited genes that are patterns of chemicals stored in the form of DNA in plant cells, just as human cultural beliefs are patterns of chemicals stored in the neurons of the brain). Environmental conditions, such as humidity, are measured by leaf cells and the tree reacts according to its genetic beliefs. Communication between cells is via chemical messengers such as hormones. The tree's chance of survival, and so reproduction, will be related to how well it performs these actions.

Tacit Knowledge

- Tacit Knowledge in society ensures task effectiveness. It also provides for a kind of creative vitality – intuition and spontaneous insight can often tackle tough problems that would otherwise be difficult to solve tacit Knowledge which is implicit. An organisation promotes the learning of Tacit Knowledge to increase the skills and creative capacities of its employees.

- Tacit Knowledge includes hands-on skills, best practices, special know-how, and intuitions. Personal Knowledge is difficult to articulate.
- Traditionally, the transfer of tacit Knowledge is through shared experience, through apprenticeship and job training.
- Tacit Knowledge is cultivated in an organisational culture that motivates through shared vision and common purpose.
- Socialisation is the sharing of tacit Knowledge between individuals, usually through joint activities rather than written or verbal instructions.

Explicit Knowledge

Explicit Knowledge is used in the design of routines, standard operation procedures, and the structure of data records. These forms of Knowledge can be found in any modern society. Explicit Knowledge is rule-based Knowledge that is used to match actions to situations by invoking appropriate rules. An organisation takes advantage of Explicit Knowledge to maximise efficiency.

- Explicit Knowledge allows enjoying a certain level of operational efficiency and control.
- Explicit Knowledge promotes equable, consistent organisational responses.

Cultural Knowledge

Cultural Knowledge belongs those ideas that are gained from experience. Although for humans, nearly all cultural ideas are stored in the brain, the cultural Knowledge of the wasp cannot be passed to other wasps (not that a wasp needs to do this). It cannot pass 'nest location' ideas to its offspring or other wasp. All its cultural Knowledge is non-transmittable. Each wasp must learn for itself all its own cultural Knowledge. Hence, we can come to the conclusion: the first cultural Knowledge that evolved was for an animal's personal use, and not for sharing with others. An organisation must adopt a holistic approach to Knowledge management that successfully combines Tacit and explicit Knowledge at all levels of the organisation. Personal Knowledge is leveraged with explicit Knowledge for the design and development of innovative products, services and processes.

Figure: The impact of cultural Knowledge on Knowledge management Behaviour

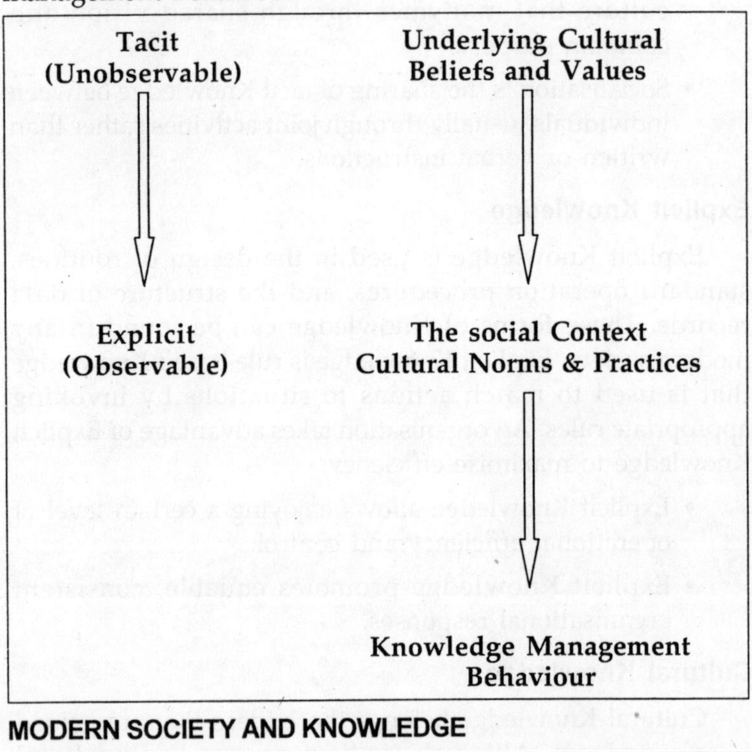

MODERN SOCIETY AND KNOWLEDGE

Modern society is an ocean of Knowledge. Only that society will survive and succeed who build themselves by understanding the dynamics of the Knowledge and create true Knowledge society. In fact, Knowledge Management is a subcomponent of Knowledge-based society or Knowledge economy. What is Knowledge-based society? A Knowledge-based society has the capacity to generate, absorb, disseminate and protect Knowledge and therapy use it to create economic wealth and social good for all its constituents. It uses Knowledge as a powerful device to drive societal transformation. A Knowledge-based society enlightens its people to take an integrated view of life. It uses Knowledge through all its constituents to enrich the people.

WHAT IS KNOWLEDGE MANAGEMENT IN MODERN SOCIETY?

Knowledge management is the transfer of knowledge from one person to another, the result of which enables the recipient to benefit from the collected wisdom of the more experienced members of a society. Knowledge management is common and generic. Knowledge management (km) has been defined as "...the process by which a society creates, captures, acquires, and uses knowledge to support and improve the performance and development of the society".

Knowledge management helps ensure the right information, gets to the right people at the right time to make the right decisions.

CHARACTERISTICS OF KNOWLEDGE MANAGEMENT

- Written theories
- Organisational agility
- Operational efficiency
- Innovation rate
- Learning
- Growth and improvement

BENEFITS OF KNOWLEDGE MANAGEMENT IN MODERN SOCIETY

- Produce and conserve New Value
- Generate new Wealth

- Improve the **Flow** of Knowledge
- Increase **Revenue**
- Improve **Decision-Making**
- Develop and implement **New Business Models**
- Build **More Profound Relationships**
- Increase **Productivity and Efficiency**
- Speed **Innovation**
- Unleash new **Ideas and Creativity**
- Help create a more **Adaptive, responsive, dynamic, flexible, organisation**
- Better prepare for and anticipate **The Future**
- **Improve and accelerate Learning**
- Enhance Team Collaboration & Coordination
- Improve the **Ability to manage Changes**
- Attract, and retain **motivated, loyal, and committed Talent**
- Maximise the use of available **collective wisdom, experience, and Brain-Power of human**
- Create a more **Knowledge aware, Knowledge friendly Culture.**
- Knowledge and Knowledge Management in Modern Society

In modern society, Knowledge and information are the most important factors in the long-term success of both an individual and society. Knowledge and Knowledge Management have emerged as a vital component. In fact, Knowledge may soon be the only source of competitive advantage for the society. One part of an organisation repeats the work of another part, simply because it is impossible to keep track of, and make use of Knowledge in other parts. A company's value depends increasingly on "intangible assets" which exist in the minds of employees, in databases, in files and in myriad documents. To manage Knowledge it must first of all be captured or acquired in some useful forms.

Knowledge management is a critical component of an organisations success. Knowledge assets are the Knowledge that an organisation owns or needs to own, to achieve its goals. Knowledge is information, extracted, filtered or formatted in some way. Every company's Knowledge requirements are a unique combination of Knowledge strategy, tools and technologies, processes and procedures. Knowledge management technologies capture this intangible element in an organisation and make it universally available. This approach is known as Knowledge management: the practice of capturing and organising information to make it more accessible and valuable to those who need it.

With the impact of globalisation, the Internet, and the rapid evolution of technology, managing Knowledge for competitive advantage has become more important than ever. Knowledge management is, therefore, an "essential ingredient of success" in the modern society.

KNOWLEDGE MANAGEMENT IN LIBRARIES

Libraries are recognised as an essential ingredient in civilized societies for the individual and for the social progress and prosperity in all human activities in the modern society. They play an important role in serving the society through its extension services. Thus there is an urgent need to study their existing conditions, positions, operations and services to identify their strength and weaknesses. This will help them in providing better services in the changing social, political and digital environment. The libraries in the states covered under study have been established long ago when education was at the developing stage. Today, the society is moving towards an electronic age. Library is a practical demonstration of democracy's faith in universal education as a continuing and life long process, in appreciation of the achievement of humanity in Knowledge and culture. Libraries provide access to recorded man's thoughts and ideas of persoris of calibre. And to make freely available to all, a public library "as organisation established, supported and funded by the community, either through local, regional or national government or through some other form of community organisation. "It provides access to Knowledge, information and works of imagination through a range of resources and services and equally available to all members of the community regardless of race, nationality, age, gender, religion, language, disability, economic and employment status and educational achievement." The public library is the local center of information making all kinds of Knowledge and information readily available to its users. The services of the public library are provided on the basis of equality of access for all, regardless of age, race, sex, religion, nationality, languages or social status. Specific services and materials must be provided for those users who cannot, for whatever reason, use the regular services and materials; for example, linguistic materials, people with disabilities or people in hospital or prison. In modern society, library is a temple of learning. Library system is an important organ of the state. Entrusted with the responsibility of maintaining and organising collection of documents in the services of storage and retrieval is a gigantic problem of today's public libraries. A library provides impartial service to all the members of a local community and serves as an auxiliary educational institution. It is a democratic institution providing information, education and culture to each according to his needs.

Libraries are information centers established in support of the mission of their parent institutions to generate Knowledge. While people equipped with Knowledge are to serve the society for the well-being of mankind. In the digital age, libraries face challenges from both within (academia) and without (the business sector). Public departments, or even faculty and students, may purchase or build their own portals to meet their Public and/or research needs.

Knowledge Management has been tooted and hyped since late 1990s, first (DiMattia, 1997) in the business sector, and then in higher education and now in library management. The impetus for embracing Knowledge Management in Public libraries is mainly from a combination of library budget shortfall and higher user expectations. Rather than adopting an often trumpeted high-tech approach, it is more practical to utilise the existing staffing, technology and management structure for Public libraries. An effective Knowledge Management programme is a long term project. How to manage Knowledge will become an important subject facing libraries in modern society. Knowledge Management in libraries should be focused on effective research and development of Knowledge, creation of Knowledge bases, exchange and sharing of Knowledge between library staffs and its users, training of library staff, speeding up explicit processing of the implicit Knowledge and at the sametime sharing and realising of its sharing. With the help of the Knowledge Management processes, libraries convert data and information stored in various sources into Knowledge and deliver the required Knowledge to users. Knowledge Management within libraries involves organising and providing access to intangible resources that help librarians and administrators carry out their tasks more effectively and accurately. Knowledge Management in libraries is the combination of different processes, such as, acquisition of Knowledge from different sources and classification, storing, indexing and dissemination of that Knowledge using people, process and technology in such a way by which library could fulfill the mission of the parent organisation in term of user's satisfaction. It is to promote relationship in and between libraries and users, to strengthen Knowledge internetworking and to quicken the flow of Knowledge. The libraries are moving from collection management to Knowledge management while the digital technologies are offering new information services and products. The application of Information Technology (IT) enlarges the scope of Knowledge acquisition, raises the speed of Knowledge acquisition as well as reduces Knowledge acquisition cost. IT is indispensable in the application and exchange of Knowledge and in other fields. It functions as a source and tool for Knowledge innovation.

CONCLUSION

The findings of our study suggest that a dominantly bureaucratic culture seems to tend toward an initial process-based KM approach. Furthermore, a bureaucratic culture seems to create the expectation among organisational members that senior management needs to provide a vision of purpose for KM before the organisational members should embark on KM activities. The members as well, view senior management support as validating any KM activities that they undertake. Innovative cultures, even if not the dominant culture at the organisational level, seem to enable subgroups to experiment with KM or create micro-KMs. In essence, in organisations having dominant bureaucratic cultures with traces of innovativeness, senior management support legitimises KM, but the innovativeness of the culture enables it to expand far beyond an organisation-wide repository. Specific KM behaviours such as ownership and maintenance of knowledge, knowledge sharing, and knowledge reuse seem to be influenced largely by the individualistic or cooperative nature of the culture. Individualistic cultures inhibit sharing, ownership, and reuse, while cooperative cultures enable the creation of virtual communities. Earley's (1994) work on organisational culture emphasized the individualistic and collectivistic aspects of culture. Organisations encouraging individuals to pursue and maximise individual's goals and rewarding performance based on individual achievement would be considered to have an individualistic culture. Whereas organisations placing priority on collective goals and joint contributions and rewards for organisational accomplishments would be considered collectivist (Chatman & Barsade, 1995; Earley, 1994). This dimension of organisational culture emerged as critical in our examination of the influence of culture on KM initiatives.

REFERENCES

Davenport, T. H., De Long, D. W., & Beers, M. C. (1998). Successful knowledge management. Sloan Management Review, 39(2), 43-57.

DeLong, D. W., & Fahey, L. (2000). Diagnosing cultural barriers to knowledge management. Academy of Management Executive, 14(4), 113-27.

Earley. (1994). Self or group? Cultural effects of training on self-efficacy and performance. Administrative Science Quarterly, 39(1), 89-117.

Enz, C. (1986). Power and shared values in the corporate culture. Ann Arbor, MI: University of Michigan Press. Gold.

A. H., Malhotra, A., & Segars, A.H. (2001). Knowledge management: An organisational capabilities perspective. Journal of Management Information Systems, 18(1), 185-214.

Gupta, A. K., & Govindarajan, V. (2000). Knowledge management's social dimension: Lessons from Nucor Steel. Sloan Management Review, 42(1), 71-80.

Hansen, M. T., Nohria, N., & Tierney, T. (1999). What's your strategy for managing knowledge? Harvard Business Review, 77(2), 106-15.

Hargadon, A. B. (1998). Firms as knowledge brokers: Lessons in pursuing continuous innovation. California Management Review, 40(3), 209-27.

Hasan, H., & Gould, E. (2001). Support for the sense-making activity of managers. Decision Support Systems, 31(1), 71-86.

Jarvenpaa, S. L., & Staples, S. D. (2001). Exploring perceptions of organisational ownership of information and expertise. Journal of Management Information Systems, 18(1), 151-83.

Johnson, G. (1992) Managing strategic change — Strategy, culture and action. Long Range Planning, 25(1), 28-36.

Kanungo, S., Sadavarti, S., & Srinivas, Y. (2001). Relating IT strategy and organisational culture: An empirical study of public sector units in India. Journal of Strategic Information Systems, 10(1), 29-57.

KPMG Management Consulting. (1998). Knowledge management: Research report.

2

Knowledge Management Practices and Electronic Resources

— *Sabita Manjari Biswal*

ABSTRACT

Knowledge Management (KM) is the way of connecting people with the best available information to facilitate the decision-making. KM is about building capacity to make more informed decisions and requires conscious efforts. Dueling challenges that information overload and information scarcity present obstacles to overburdened health workers, managers and policy-makers. Successful KM initiatives incorporate knowledge-seeking and sharing into a workflow, allowing users of the KM system to work more productively with better quality information. KM does not come in a one-size-fits-all model.

INTRODUCTION

The Knowledge management (KM) is defined and addressed by many ways. Knowledge management (KM) has rapidly moved beyond the stage of a trend and has established itself as a key part of many libraries' knowledge strategy. The concept and name "Knowledge Management" was started and popularised in the business world during the 20th century. It was the business world that first recognised the importance of knowledge in the "global economy" of "knowledge age". The applications of knowledge management have now spread to other organisations including government agencies, research and development departments, universities and others. Knowledge-embedded organisation's business processes and employee's skills provides the firm with unique capabilities to deliver a product or service to the customers. Knowledge-management is a form of expertise-centered management which draws out tacit knowledge making it accessible to specific purposes to improve the performance of organisations. Successful application of knowledge management practices involves understanding and constructively utilising information for organisational learning. Social science institutions, government and non- government organisations, etc. are knowledge intensive and the use of advanced technology may transform these institutions and organisations in the future.

Knowledge management caters to the critical issues of organisational adaptation, survival and competence in the face of increasingly discontinuous environmental change. Essentially, it embodies organisational processes that seek synergistic combination of data and information processing capacity of information technologies, and the creative and innovative capacity of human beings. (Malhotra, 2000).

Knowledge management is a systematic approach that ranges from technology-driven methods of accessing, controlling, and delivering information to massive efforts in transforming corporate culture. KM is not only about managing knowledge assets but managing the process including developing knowledge, preserving knowledge, using knowledge and sharing knowledge (Vinitha & Mymoon, 2005). KM involves the systematic process of finding, selecting, organising, distilling and presenting information in a way that improves an employee's comprehension in a specific area of interest. KM is a conscious strategy of getting the right knowledge to the right people at the right time and helping people to share and put information into action in ways that strive to improve organisational performance.

KNOWLEDGE MANAGEMENT (KM) IN E-RESOURCES

As a learning organisation, libraries should provide a strong leadership in knowledge management. Libraries should improve their knowledge management in all the key areas of library services. To cope with the exponential growth in human knowledge, libraries need to develop their resources, access and sharing strategies from printed to electronic and digital resources. Limited by funding, technology, staff and space, libraries must carefully analyse the needs of their users and seek to develop cooperative acquisition plans to meet the needs of the users. Libraries should develop and maintain an integrated Online Public Access Catalogue (OPAC) with both internal and external resources as well as printed and other formats of knowledge. Useful websites and knowledge sources should be regularly searched and selected in and from the internet and included in OPACs. In the current digital and networking knowledge age, the size of information sources on the web is growing exponentially. No one really knows exactly how many web pages are on the internet, because new web pages are added every second. Universities and research organisations are knowledge reservoirs. These highly valued intellectual assets, regardless of whether they are explicit or tacit, should be inventoried, archived, indexed, frequently updated and made accessible to digital form. Other familiar territory for professionals exists in the KM field as well; this includes a continuing need for expertise in information management and high levels of support for teams engaged in innovative pursuits (Cheng, 2001).

The tools and help components in KM:

THE INTERNET

Internet can provide comprehensive information in a diversity of subjects for a variety of needs and to various categories of users at any point of time. Internet is the largest single resource of information available on a network of computers, which can be accessed anytime through any

Internet-connected computer irrespective of its location. The Internet is changing the roles of information professionals and the way we process and transfer information. Identification, location and selection of worthwhile and useful digital collections have become one of the important jobs of modern professional librarians.

WORLD WIDE WEB (WWW)

With the digital revolution, data and information can now be transmitted to all corners of the world, and that is significant for almost all humanity, and it is significant for libraries. The World Wide Web has many features of a digital library, and if the web did not exist, our conception of digital libraries would be very different. The web is undoubtedly the means via which most digital libraries are accessed, but it is not a digital library itself as it lacks characteristics of a digital library.

ELECTRONIC INFORMATION SERVICE (EIS)

To establish a successful electronic information service (EIS), it is essential that you define the scope of the service you are establishing. This requires strategic planning, including an information audit of needs of the customers and management, which requires consultation with customers, both current and potential. You need to agree who the users are, so as to be able to cater adequately to their information needs now and in the future. Your users need some help in identifying how their needs can be met from electronic sources. Digital libraries offer new levels of access to broader audiences of users and new opportunities for the library and information science field to advance both theory and practice. Digital libraries can help move the nation towards realising the enormously powerful vision of 'anytime, anywhere' access to the best and the latest of human thought and culture, so that no classroom, individual or a society is isolated from knowledge resources. Digital libraries bring the library to the user, overcoming all geographical barriers.

DIGITAL LIBRARIES

Digital revolution has transformed the intellectual function of traditional libraries. Digital libraries are providing the base for a set of distributed activities. It is also providing 'a one step solution' for speedy delivery in a reliable fashion. Libraries are being digitised and patron demand is growing as the concept of content management has been adapted to the library world. More libraries are providing virtual references via the web. The greatest challenge for the information manager today is to create an organisation that can share knowledge. Quality library services are imperative in knowledge society as it inspires the knowledge workers to be innovative, viz. think globally and design locally.

METADATA

This is defined as 'data about data' or 'information about information'. In other words, metadata is the data that describe information resources (Safari, 2004). A short descriptive note on a book, an informal description of search hits by search engines, a catalog and MARC (Machine Readable Cataloging) record, are data that describe information resources and hence metadata. To refine this popular definition, metadata is considered "structured" data about data. Metadata is any data that supports the effective use of data, including information that can facilitate knowledge management, knowledge access and analysis.

SEMANTIC WEB

The next generation of web, called semantic web, is based on the machine-processable semantics of information, stored in the machine processable metadata. This is not a separate web but an extension of the current web in which the information is given well-defined meaning, better enabling computers and humans to work in cooperation (Berners-Lee, 1998).

ONTOLOGY

Ontology is a concept borrowed from philosophy where ontology is a systematic account of existence. This term has a different meaning in the context of knowledge representation: an explicit specification of conceptualisation (Gruber, 1993).

THE KNOWLEDGE MANAGEMENT PROCESS

Knowledge Management occurs naturally in every organisation whether or not specialised information systems are in place to support it. Cognitive and social demands impel people to devise strategies for building and categorising pieces of knowledge that are valuable to them. They also push people to leverage knowledge held by others. To promote the distribution of knowledge, many organisations encourage or even expect subject-matter experts to advertise and share their expertise with others, either informally or through structured communication means, such as seminars, presentations, or in written form. Efforts to highlight knowledge that might be important and to promote its capture and distribution are also common.

KNOWLEDGE MANAGEMENT EDUCATION AND RESEARCH

To be successful, the education process should generate value of the knowledge disseminated or created. That introduces the role of knowledge application; this essentiality covers the knowledge cycle. The end products of universities are knowledge and the knowledge workers that society and business need. As a result, the education system should be in tune with economic development, in particular, local economic development. In the perspective of the above discussion, university curricula and the professorial body are to be sure that some criteria should be observed.

KNOWLEDGE MANAGEMENT: THE INFORMATION PROCESSING PARADIGM

The evolution of the information-processing paradigm over the last four decades to build intelligence and manage change in business functions and processes has generally progressed over three phases:

1. Automation: increased efficiency of operations;
2. Rationalisation of procedures: streamlining of procedures and eliminating obvious bottlenecks which are revealed by automation for enhanced efficiency of operations; and,
3. Re-engineering: radical redesign of business processes that depends upon information technology, intensive radical redesigns of workflows and work processes.

THE VALUE OF KNOWLEDGE MANAGEMENT

In an organisational context, data represents facts or values of results, and relations between data and other relations have the capacity to represent information. Patterns of relations of data and information and other patterns have the capacity to represent knowledge. For the representation to be of any utility, it must be understood, and when understood the representation is information or knowledge to the one that understands. Yet, what is the real value of information and knowledge, and what does it mean to manage it?

MYTHS AND KNOWLEDGE MANAGEMENT

The information-processing view of knowledge management has propagated some dangerous myths about knowledge management. Simplistic representations of knowledge management that often appear in popular press may often result in misdirected investments and system implementations that never yield expected returns (Strassmann 1997, 1999). Given the impending backlash against such simplistic representations of Knowledge Management (Garner 1999), it is critical to analyse the myths underlying the 'successful' representations of knowledge management that worked in a bygone era. There are three dominant myths based on the information-processing logic that are characteristics of most popular knowledge management interpretations (Hildebrand 1999).

CONCLUSIONS

In a digital environment librarian should be familiar with search engines such as Google, Yahoo etc. And relevant websites according to the users' needs. In a traditional library system, librarians are used to compile cumulative indexes for the benefit of their users. But in a digital system librarians can use various databases, library networks, search engines, websites etc. for the search of information. In the Regional Centre for Strategic Studies (RCSS) library, we use traditional and non-traditional knowledge organisation systems for content organisation. In the digital environment, we use classification systems to organise knowledge. And we also use traditional card catalogue as well as electronic database. In a developing country like Sri Lanka, we have to face electricity failures and at that time physical catalogue is very useful. There are a few basic changes that pose challenges to modern libraries towards acquiring and managing larger and larger bodies of knowledge; they are: globalisation, decentralisation, customisation and acceleration. Modern libraries are dependent on technology, which is highly diversified in their products and services they offer.

REFERENCES

Berners-Lee (1998). Semantic Web Road Map. http://www.w3.org/Design Isuues/Semantic.html.

Blair DC (2002). Knowledge management: hype, hope or help? J. Am. Soc. Inf. Sci. Technol. 53(12): 1019–28.

Cheng G (2001). The shifting information landscape: re-inventing the wheel or a whole new frontier for librarians. New Library World. 102(1160/1161): 26–33.

Garner, R. "Please Don't Call it Knowledge Management", Computerworld, August 9, 1999.

Gruber, T.R. (1993). Toward Principles for the Design of Ontologies used for Knowledge Sharing. In: Roberto Poli Nicola Guarino (Ed.), International Workshop on Formal Ontology, Padova, and Italy,1993.http://ra.crema.unimi.it/lenya/turing/live/know/knowpubs/gruber93toward.pdf.

Hildebrand, C. "Does KM=IT?" CIO Enterprise, Sep. 15, 1999. Online version accessible at:http://www.cio.com/archive/enterprise/091599_ic.html.

Malhotra, Yogesh (2000). Knowledge Management & New Organization Forms: A Framework for Business Model Innovation. Information Resources Management Journal, 13(1), 5-1.

Safari, Mehdi (2004). MetadataAndthe Web.http://eprints.rclis. org/archive/00005845/01/Metadata_and_the_Web.pdf.

Strassmann, P.A. "The Knowledge Fuss", Computerworld, October 4, 1999.

Strassmann, P.A. The Squandered Computer: Evaluating the Business Alignment of Information Technologies, 1997, Information Economics Press, New Canaan, CT.

Vinitha, K. and Mymoon, M. (2005). Knowledge Management: Emerging challenges for Library and Information Professionals. In:Proceedings of the National Convention on Library and Information Networking (NACLIN 2005). Eds. H.K.Kaul and Gayathri Sen, (pp. 122-35).

3

Application of Knowledge Management in Modern Libraries

— *Dr. Kanchan Kamila*

ABSTRACT

Knowledge has become the driving force for social development and its identification, acquisition, development, resolution, use, store and share are called Knowledge Management (KM). The present paper also depicts the division of knowledge, definition, processes of KM, contents of KM, tools and techniques of KM, its characteristics and necessity of Human Resource Management for its effective application in libraries, impact of IT & ICT on KM, essentials of KM in digital environment, problems with conventional KM and concludes that effective KM is the key to success in ICT enabled modern libraries.

Keywords: *Implicit Knowledge, Tacit Knowledge, Explicit Knowledge, Cultural Knowledge, Contents of KM, Process of KM, Tools of KM*

INTRODUCTION

In the digital era, 'management' refers to effectively identify, acquire, develop, resolve, use, store and share knowledge, to create an approach to transforming and sharing of tacit and explicit knowledge, and to raise the emergency and innovation capability by utilising the wisdom of the team. Since knowledge has become the driving force for social development, the attention of the society to information and knowledge is rising and people's demands for information and knowledge are increasing step by step. This has provided a good environment for library development. Knowledge management in libraries should be focused on effective research and development of knowledge, creation of knowledge bases, exchange and sharing of knowledge between library staff (including its users), training of library staff, speeding up of the implicit knowledge and realising of its sharing.

KNOWLEDGE AND ITS MANAGEMENT

Division of Knowledge

Knowledge can be divided into three types which are required to be captured:

Implicit Knowledge: This is personal knowledge—the human mind, hard to formalise, and often difficult to communicate. This is the knowledge of experience, which is also known as simultaneous knowledge, mostly known as implications. It has two dimensions, technical and cognitive dimensions.

Explicit Knowledge: Explicit knowledge can easily be written down and codified. This is a simple form of knowledge, which is formal and easy to communicate and document. This is the knowledge of rationality i.e. policies, rules, specifications and formulae. This is also known as declarative knowledge or sequential knowledge.

Cultural Knowledge: It is the knowledge which includes assumptions, and beliefs that are used to understand, describe, and explain the reality, as well as conventions, values and significance to new information. These shared beliefs, norms, and values form the frame work in which organisational members construct reality, recognise the new information, and evaluate alternative interpretations and actions.

Knowledge Management

Knowledge management (KM) is the process of capturing, organising, and storing information and experiences of the workers and groups within an organisation and making it available to others. By collecting those artifacts in a central or distributed electronic environment (often in a database called a knowledge base), KM aims to help a company gain competitive advantage.

Knowledge management refers to the critical issues of organisational adaptation, survival and competence against discontinuous environmental change. Essentially, it embodies organisational processes that seek synergistic combination of data and information processing capacity of information communication technologies, and the creative and innovative capacity of human beings.

Knowledge Management (KM) is more about the pragmatic and thoughtful application of any concept or definition, as it is not in the definition but in real world execution where opportunities and challenges lie.

Therefore, knowledge management involves an organisation recognising and mapping its intellectual assets, creating knowledge for competitive advantage, making large amounts of business information available, and allocating the best practices and technology that facilitates all of the above, including groupware and internet. Four steps in getting started in knowledge management are described:

- Making knowledge visible
- Building knowledge intensity
- Developing a knowledge culture
- Building knowledge infrastructure

KM is also related to the concept of intellectual capital.

PROCESS OF KNOWLEDGE MANAGEMENT

Knowledge management is a complex process, which deals with knowledge creation, acquisition packaging, and application or reuse of knowledge. Knowledge management basically consists of:

Creating and Discovering/Knowledge Collection

- Creativity Techniques
- Data Mining
- Text Mining
- Environment Scanning
- Knowledge Elicitation
- Business Simulation
- Content Analysis

Sharing and Learning

- Communities of Practice
- Learning Networks
- Sharing Best Practice
- After Action Reviews
- Structured Dialogue
- Share Fairs
- Cross Functional Teams
- Decision Diaries

Organising and Managing

- Knowledge Centers
- Expertise Profiling
- Knowledge Mapping
- Information Audits/Inventory
- IRM (Information Resource Management)
- Measuring Intellectual Capital

TOOLS AND TECHNIQUES FOR KNOWLEDGE MANAGEMENT

A large number of tools and techniques are given below which is effective in managing and handling knowledge and thereby maintaining the knowledge base organisation:

- Intranets/Extranets
- Groupware
- Electronic Data Management
- Information Retrieval Tools
- Workflow Management Integration of Systems
- Data Analysis
- Data Warehousing/Data Mining
- Agent Technologies
- Help Desk Technologies
- Machine Learning
- Computer based Training – CBT
- Geographic Information System – GIS
- Meta data
- Ontology (Computer based)

Information technology is a tool for knowledge management in libraries. Knowledge acquisition is the starting point of knowledge management in libraries. The application of information technologies enlarges the scope of knowledge acquisition, raises knowledge acquisition speed and reduces knowledge acquisition cost. It is impossible to accomplish such important tasks by using man's brains only in the modern society in which the knowledge changes with each passing day. It will be possible to link closely knowledge sources and knowledge workers by computer networks, thus constructing knowledge networks in libraries based on realisation of single-point information.

The knowledge acquired must be accumulated and converged into knowledge warehouses of libraries. The priority of information technologies in the field of knowledge storage not only finds expression in quantity, but also in retrieval, sorting and security of the knowledge. Information technology is also indispensable in the application and exchange of knowledge and other fields. It functions as a source and tool for knowledge innovation.

KNOWLEDGE MANAGEMENT IN LIBRARIES: CHARACTERISTICS AND HUMAN RESOURCE PERSPECTIVE

The role of knowledge management in libraries will become more and more important along with the development of knowledge economy. It is a new management mode, boasts of the following superiority and characteristics incompatible with conventional management.

Knowledge management in libraries is to promote relationship in and between libraries, between library and user, to strengthen knowledge internetworking and to quicken knowledge flow. In the knowledge economy era, libraries carry out researches on development and application of information resources, construction of virtual libraries, protection of intellectual property rights in the electronic era etc., thus founding the base for knowledge innovation.

The most important resource in the knowledge economy system is the talents who grasp knowledge. The talent competition has become the focus of market competition in the knowledge economy era. In the knowledge economy era, the libraries attach importance to vocational training and lifelong education of library staff to raise their scientific knowledge level and ability of acquiring and innovating knowledge. They also fully respect the human value, guide and bring into play wisdom potentialities of library staff, take developing knowledge resources in the brains of library staff as an important way for rising work efficiency. An all-round improvement of library staff's quality and positioning of the human value become have/the important objectives of knowledge management in libraries.

Human resource management takes it as its basic starting point to train high quality specialised talents and to revitalise the library undertaking. In practice, full attention is being paid to diversity and variation of library staff requirements, strengthened management of different library staff by applying contingency management approach. That is, to some people, rigid management method is applied, rigorous supervision and control imposed, and quantity and quality requirements of work according to regulations and procedures are made clear. And, to the rest of people, more flexible management method is applied to let them participate in decision-making and consultation and undertake more jobs so as to bring their management abilities into full play and realise organisational and personal objectives. Doing well in continuous engineering education of specialised staff, which should not only focus on the theory of library science and related disciplines, but also cover the latest technical knowledge and strengthening professional ethics education.

PROMOTION OF KNOWLEDGE INNOVATION IN LIBRARIES THROUGH KNOWLEDGE MANAGEMENT

Knowledge innovation is the core of knowledge economy society. As bases for collection, processing, storage and distribution of knowledge and information, libraries represent an indispensable link in the scientific system chain, an important link in the knowledge innovation. *Secondly*, libraries take part in scientific research process directly. The library work is a component of knowledge innovation. *Thirdly*, libraries must pay attention to diffusion and conversion of knowledge. They act as bridges for turning the results of knowledge innovation into realistic productive forces. Knowledge management in libraries is to promote relationship in and between libraries, between the library and the user, to strengthen knowledge internetworking and to quicken knowledge flow. In the knowledge economy era, libraries are to carry out researches on development and application of information resources, construction of virtual libraries, protection of intellectual property rights in the electronic era etc., thus founding the base for knowledge innovation.

CONTENTS OF KNOWLEDGE MANAGEMENT IN LIBRARIES

As a completely new method of management, knowledge management in libraries leaves much to be desired in its theoretical system.

Knowledge management in libraries should include such respects as given below.

Knowledge Innovation Management

Knowledge innovation management in libraries refers to the management of production, diffusion and transfer of knowledge as well as of the network systems constructed by related institutions and organisations. It includes three aspects, namely, theoretical innovation management of knowledge, technical innovation management and organisational innovation management.

Theoretical innovation management is to enrich and enlarge the theoretical and practical research fields of library science and information science through pursuing the latest development trends in library science the world over. Technical innovation management is to manage the network systems constructed by institutions and organisations that relate to the full course of technical innovation. In their evolution from conventional libraries to electronic libraries, or digital libraries, Libraries should make technical breakthrough and progress and build up technical facilities to support knowledge management. Organisational innovation management is to create a set of effective organisational management systems adaptable to the requirements in the electronic library era to support and strengthen knowledge management activities, by optimising the functional departments and operation procedures of libraries.

In these systems, it firstly requires that leaders who take charge of knowledge management activities should undertake to formulate the management plans and coordinate all knowledge management related activities. Secondly, it requires establishment of special leading groups of knowledge flow for accomplishing all tasks relating to knowledge management activities. Electronic resources committees are composed of various types of specialists to take charge of evaluating, procuring and creating the electronic resources on the one hand, and coordinating activities of business departments and spurring them on to close cooperation in such fields as procurement and organisation of the electronic information resources as well as providing services on the other hand.

Knowledge Dissemination Management

Libraries may use diverse media and channels to disseminate various new knowledge. In the 21st century, the Internet, with its mass information and extensive contents, will provide people with the main approach to searching knowledge and acquiring information.

It is necessary to strengthen knowledge dissemination management in libraries as follows:

- Uninterruptedly strengthening the creation of libraries' own document resources and solidifying the development of document information resources;
- Continuously raising the quality of library staffs and strengthening continuous engineering education of the working staff;
- Giving full support to the special role of the expert system in knowledge dissemination; and
- Making a comprehensive utilisation of all media to ensure security of operation of networks, and prevent online criminal activities and online dissemination of inappropriate information.

Knowledge Application Management

In the 21st century, libraries should also attach importance to provision of services for people to acquire knowledge and achieve maximum functions and efficiency of knowledge information. Therefore, knowledge services based on high-speed information networks should be carried out by:

· Setting up virtual libraries or information centers for enterprises, governments, public organisations and scientific research institutions is difficult. It is difficult for an enterprise or a social organisation to put sufficient manpower, material and financial resources on information gathering, organising and developing. It is also impossible and unnecessary to spend a large amount of funds on information resources for their own use. Libraries can create virtual libraries or information centers for these organs separately according to their respective information requirements by using abundant information resources on the high speed information networks.

· Setting up digitised knowledge services is actually a development trend of libraries in the 21st century. This presupposes: creating step by step the users-oriented information service systems, such as, information dissemination, information search and special supply of information; quickening the creation of digitised libraries; studying the methods, means and techniques of information distribution and search with the Internet as the base and web technique as the core.

· Digitising libraries' resources. The electronic libraries or digitised libraries are the technical modes and development trends of libraries in the knowledge economy era. The knowledge services of libraries in the future will start with the creation of databases comprising electronic journals and books in different languages that have discipline features and can operate on high-speed information networks. Great efforts should be made to transform all existing large non-electronic information resources into electronic information and integrate them into electronic libraries.

IMPACT OF IT & ICT ON KNOWLEDGE MANAGEMENT

Impact of IT on Knowledge Management

One of the aims of knowledge management in libraries is to promote the knowledge exchange among library staff, strengthen innovation consciousness and abilities, and raise the library staff enthusiasm and abilities for learning, making the knowledge most efficiently applied to business activities of the library, and rebuilding the library into a learning organisation. Therefore, the main train of thought in realising knowledge management of libraries is a rational design of the organisational structure and business procedures of libraries, and cultural fostering, as well as modernised information support, whereby creating an environment and incentive mechanism for innovation, exchange, study and application of the knowledge.

The principal information technologies (IT) relevant to knowledge management includes: Internet, Intranet and Extranet, storage architectures, database management systems, metadata, data acquisition and gathering, dissemination, messaging, push and pull, information retrieval, information resources sharing, groupware, middleware, on-line analytical processing, multidimensional analysis and data mining. How to convert data to the object of knowledge management – knowledge is also relevant to some basic information technologies, mainly including data processing, reporting, network communication, document management, information search and retrieval, relational and object oriented databases, electronic publishing, work flow and help desks.

In addition, because of the differences in architecture, usage and characteristics between information and knowledge, the storage and management of knowledge are more complicated than those of information. The storage architecture technology, database management system technology and metadata are also the key technologies in knowledge management.

Impact of ICT on Knowledge Management

The various needs of users and unrestricted flow of knowledge are the main reasons for the use of Information and Communication Technology (ICT) in modern libraries.

Now a day the emphasis in libraries is shifting from collection to contact (access). To cope with the time, use of ICT plays a very important role. KM provides an efficient and professional approach to the management of ICT service provisions. Adopting its guidance offers users a huge range of benefits that includes:

- Reduced service costs
- Save the time of users as well as staff
- Quality and quantity progress
- Improved user services
- Improved customer/user satisfaction
- Improved productivity
- ICT helps to maximize the benefits
- Provides confidence to manage and cover risk to achieve the organisational goal
- Faster and easier recovery of data and dissemination of information
- Reducing risks and errors

CHIEF KNOWLEDGE OFFICER (CKO) SYSTEM FOR ORGANISATION STRUCTURE, BUSINESS PROCESSES AND CULTURE OF LIBRARIES

The Chief Information Officer (CIO) is conspicuously a high management position that has emerged successively in the government departments and large organisations in Western countries since 1980s. The Chief Knowledge Officer (CKO) is the highest ranking person in charge of knowledge management, which has evolved from CIO along with the transition of information research management into knowledge management. The CKO system represents the latest development trends of the information management system of the organisations, and marks the transition of information management from the stage of information resources management to that of knowledge management.

Realising seamless combination of library business management with knowledge management during the business process reorganisation of libraries, knowledge management integrates itself with the whole process of knowledge exchange, sharing, innovation and application of the organisation, and becomes the key driving force for the knowledge innovation, exchange and application of the organisation. The implementation of knowledge management will inevitably give rise to organisation of library business process. This reorganisation will also be the process of further combination of library business management with knowledge management.

REBUILDING THE LIBRARY CULTURE BY USING THE THEORY OF KNOWLEDGE MANAGEMENT

Knowledge management will inject new blood into library culture. The main contents include: Mutual trust, open exchange, studying, sharing and developing knowledge operation mechanism of libraries, enjoying the knowledge management process. In a word, to make full use of knowledge, it is necessary to foster a new type of library culture suitable to its requirement. This is a high level requirement of realising technology of knowledge management.

ESSENTIALS OF KNOWLEDGE MANAGEMENT IN DIGITAL ENVIRONMENT

- Service areas are increasingly competitive and the rate of innovation is on the rise:
- Reductions in staffing create a need to replace informal knowledge with formal methods;
- Competitive pressures reduce the size of the work force that holds valuable business knowledge;
- Early retirements and increasing mobility of the work force lead to loss of knowledge;
- Changes in strategic direction may result in the loss of knowledge in a specific area;

- Most of our work is information based;
- Organisations compete on the basis of knowledge;
- Products and services are increasingly complex endowing them with a significant information component;
- The amount of time available to experience and acquire knowledge has diminished;
- Competitive marketplace; and
- Accelerating rate of innovations that need to be assimilated at an even faster rate.

KNOWLEDGE MANAGEMENT SUPPORT TO DIGITAL ENVIRONMENT

- **People Aspects**: By training development, recruitment motivation, retention, organisation, job design, cultural change and encouraging thinking and participation.
- **Process Aspects**: By process innovation, re-engineering both for radical and continuous improvement.
- **Technology Aspects**: By information and decision support systems, knowledge based systems and data mining systems.
- **Knowledge Management in Academic Settings:** It must encompass the community of scholars in a given discipline and must be able to integrate publications, data sets, tools for manipulating such data, connections to databases of pictures and images and much more.
- **Systematic Approaches to Knowledge Management**: It retains the traditional faith in rational analysis of the knowledge problem.

Problems with Conventional Knowledge Management

Some experts are not that great at cooperation. They like to figure things out for themselves and can't be bothered with passing on their knowledge to others. Many such brilliant people also hate the organisation associated with having to document everything they do. Then there is the old saying "knowledge is power". Just as knowledge gives organisation a competitive advantage, individual knowledge workers also know that the uniqueness of their expertise enhances their marketability. Every library professional who works in modern libraries wants to use the techniques of knowledge management to achieve the organisational goal and provide better service to its users but due to some following problems they are not able to use that:

- There is no cooperation between the senior and the junior staff
- Generally the junior staff cannot share their knowledge and ideas
- Every library cannot participate in terms of modern technology
- Lack of communication skills
- Lack of sufficient budget/funds
- Lack of centralised policy for library cess
- Lack of staff training
- Lack of tool and technologies

CONCLUSIONS

Today, we are all in agreement that the world is becoming increasingly as is evidenced by the big role it is playing. Now we can say that knowledge management is an effective approach being adopted by globalised modern libraries. Knowledge management can offer improved global integration, knowledge implications, wide applicability and knowledge sharing (rather than information) etc. There is a growing need for developing KM based supply chains and their demo models to promote the benefits of knowledge sharing and knowledge advancements. We suggest efforts to improve effective KM based supply chain thinking that aims to promote collaborative knowledge sharing for performance improvements in modern libraries. Application of ICT in modern libraries is helpful to obtain the right information at the right time, in the right place and at the right cost, while improving the status of library and reducing the work load of the library professionals.

REFERENCES

Cao, Yi. 1999. The Reorientation of libraries in the knowledge economy era. *Library Work & Research*, 3, pp. 24-26.

Chand, Banka Bihari. 2001. Knowledge management: Tools and techniques for librarians. *Journal of Library and Information Science*, 26, pp. 75-186.

Chen Rui. 1999. Thoughts and technologies of knowledge management. *Information Knowledge in Libraries*, 1, pp. 10-13.

Davenport, Thomas H. The future of knowledge management. http://www.cio.com/archive/010196-davenport-content.html

NACLIN 2003 Proceedings.

Oracle Magazine. 1998. Knowledge management in the information age, May 1998.

Prusak, L. 2001. Where did knowledge management come from? IBM Systems Journal, 4.

Sheng, Xiaoping. 1999. Knowledge management of libraries in the 21st century. *Library Magazine*, 8, pp. 29-32.

Sreekumar, M.G. et.al. eds. 2006. Digital libraries in knowledge management. New Delhi: Ess Ess Publishers.

Wang, Delu. 1999. The collection and processing of knowledge. February 4.

Wang, Yunhua. 1999. Knowledge economy and the development of the library. *Library Work & Research*, 6, pp. 17-19.

www.aiai.ed.ac.uk

www.computerworld.com

www.media-access.com/whatishtml

www.sveiby.com.au

4

Knowledge Management: Opportunities and Challenges

— *Mr. Sambhaji G. Patil*
— *Dr. Shamkant Deshmukh*

ABSTRACT

India has been the germination ground for the Outsourcing business and many global organisations have tapped the country's ample human capital to effectively outsource critical business functions. The variety of processes within each one of the functional domains has triggered off increased interest in capturing best practices, processes and learning from each project that is outsourced. This is aimed at saving time, money and effort while training and setting up similar processes or ramping up an existing process / project. This has led to an increased interest in the Knowledge Management (KM) discipline, which deals with leveraging existing knowledge, capturing tacit elements and preserving knowledge assets for use in the future. Though the initiatives may be implicit and not necessarily be known as Knowledge Management in all organisations, it is present in some form or the other.

Trends and surveys indicate that all organisations have begun to realise the importance of KM. However, most of them face the challenge in collating and assimilating all information and experiences, which may, in the case of some organisations, be spread across geographical boundaries. Even if knowledge is captured, getting people to contribute and utilise stored knowledge assets is a challenge. With these come further challenges, which are precipitated either because people are not aware of the involved technology or are not cognisant of the benefits of such an exercise. Our goal in this paper is to explain the value of a Knowledge Management System and impart an understanding of how such a system can be used to impact customer satisfaction and corporate value.

DEFINITION OF KNOWLEDGE MANAGEMENT

Data are facts, and information is interpreted data. Knowledge is created and organised by flows of information, shaped by their holder. It is tacit or explicit. Tacit knowledge is no verbalised, intuitive, and unarticulated knowledge that people carry in their heads. It is hard to formalise and communicate because it is rooted in skills, experiences, insight, intuition, and judgment, but it can be shared in discussion, storytelling, and personal interactions. It has a technical dimension, which encompasses skills and capabilities referred to as know-how. It has a cognitive dimension, which consists of beliefs, ideals, values, schemata, or mental models. Explicit knowledge is codified knowledge that can be expressed in writing, drawings, or computer programs, for example, and

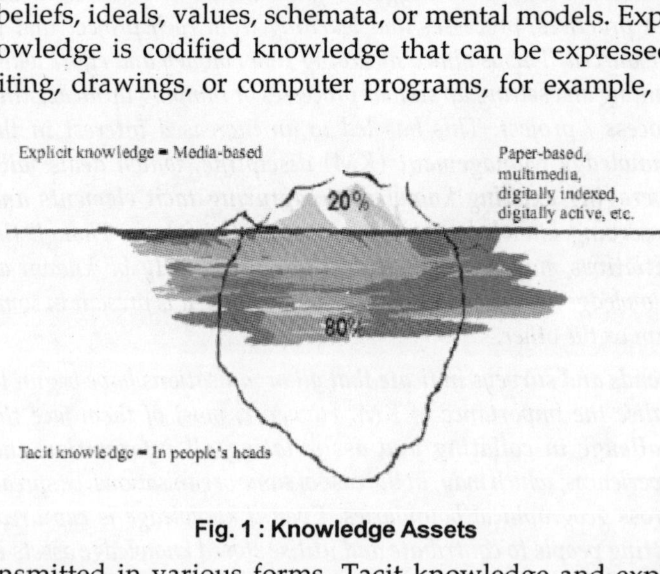

Fig. 1 : Knowledge Assets

transmitted in various forms. Tacit knowledge and explicit knowledge are mutually complementary forms of meaning.

KNOWLEDGE AGENTS

Most models of knowledge management assume four agents of knowledge, namely the individual, the group, the organisation, and the inter-organisational domain. They view knowledge and its creation as a spiral process from the individual to the group, the organisation, and sometimes the inter-organisational domain.

	Individual	Group	Intra-Organisational Domain	Inter-Organisational Domain
Tacit knowledge	Cross-cultural negotiation skills	Team coordination in complex	Corporate culture	Customer's attitude to produces and expecttions
Explicit knowledge	Knowing calculus	Quality circle's documented analysis of its performance	Organisation chart	Supplier's patents and documented practices

Fig. 2 : Knowledge Management Model

MODES OF KNOWLEDGE CREATION

In large organisations, knowledge is created through continuous dialogue on tacit and explicit knowledge via four patterns of interactions: socialisation, externalisation, combination, and internalisation.

Figure 5 frames the process of knowledge creation. Socialisation is the process of creating common tacit knowledge through interactions including observation, imitation, or apprenticeships. Externalisation is the process of articulating tacit knowledge into explicit knowledge by means of metaphors, analogies, or sketches. Combination is the process of assembling new and existing explicit knowledge into systemic knowledge such as a set of specifications for the prototype of a new product. Combination involves combining explicit knowledge through meetings and conversations or using information systems. Internalisation converts explicit knowledge into tacit knowledge. Externalisation converts tacit knowledge into explicit knowledge.

	Tacit knowledge	Explicit knowledge
Tacit knowledge	Socialisation	Externalisation
Explicit knowledge	Internalisation	Combination

Fig. 3 : Modes of Knowledge Creation

KNOWLEDGE MANAGEMENT ARCHITECTURE

The architecture of knowledge management must be strengthened in support of organisation-wide initiatives. Figure 7 shows its four pillars to be leadership, organisation, technology, and learning. Figure 8 exemplifies the need to seek balanced interconnectivity.

Leadership: Leadership develops the strategies necessary to position for success in an environment. Those strategies determine vision and must align knowledge management with business tactics to drive the values of knowledge management throughout the organisation. Focus must be placed on building executive support. Successful implementation of a knowledge management strategy requires champions at or near the top of an organisation.

Organisation: Respect for knowledge must pervade an organisation. Introducing knowledge management requires organisational change, and knowledge management inevitably acts as a catalyst to transform the organisation's culture. The increasing value placed on capable people, rising job complexity, and the universal availability of information on the Internet are fundamental changes contributing to attempts to leverage knowledge management solutions. To begin to change an organisation, knowledge management must be integrated into business processes and connected to changes in organisational culture.

Technology: Knowledge management tools are essential for achieving knowledge management strategies. However, any technical solution must add value to the process and achieve measurable improvements. Properly assessing and defining information technology capabilities is essential, as is identifying and deploying best-of-breed knowledge management tools to match and align with the organisation's requirements. The ten processes that must be built collectively make up full-function knowledge management: capture and store, search and retrieve, send critical information to individuals or groups, structure and navigate, share and collaborate, synthesize profile and personalise, solve or recommend, integrate, and maintain.

Learning: People are responsible for using knowledge management tools in support of organisational performance. Organisational learning must be addressed with approaches such as increasing internal communications, promoting cross-functional teams, and creating a learning community. Learning is an integral part of knowledge management. In this context, learning can be described as the acquisition of knowledge or a skill through study, experience, or instruction. Organisations must recognise that people operate and

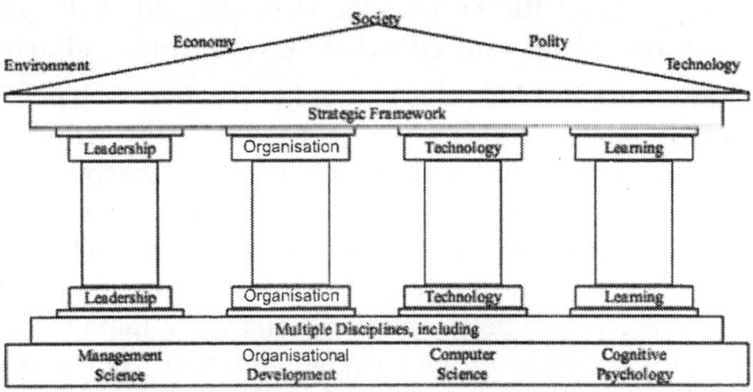

Fig. 4 : Knowledge Management Architecture

communicate through learning that includes the social processes of collaborating, sharing knowledge, and building on each other's ideas. Managers must recognise that knowledge resides in people and that knowledge creation occurs through the process of social interaction.

CORE KNOWLEDGE ACTIVITIES

Knowledge management activities can be described in relation to many different disciplines and approaches but almost all focus on five basic activities: identify, create, store, share, and use. Figure 9 interprets the routine associated with core knowledge activities.

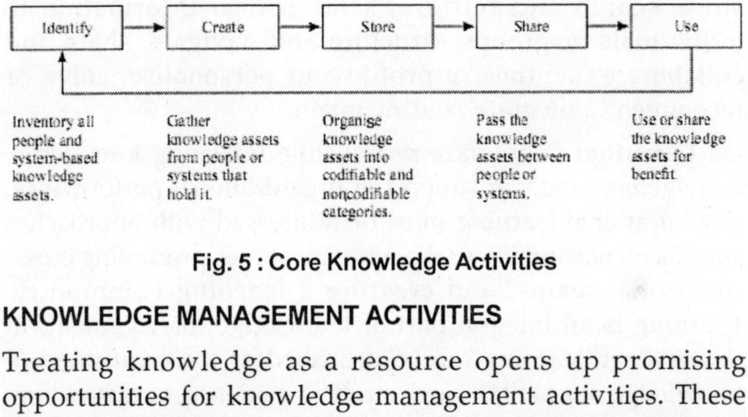

Fig. 5 : Core Knowledge Activities

KNOWLEDGE MANAGEMENT ACTIVITIES

Treating knowledge as a resource opens up promising opportunities for knowledge management activities. These can be split into four categories, each impacting a particular time segment of the knowledge management cycle. They relate to **reviewing, conceptualising, reflecting, and acting.**

Reviewing involves checking what has been achieved in the past and what the current state of affairs is. Conceptualising entails sitting back, trying to grasp the state of knowledge in the organisation, and analysing the strong and weak points of its knowledge architecture. Reflecting calls for directing toward improvements by selecting the optimal plans for correcting bottlenecks and analysing them for risks that might accompany their implementation. Acting is the actual effectuation of the plans selected. Figure 10 delineates the knowledge management cycle and the methods and techniques that drive it.

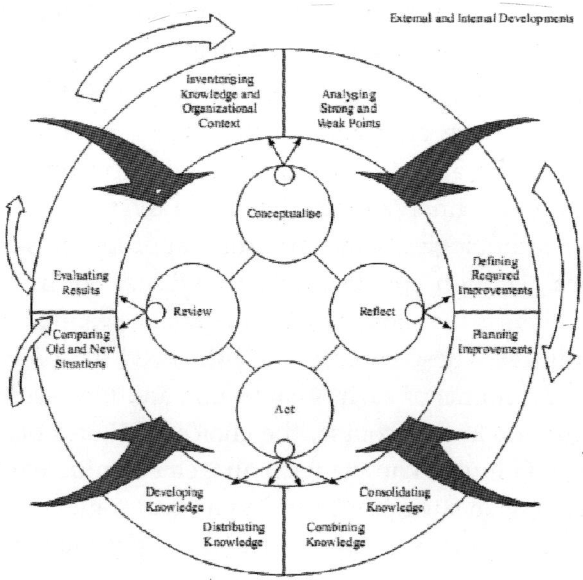

Fig. 4.6 : Knowledge Management Cycle

Most of the time, actions will be one or a combination of generic operations that involve developing knowledge, i.e., buying knowledge, establishing learning programs; distributing knowledge, i.e., channeling knowledge to the points of action, preparing manuals, connecting networks; combining knowledge, i.e., finding synergies, reusing existing knowledge; and consolidating knowledge, i.e., preventing knowledge from disappearing, instituting tutoring programs, establishing knowledge transfer programs.

CULTURAL ROADBLOCKS TO KNOWLEDGE MANAGEMENT SUCCESS

Culture has been characterised as the glue that holds organisations together. It can, for instance, be a critical factor in the execution of strategy. It can play a crucial role in determining the success or failure of operations. At the micro level, there are close relationships between organisational culture, employee satisfaction, and job commitment and turnover. As one might expect, organisational culture plays a pivotal role in knowledge management.

Organisational culture is shaped by many factors, some of which can be changed while others are intractable. Organisations adapt to their external environments by designing responsive structures and systems, adopting relevant technologies, and harvesting appropriate skills and qualities. Though constrained by external environments, organisations make choices that, collectively, eventually define their cultures. These choices are influenced by the mission, values, and norms of each organisation and the assumptions of its leaders. In due course, the choices will also define the success or failure of knowledge management initiatives. Thus, knowledge is inextricably bound to human cognition, and its management occurs within a structured psychological and social context.

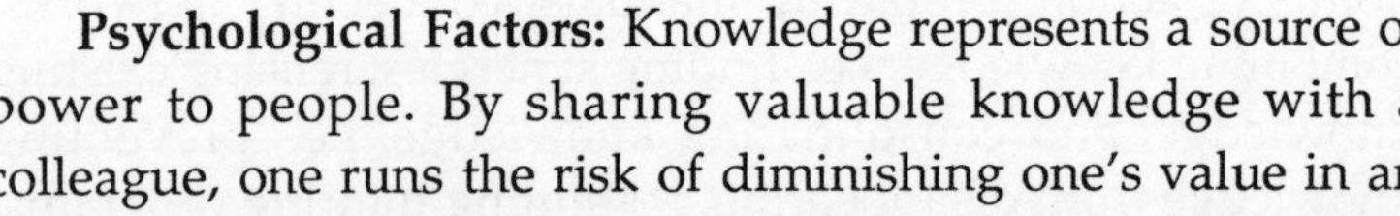

Fig. 7 : Barriers affecting Knowledge Sharing

Psychological Factors: Knowledge represents a source of power to people. By sharing valuable knowledge with a colleague, one runs the risk of diminishing one's value in an organisation; potentially, one is no longer indispensable. There are three conditions under which, as an employee, one will share knowledge: reciprocity, repute, and altruism. One's time and energy are finite and one will more often than not take the time to help a colleague if one is likely to receive valuable knowledge in return, either now or in the future. In addition, it is in one's interest to be viewed as an expert in an organisation; if one does not have a reputation for expertise, one's knowledge cannot represent a source of power. Likewise, before sharing, one needs to be certain that colleagues will acknowledge the source of knowledge and will not claim credit for it. But, in a process akin to self-gratification, there is also the need to talk to others about subjects that one finds fascinating and important.

Following resource-based views of organisations, which identify knowledge as potentially the primary source of sustainable competitive advantage, one can imagine that there are internal markets for knowledge within organisations. Knowledge is exchanged between buyers and sellers, with reciprocity, repute, and altruism functioning as payment mechanisms. Trust, however, is an essential condition to the smooth functioning of such a market. This trust can exist at an individual level, through close working relationships between colleagues, or at group and organisation levels, by the creation of a cultural context that encourages and rewards knowledge sharing and discourages and penalises knowledge hoarding.

Social Factors: Organisational culture, and the social networks that frame it, is the most frequently cited roadblock to knowledge management success. Based on understanding of psychological factors, the onus is on leadership to drive people-focused knowledge management and move from old to new knowledge management paradigms. People are more likely to understand and energetically support an initiative when they observe leadership behaviour that is both credible and supportive.

RISK FACTORS /MAJOR CHALLENGES

(1) Information is crucial to both offensive and defensive competitive moves. Sometimes selective release of information can serve very useful purposes, but often information about plans or intentions can make it a

great deal easier for competitors to formulate strategy. For example, if an impending new product is disclosed in detail, competitors will be able to focus their resources in preparing a response.

(2) Not many Companies have published their ROI on KM projects. Therefore, having a clear vision, objectives, and planning and steady one-step-at-a-time path will help companies achieve good results in KM implementation.

(3) People may not be receptive to share the knowledge. Therefore, creating an environment and policies that enable knowledge sharing culture is important.

(4) Change Management: Resistance to participate and contribute knowledge to the KM database. Because employees might think they may lose their importance in the organisations. One should make it clear that KM will enhance their understanding and help them think differently from the present. KM is to enhance their understanding, not replace it.

GETTING RESULTS FROM KNOWLEDGE MANAGEMENT

First and foremost, knowledge management is about results. Figure 2 describes the typical model of learning progression under which data are analysed to generate information, information is placed in context to produce knowledge, and evaluated knowledge begets wisdom (or informed actions). However, there are limits to looking upstream and concentrating on the supply of knowledge. It can result in the creation of unfocused data and information whereby strategy is blindly driven by technology. It is also helpful to examine the desired results and deduce what knowledge will be required to accomplish them. Figure 13 demonstrates how awareness of the stages in human learning can be exercised to imbed the relationships into forms of meaning to focus on results. It reinforces the idea that knowledge management is primarily a matter of people, process, and outcome orientation.

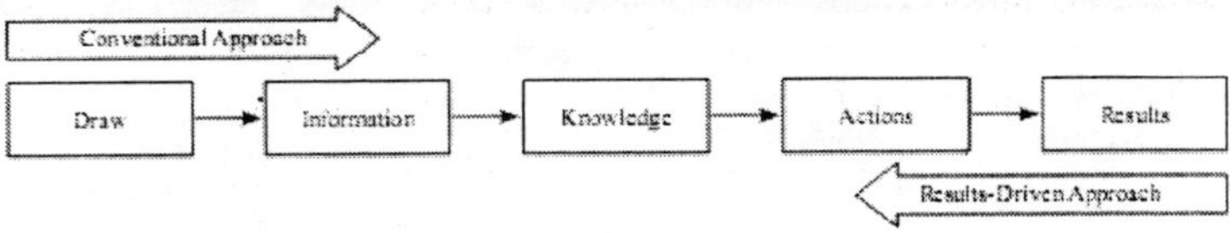

Fig. 8 : A Results-Driven Knowledge Management Model

BUILDING COMMITMENT

As a part of an approach to managing change programs, it is helpful to observe the stages that people live through before committing to a new way of working. From simple awareness, they must first hear, and then understand the change. Based on the actions of leaders and peers, they then opt to support the change and can be seen to act in the desired manner. Commitment is built when they use the new way of working in regular activities and finally own the change in their environment. At every stage, commitment is fragile and invokes active sponsorship from leaders. Figure 14 illustrates the process of committing to change.

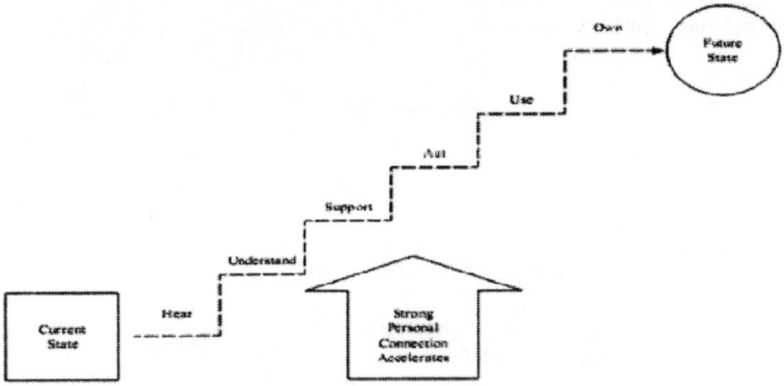

Fig. 9 : A Results-Driven Knowledge Management Model

KNOWLEDGE FRAMEWORK

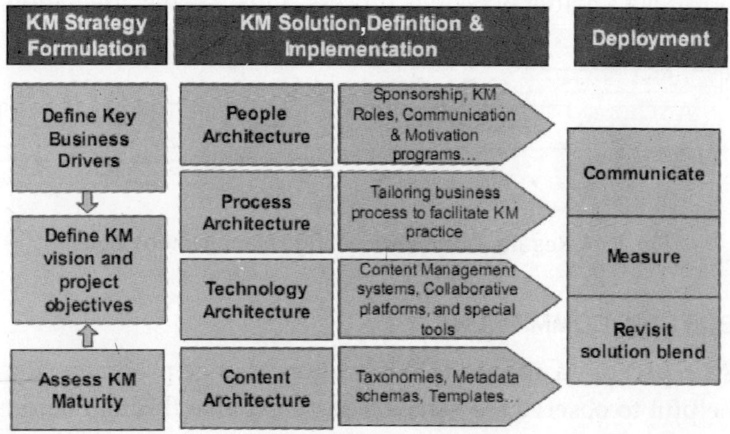

Fig. 10 :

PRODUCT COMPONENT

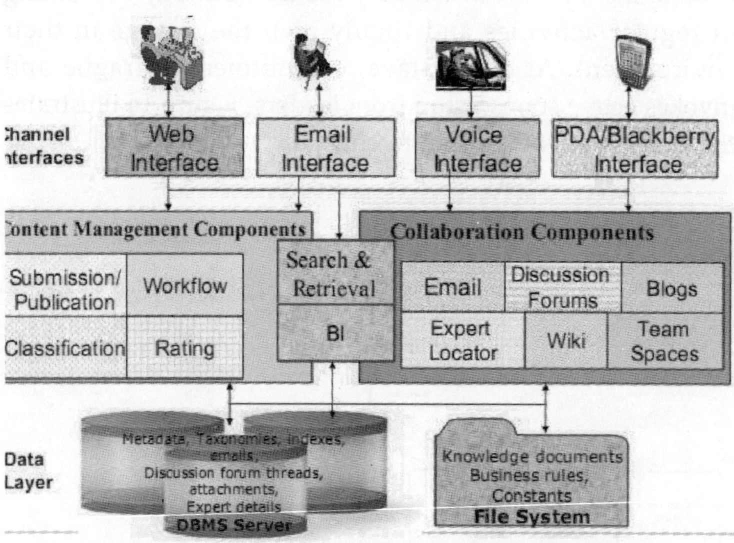

Fig. 11 : A Results-Driven Knowledge Management Model

EXAMPLES OF KNOWLEDGE MANAGEMENT

K Mail: It is a system for facilitating real-time collaboration amongst communities with the aid of automated query-response features.

Advantages of K Mail are:

- It can provide answers to questions that are previously answered in mailing groups.
- It can intelligently act as an intermediary by keeping track of queries and replies.
- It can automatically capture content and build its repository.
- It does not expect a major behavioral change among users.

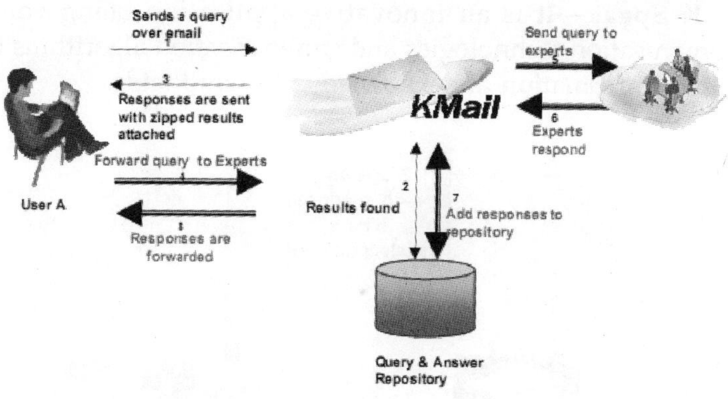

Fig. 12 :

K Agent—It is a proactive, semi intrusive agent which understands user contexts and delivers information and knowledge feeds at desktops.

Advantage of K Agent are:

- Broadcast and Delivery of knowledge available in the intranet universe.
- Proactive, resulting in time and effort saving for end-user.
- K-Feed based on user profile and work context.

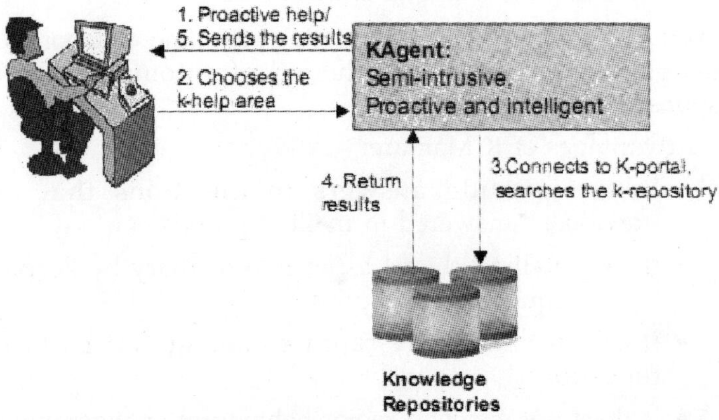

Fig 13:

K Speak—It is an innovative application using voice reorganisation technologies and summarisation algorithms to deliver information and knowledge to handhelds.

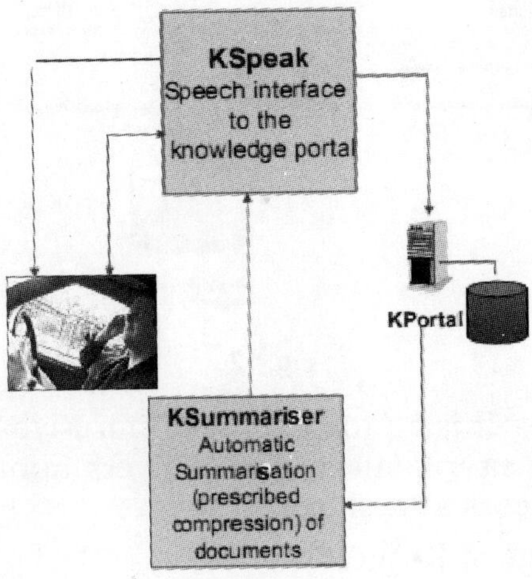

Fig. 14:

Advantage of K speak are:

- Voice recognition
- Text to speech conversion

Advantage of K summarise are:

- Focused summaries of business and technical information
- Condensed text for mobile users
- internally developed extraction-type summarisation algorithm

K Search—It is a tool that the user to search multiple information and knowledge stores from the comfort of MS Office applications.

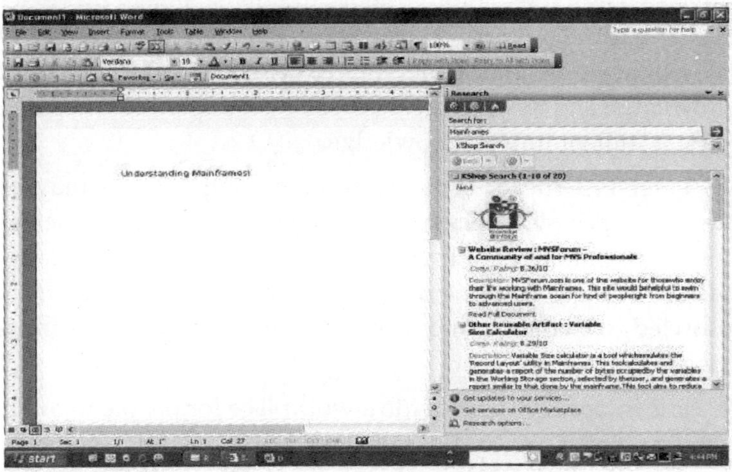

Fig. 15 :

Measuring Return on Investment (ROI)

Parameters on which ROI is measured are:

- No. of unique contributors
- No. of knowledge artifacts
- Artifact download rate (per day)
- No. of experts
- No. of discussion forums
- No. of knowledge areas

CONCLUSION

Knowledge Management is a system of technologies focused upon the delivery of strategically useful knowledge and expertise, the availability of which facilitates effective collaboration and timely decision-making. The strategically literate employee, armed with the best and most up-to-date knowledge, delivered in a timely manner, will produce work that results in more satisfied customers, increased success and corporate value. Knowledge Management or learning organisation can't be built overnight. It's a product of carefully cultivated attitudes, commitments and management processes that are accrued steadily over time. It's the responsibility of the management and leadership to create an environment of knowledge and technology! Because next millennium is going to be a millennium of knowledge.

Peter F. Drucker says "to remain competitive - may be even to survive - businesses will have to convert themselves into organisations of knowledgeable specialists." In Bill Gates' words, "Power comes not from knowledge kept, but from knowledge shared." And value of the knowledge lies in its usage.

It is imperative to provide a workplace for people to think, imagine, innovate and create new solutions and methods. These new additions will add more value to your Knowledge Management database.

According to Michael Porter's competitive strategy, there are five forces that drive the industry competition: Suppliers, Buyers, Potential Entrants, Substitutes and Industry Competitors. Therefore, to survive and compete in global market, organisations need to develop knowledge and intelligence on all the competitive forces of value-chain. Knowledge Management is a symphony of ideas, thoughts, insights, processes, strategies, structures, and best practices - and that is the mantra for competing and winning in the 21st century.

REFERENCES

Bill Gates. Business @ The Speed of Thought, Using a Digital Nervous system; Warner Books, Ed 1999; pp: 200-261.

Michael E. Porter (1998). Competitive Strategy - Techniques for analysing industries and competitors, Free Press, p. 107.

Peter F.Drucker (1998). The coming of the new organisation, Harvard Business Review on Knowledge Management, pp. 1-11.

Prabhakara, C.S. (1999). Unleash the cerebral power, Financial Times By Times Publishing House Limited.

Ray Stata (1989), "Organisational learning - The Key to Management Innovation", Sloan Management Review.

www.kmworld.com , accessed on 24/01/2011.

www.knowledgebusiness.com , accessed on 24/01/2011.

REFERENCES

5

Knowledge Management: The New Challenges for Libraries in Digital Era

— *Surbhi Saini*

ABSTRACT

This paper will briefly discuss about data, information, knowledge and also knowledge management. It will compare the difference between tacit and explicit knowledge and also the type of knowledge management. This paper also throws light on the basic difference between Knowledge Management System (KMS) and Data warehouse. Not only this, it also describes about the knowledge of engineering and quality of knowledge engineer. It also highlights the knowledge management capacity of system. The paper attempts to highlight the knowledge management in the changing context of digital environment as well as current and common challenges in knowledge management and its probable solution while highlighting the role of library and information professionals.

INTRODUCTION

Knowledge is actionable information. Actionable refers to the information of relevant, and nothing but the relevant information being available in the right place at the right time, in right context, and in the right way so alone can make decisions being made every minutes. Knowledge is the key resource in intelligent decision-making, forecasting, designing, planning, diagnosing, analysing, evolutionising and judgment making. It is formed in and shared between individual and collective minds. The term 'knowledge engineering' has emerged recently and is now commonly used to describe the process of knowledge management. The term data, information and knowledge are inter-related. The transition from one to the other is not always clear-cut, these are concepts from a consortium. Data means the individual facets that are found everywhere. Data alone is meaningless. When data is relevant and fulfils a goal, then it becomes information. When data is selected, organised and analysed, then they are known as information. Information also consists of symbols as text or numbers, but here there is some meaning associated with the symbols. Because of this added meaning, the information now has some use or value.

CATEGORIES OF KNOWLEDGE

Knowledge can be classified into two broad categories:

1. **Tacit Knowledge:** Tacit Knowledge is personal, context-specific knowledge that is difficult to formalise, record, or articulate. It is stored in the hands of people. The tacit component is mainly developed through a process of trial and error encountered in practice.

Table 5.1 : Tacit vs Explicit knowledge

S.No.	Objects	Tacit Knowledge	Explicit knowledge
1.	Communication	Unable to communicate and personal	Communicate easily to others
2.	Use	Difficult to use	Easy to use
3.	Accuracy	Not accurate error may be possible	Errorless and systematic
4.	Form	Ideas, experience, and action	Human knowledge is externalised
5.	Availability	It not available in text	It is available in various forms, eg: documents, journals, books

2. **Explicit Knowledge:** Explicit Knowledge is the component of Knowledge that can be codified and transmitted in a systematic and formal language like documents, databases, webs, E-mail, chats, etc.

TYPES OF KNOWLEDGE

Tacit and explicit knowledge interact in these types:

1. **Externalised Knowledge:** It is cognitive dimension that comprises beliefs, ideas, values and mental models.
2. **Multi locational Knowledge:** It might be resident both within the organisation and outside it. Knowledge management encompasses activities surrounding the integration of this knowledge from different sources in different forms and maintaining it.
3. **Migratory knowledge:** It is independent of its owner or creator. As knowledge becomes more and more extensively codified to more increase in documents, databases, picture, illustration, disk, video tapes, E-mail or on a web-page.

Difference between Knowledge Management System (KMS) and Data warehouse

There are few key points which differentiate the Knowledge Management System (KMS) and Data warehouse, are as follows:

Table 5.2 : Knowledge Management System (KMS) and Data warehouse

S.No	Knowledge Management System(KMS)	Data warehouse
1	2	3
1.	It needs to support both informal and formal contents and everything in between	It focuses more on highly structured content.

1	2	3
2.	In the KMS, the information stage is condensation. So, size requirements for pure content are low.	It focuses on clean, structured and organised data; the size of the data warehouse is always large. Raw data is in its native form; so it must be stored in high storage capacity.
3.	The content focus of the KMS is on highly filtered information and on knowledge.	The content focus of the Databases is on scrubbed, raw, clean and organised data.
4.	The live network is imperative for a KMS i.e. trying to draw from resources available in the entire world.	It does not need to be on a live network to function properly.
5.	The computing power needed for a KMS is much higher because of the complex nature of retrieval and classification requests that a KMS must be able to handle successfully	In data warehouse, the computing powers requirement is much lower.

KNOWLEDGE ENGINEERING

Knowledge engineering is software engineering applied to the design of a knowledge-based system.

Knowledge engineering includes:

1. **Knowledge acquisition:** Knowledge acquiring from the experts.
2. **Knowledge representation:** Choosing an appropriate method of representing the knowledge in a symbolic form.
3. Software Design.
4. Implementation in an appropriate computer language.

QUALITY OF THE KNOWLEDGE ENGINEERS

1. Knowledge engineers are expected to have a number of human & interpersonal skills in order to deal with experts, users and also members of the project team.
2. Knowledge engineers should play an integral part as Project Management.
3. Knowledge engineers have to be a knowledge-based system champion, to both user and to management.
4. Knowledge engineers are also expected to be creative, have the ability to think logically and possess enough experience to enable them to solve real problems.
5. Knowledge engineers must possess skills in different areas like management creativity, analysis, verbal skills, human skill, fact finding and knowledge representation techniques.
6. Knowledge engineers have to be able to elicit knowledge from experts through interviews and the application of other techniques, so that they can understand problems as well as real experts do. They must also be able to translate this knowledge into a form in system. This means that a thorugh appreciation is vital, together with an awareness of current trends.

KNOWLEDGE MANAGEMENT SEARCHING CAPACITY OF SYSTEM

There are four types of navigation strategies by which a user can search relevant knowledge from the system as follows:

1. **Meta Searching:** The Meta search function is to minimize the time spent in locating a general category for a piece of potential knowledge within a repository.
2. **Hierarchical Searching:** If the user successfully identifies the broad categories, the user can follow or traverse links within such a structure to efficiently locate the right knowledge element in a timely manner.

3. **Attribute Searching:** Searching by attribute uses a value input by the user. This attribute value is matched against closely related values attached to documents and pointers like skills databases. Those that closely match are returned as the final search result.
4. **Content Searching:** Content Searching is the least efficient search strategies. The user enters an arbitrary search term, keyword or text string. All items that match are returned with a relevant score.

WHY KNOWLEDGE MANAGEMENT IS NEEDED IN DIGITAL ENVIRONMENT

1. Service areas are increasingly competitive and the rate of innovation is rising.
2. Reductions in staffing create a need to replace informal knowledge with formal methods.
3. Competitive pressures reduce the size of the work-force that holds valuable business knowledge.
4. Early retirements and increasing mobility of the work-force lead to loss of knowledge.
5. Changes in strategic direction may result in the loss of knowledge in a specific area.(Ms. Macintosh's observations, 2004)
6. Most of our work is information based. Organisations compete on the basis of knowledge.
7. Products and services are increasingly complex endowing them with a significant information component.
8. The amount of time available to experience and acquire knowledge has diminished.
9. Competitive marketplace.
10. Accelerating rate of innovations that need to be assimilated at an even faster rate (Das 25).

Services in knowledge management information network in India

The Library Information Systems and Services (LISS) in India could play a vital role in the educational, scientific, industrial and over-all socioeconomic development of India. The need for developing these systems and services became more essential because of certain factors such as: Firstly, vast proliferation in the universe of information and knowledge and the resultant document/information explosion in the world and secondly, the varied and complex needs of users for information in Research and Development activities, educational and research programmes and various other fields of human activities. The developments in different types of libraries, documentation/information centers etc provide the more and more library services to the users such as bibliographical services, Selective Dissemination Service (SDI) Current Awareness Service etc. Today popular library and information networks at local level are DELNET and CALIBNET and at the national level such as ENVIS, NISSAT and INFLIBNET and others are being developed. Access through information networks such as NICNET, ERNET, SIRNET, INDONET and several others are being utilised in the LISS in the country for services such as CAS and SDI. INTERNET facilities are being used in many libraries and information systems for the benefit of the users. Management Information System (MIS) can be defined narrowly as the automating of routine and structured tasks to support decision- making. It supports decision-making at all levels of management processes. MIS are made of people, computers, procedures, databases, interactive query facilities. MIS is an integrated information system which provides the information for making decisions regarding the integration of the organisation through the process of management (Sharma 29).

KNOWLEDGE MANAGEMENT SOLUTION IN DIGITAL INFORMATION SYSTEM

1. People Aspects: Training development, recruitment

motivation, retention, organisation, job design, cultural change and encouraging thinking and participation.

2. Process Aspects: Process innovation, re-engineering both for radical and continuous improvement.

3. Technology Aspects: Information and decision support systems, knowledge based systems and data mining systems.

4. Knowledge Management In An Academic Setting: It must encompass the community of scholars in a given discipline and must be able to integrate publications, data sets, tools for manipulating such data, connections to databases of pictures and images and much more.

5. Systematic Approaches To Knowledge Management: It retains the traditional faith in rational analysis of the knowledge problem. The problem can be solved, but new thinking of many kinds requires some basic assumptions:

(a) A resource cannot be managed unless it is modeled, and many aspects of the organisation's knowledge can be modeled as an explicit resource.

(b) Solutions can be found in a variety of disciplines and technologies and traditional methods of analysis can be used to re-examine the nature of knowledge work and to solve the knowledge problem.

(c) Cultural issues are important, but they too must be evaluated systematically. Employees may not have to be "Changed" but policies and work practices must certainly be changed and technology can be applied successfully to business knowledge problems.

(d) Knowledge management has an important management component, but it is not an activity or discipline that belongs exclusively to managers (Das 28).

ROLE OF LIBRARY AND INFORMATION PROFESSIONALS IN THE KNOWLEDGE ENVIRONMENT

Librarians are forced to adapt with the fast growing technology. The tremendous changes has taken place in the library services such as infrastructure, content creation, collection development, user interface, information and knowledge management strategies etc. Digital libraries are the libraries without physical boundaries. Users could access the information at any place, any time, anywhere and in any format. In the changing knowledge environment the expectations from the users have gone up into a high level that the librarians are trying to meet with continuous learning.

The new faces of librarians are as follows:

1. **Information Manager:** The work of librarians is increasingly varied as it expands to keep up with the flow of information. Librarians work with the computer experts to create and manage web sites and intranets for the library. Librarians have to analyse, describe and organise the digital resources such as e-books, scanned images etc for efficient retrieval by the users. The librarian is responsible for managing the information resources, the infrastructure and staff to meet the information needs of the users.
2. **Facilitator/ Trainer:** Librarians also play the role of information facilitators/trainers. Their main business is to enhance the information literacy among the users of an organisation. In addition to training, other activities such as the development of support tools and services would be incorporated to help facilitate the ease with which users can access information more efficiently and effectively.
3. **Network manager:** The library and information professionals must often be network specialists. This includes not only the physical networking technology to connect computers, workstations and peripherals with the central institutional computer , with CD-ROM

and other physical information servers at the institutional level and also the integration of various computer technology within an institutional network. It also includes the networking technology of the Internet Protocol (TCP-IP) and various other aspects of virtual connections with the world-wide network of information sources. In smaller institutions, the librarian may be required to setup or maintain the web server, produce HTML-pages both for the library and the institution itself, and set up Internet services like training sessions, trouble-shooting, and specialised information services like RSS and blogs. A close interaction with organisational network administrators will help to enhance the knowledge and ensures sustained information services to the users.

4. **Frontier of latest technology:** Librarians and information professionals will have to be familiar with key Internet resources and even provide their own content. Library 2.0 has become the buzz word. Librarians have to start to migrate to become Librarian 2.0. This requires them to know several web 2.0 technologies such as RSS (Really Simple Syndication), Wikis, Blogs, Web tools, Technology standards and protocols. Librarians are familiar too with the latest technology and Information resources from the Internet, influence the content of the library's collection policy and require inclusion of electronic journals, current awareness services, document delivery and even ephemeral information resources from the Internet.

5. **Knowledge Manager:** The Librarian will be the person to manage the knowledge of the organisation. The Knowledge Manager means that creating value to the firm by facilitating access to high quality information and by networking people and their ideas together using the technological infrastructure. The emphasis will shift from technical skills in the library to

communication, facilitation, training and management skills such as strategic and marketing management (Soundararajan, Jayakumar, and Somasekharan, 10-12).

CONCLUSION

Project management is the area which is often overlooked by the knowledge engineer. This area covers the organisation of resources including people, time, money and equipment. It requires skills of planning and motivation, knowledge management initiatives that support active and complete transfer of knowledge from successful projects to new ones, could reduce the extent of repeated wasteful expenditure for resources and effort put into solving problems that might have already been solved. Today, the tools and techniques are continuously appearing to improve the way in which knowledge based systems are built. The innovative techniques may help the knowledge engineers, so that they can provide the better services to the user and also save the time of the user, which fulfill the goal of the knowledge management. Libraries, with limited budget and human resources, should utilise the current management structure and technology to implement KM, either bottom-up or top-down. With an effort, KM will help to increase libraries' operational efficiency and later to the ever-increasing needs of our users.

REFERENCES

Di Mattia, S and Oder, N. "Knowledge management: hope, hype or harbinger?" *Library Journals*, 122.15(1997): pp. 33-36

Kumar, P.S.G. *A Student's manual of library and information Science*. Delhi: B.R. Publishing, 2002.

Smith, P. *An introduction to Knowledge engineering*. Thomas Computer Press, 1996.

Tiwans, A. *The Knowledge management tool-kits: Practical Techniques for building a knowledge management system*. New Jersey: Prentice Hall, 2000.

Wiggins,Bob. *Effective Document Management: Unlocking corporate knowledge*. Hampshire: Gower, 2000.

Sharma, Ajay Kumar. *Knowledge management and new generation of libraries information services: A concepts*. 7 March.2011.< http://academic journals.org/IJLIS/PDF/pdf2010/Mar/Kumar.pdf>

Soundararajan, E, Jayakumar, C, and Somasekharan, M. *Role of library and information professionals in the knowledge environment*. 8 March.2011.< http://library.igcar.gov.in/readit2007/conpro/proceedings.pdf>

Das, Subarna K. *Knowledge Management in Digital Management System and the role of library and Information Centres with special reference to India*. 8 March 2011.< http://library.igcar.gov.in/readit2007/conpro/proceedings.pdf>

Knowledge engineering. 7 March.2011. <http://en.wikipedia.org/wiki/Knowledge_engineering>

Schreiber, *Guus, et. al. Knowledge Engineering and Management: The Common KADS Methodology*. 8 March. 2011 <http://mitpress.mit.edu/catalog/item/default.asp?ttype=2&tid=3603>

6

Knowledge Management of Libraries in Digital Environment Era

Mahipal Sharma
Daizy

ABSTRACT

This paper deals with the marketing of library and information services in the global era. It discusses about the marketing concept of today's library and information centers covering various topics such as management of libraries and commitment to customer's satisfaction. It also defines the marketing and its current approach to library and information services at the global level. It also describes customer/user's topic such as customers' priorities, customers' expectations, individuality responsiveness, relationships, quality of services, professional skills and competencies and value added services. The 5 Ps of marketing mix, i.e. product, pricing, place, promotion and person (staff) have been discussed. The marketing should aim at effective library and information services. The "service trinity", i.e. users (customers), the staff (service provider) and information resources and system should be taken care of from the point of view of these services. In the modern age, the library and information services (LIS) are customer (user) oriented. The ultimate objective of the marketing of library and information services should be the dissemination of the right information to the right customer (user) at the right time.

Keywords: *Library services; Information services; Marking; Market; Management*

INTRODUCTION

The interest in marketing has tremendously increased over the past few decades in libraries like other service centers; education, health, transportation, insurance, banking, etc.

For a long time, we (librarians and information professionals) had enjoyed a supplier's market and we lost our interest in working for our customers, and yet we want customers to come back. However, we should always keep in mind that only satisfied customers come back and there are greater chances that a dissatisfied customer will find some other suppliers of information to meet his information need. Hence, there are some unique reasons that require marketing orientation in library and information services and it will help us in:

1. **Management of Libraries**: Due to explosion of information at global level, the more information available in the market, therefore, management of libraries is necessary to meet information needs of the users. "The world in which libraries exist has changed dramatically. It moves faster, relies on technology and competes more intensely."
2. **Commitment to Customer Satisfaction**: In particular to library services area, the users are fund providers, patrons, employees, etc. As such, satisfaction of the customer is of primary concern in the marketing process and the entire ethos and shared values of the organisation owe the responsibility of satisfying the customer. The library and information center is not a profit-oriented organisation in marketing.
3. **Understanding Customers**: When we talk about customers, we have some very fundamental questions to ask, questions that affect any and everything else we do. Such questions include: Who are the customers? Whom are we trying to serve? What is the

interest area? What can we provide to serve these interests? What are the conditions for offering information services and products? How well do we communicate with our users and how they communicate their needs to us? There is a common understanding that he/she who knows better about the library then he/she knows better about its resources, facilities, services, and products particularly in the information era. The most important role of marketing in library and information centre is to find information/products for the customers, not customers for the information/products.

4. **Libraries need to grow**: According to Ranganathan's 5th law *"Library is a growing organism"*. Due to global information explosion, more information comes every second and today's information is old very fast for tomorrow. Libraries continue to face continuing changes in the environment strategies and outcomes. Good marketing efforts take care of all resources and how it can be done in an efficient way.
5. **Improving our Image**: In today's business environment, "Librarians who take marketing seriously will earn *"street creed"* in their organisation. This will be benefited to them in career terms, but will also help to accelerate the death of the old buddy-duddy image and herald the arrival of the focused, business-like, customer led librarian" A good reputation may involve cordial relations with the community, good facilities, high service standard, good discipline, a well-qualified staff and good results. As such, marketing efforts can help us in improving our image through improved services.

MARKETING – MEANING

There is a new meaning of marketing in library and information sector. There is still considerable misunderstanding in most of the libraries and information sectors as to what constitutes effective marketing. To some, it is still primarily equated with selling and the pursuit of sales, rather than customer satisfaction. Many libraries are still reluctant to make the change necessary to focus on the marketplace, even when the need for more active marketing is generally agreed. As such, the developing marketing initiatives of libraries and understanding of the total marketing concept among library and information professionals need some basic marketing frameworks that they have taken so far.

Broadly, the concept of marketing is depicted as follows:

6. Marketing as a set of techniques: Generally, it is viewed as a set of techniques involving a number of processes. An organisation that embraces the marketing concept tries to provide products and satisfy customer needs through a coordinated set of activities and that also allows the organisation to achieve its goals' in such approach marketing, planning to work together. The key activities of such concept are:

- An assessment of the customers are, the services they want and the benefits they are looking for.
- Analysis of the librarys' strength, weakness, opportunities and the services it provides.
- Assessment of the strengths and weaknesses of competition.
- Understanding what the real differences are between the library and the competition.
- A practical action plan which draws on this understanding of the market place and sets out measurable actions to achieve the current objective.

7. Marketing as a philosophy: It was less than three decades ago that marketing came into the field of library and information services as thinking and orienting library and information services business/library and information services in marketing term. Integration of marketing into library philosophy is helpful in reinforcing and reiterating the basic values of the profession in a changing environment. In one sense, it implies commitment to shared professional beliefs. The most widely agreed beliefs are about library services *"to provide the right information to the right user at the right time"*. This involves reducing barriers to access and use information and empowering users in making use of their own, particularly with the use of modern technologies.

Marketing help us the following aims of the library and information services:

- A focus on the users own purpose and on helping the individual user to articulate these at every level.
- A focus on the users, giving them an environment in which they can sit, study, work and on giving them an experience of good service.
- A belief that every individual user has different needs, requirements and expectations when he/she visits/approaches the library.
- A commitment to help the user in acquiring skills in obtaining the information from various sources and means.

Marketing should first of all, be an attitude of mind. This is the foundation of successful marketing.

8. **Marketing as an Approach**: There are exploited symbolic dimensions to human and physical resources while serving the user. In this approach everything, human skills, service attitude and information resources are put more closely to serve the customers' information needs.

According to Ranganathan, *"service trinity"* has great relevance with such approach in the case of libraries. Ranganathan considers:

1. Users (customers)
2. The staff (service providers)
3. The information resources and system (different types of material, systems, procedures, etc.) have greater relationship with each other in library and information services.

DEFINITION OF MARKETING

Let us try to search answers to the following questions. What is marketing? What does it mean? Why is it so important in the current scenario? How does marketing relate to information service?

Kotler (1994), a professor of marketing, adopted the following definition of marketing:

> "Marketing is the analysis, planning, implementation and control of carefully formulated programs designed to bring about voluntary exchanges of values with target markets for the purpose of achieving organisational objectives. It relies heavily on designing the organisation's offering in terms of the target market's needs and desires and as using effective pricing, communication, and distribution to inform, motivate and serve the markets."

There are 6 major points to be emphasized in the above definition:

1. Marketing is a managerial process involving analysis, planning, implementation and control.
2. Marketing is concerned with carefully formulated programmes, not random actions designed to achieve the desired responses.
3. Marketing seeks to bring about voluntary exchange.
4. Marketing selects target markets and does not seek to be all people.
5. Marketing is directly correlated to the achievement of organisational objectives.

6. Marketing place emphasis on the target market's (consumer's) needs and desire rather than on the producer's preferences.

CUSTOMERS– TOP PRIORITY

The new customers do not know about library rules and regulations, therefore it is the duty of library staff to give orientation for maximum utility of library. They do not care about rules and ways of doing business. They care to adapt its products and services to fit their problems. This represents the evolution of marketing to the customer-driven. We must always remember the following points:

- Customers are the most important people to be served in library and information centers.
- They are not dependent on the library; rather the library depends on them.
- They are not just from outsiders but part of the library.
- They are not just statistics, but also they are human beings.
- They are the people who bring their wants and needs and we are there to meet their information needs exceedingly.

CUSTOMERS – EXPECTATION

Library and information professionals should strive hard to gain a far vision of 'who our customers are', 'what they want', and 'what are their social characters, values, desires, and aspiration'. The advancement of information and communication technologies (ICTs) has enabled education and technology in self-help and do-it-yourself activities in libraries. The 21st century customer will place high value on self-reliance, adaptability and survival under difficult conditions and the ability to do things of his/her own.

INDIVIDUALITY

The new generation customer is a global citizen who is more demanding and individualistic, seeking change and is value conscious. He/she shares a consistent set of tastes, preferences and has a growing commonality of his or her task across the globe.

RESPONSIVENESS

It is the willingness to help customers and to provide prompt service. This dimension emphasises attentiveness and promptness in dealing with customers' requests, complaints and queries. Responsiveness is demonstrated in terms of accessible employees, least waiting time and attention to problems.

RELATIONSHIP

To measure customer satisfaction, the relationship between the customer and the library must be understood. A customer relationship comprises of a hierarchy of encounters through facilities, resources, services and service providers.

To serve the customer, the library should serve as host, as advocated by (Ranganathan, 1961), considers that like a host, the library should provide full hospitality to a user – as a supreme guest at the premises of the library. According to Ranganathan (1961):

- Give service with full attention and sincerity.
- Give him/her service to the best capacity at your command.
- Give him/her service in all modesty and in full freedom from any touch of prestige or ego.
- Give him/her service in full measure; there should not be any offence to the laws of library science.
- Acquire the best knowledge and information for giving him/her your best service. We cannot retain customer unless given prompt and relevant service in a personal way. He/she is human; and human

personality alone can keep good humor, make the appreciation of the value of books which blossom in him/her and transform him/her into a willing beneficiary of the library.

QUALITY SERVICES

The user of the service is the ultimate judge of the quality. He/she weighs the value he/she receives from a service organisation against the time spent and/or the efforts involved besides the monetary burden in getting the desired service and thus decides the quality. Users seldom define the quality of the library and its services in terms of stock size, annual budget, physical facilities, staff and the mere number of services. No doubt, these are some of the essential criteria for providing quality services; it benefits the service itself that users look for. Quality service in part depends on how well various elements function together in a service system (see Figure 1). These elements include the people who perform the specific service in the service chain, the equipment that supports these performances and the physical environment in which the services are provided. The management concept achieving service excellence is termed as Total Quality Management. It is a customer need driven management process. It emphasizes on identifying customer's needs expressed in customer's own words and then linking customers' perceived quality into internal processes and measuring the impact of quality measurement on the market place.

RELATIONSHIP WITH USERS

The relationship with users mainly depends upon the commitment of the organisation and its people towards customers, intimacy between them, and the trust of customers for the products and services. The relationship is fairly a complex issue for library and information services (LIS) managers, for them it is a strategic issue, but for customers it is just a communication process. LIS managers need to break the ice and take responsibility to initiate, nurture, and forge sustainable relationship with customers offering services in a more satisfying manner to succeed in the new millennium.

PROFESSIONAL SKILLS AND COMPETENCIES

Libraries do not require a good marketing person to run marketing operations, like a business firm, that person would immediately hire an advertising agency, change the ad campaigning, redesign company logo, design the brochures, train the sales force, retain a high powered public relation firm and alter or otherwise reposition the company's complete image. On the contrary, marketing is nothing but a way of doing business, which does not require good marketing persons, but certain skills or attributes, which are in no manner different from other service organisation (1994). Marketing is:

- a belief in service and trying to achieve customer's satisfaction;
- a clear understanding of their organisation's overall aims and objectives;
- an ability to assemble and interpret information for the benefit of the customer;
- good communication skills, both oral and written;
- enthusiasm and commitment; and
- Ability to take criticism, not always constructive.

These attributes are very much desired for the successful information service providers. Thus, skills, attitude and judgment of the service providers are important while marketing in library and information services.

VALUE ADDED SERVICES

Marketing today embraces an integrated value proposition. This in effect, would mean that with making a decision about using a particular service or evaluating a marketing relationship, a customer not only looks at the product or value related to it, but He/she also evaluates the process, the total transaction cost. To a customer, value is the benefits received from the burden endured. Benefits may be product quality, personal service and convenience. Cost includes price and non-monetary cost as time, energy and efforts. In the process He/she interacts with the people, technology, methods, environment and the materials used to serve the customers in the library. In the marketing oriented library, the process depends on the customer preferences and cues to their requirements. Even the customers are an important partner to the process and in libraries most of the time, they put forward their views to overcome their problems and work with the staff to solve them.

By simply shedding long standing stereotypes, librarians have been able to take the 5P's of the traditional external marketing mix and use them to paint a more accessible service-oriented picture of library offerings for their customers. By staff and security devices, a treasure house where the borrower is a nuisance or a potential thief. The new-age library ought to be a true service organisation, a group of professionals who quickly identify in the vast ocean of knowledge the kind of information that different customers need and help them access it with the least waste of time and effort. A library that can survive and thrive in the Internet age is a knowledge-based social structure.

MARKETING INFORMATION SERVICES GLOBALLY

There have been so many new methodologies for promoting information services of a library. Some are mentioned below:

OPAC – An online public access Catalogue (OPAC) is a computerised online catalogue of the materials held in a library, or library system. The user in the library can search the bibliographic database and find specific information online. The search facility also apprises the user about the availability of each item for circulation, including current status of individual copies of a title and reserve status. The scope of these services includes :

Online Catalogues: The catalogues of title, author, subject, classified, KWIC Index, Publisher, etc are available online.

Current Serials: To provide online information holdings of current serials including recent issues received in library.

Recent Additions: To make available new additions to the library, to the users.

Multiple databases: To support the definition of multiple databases based on types of documents for searching in OPAC.

Web OPAC – Web OPAC is a web based search platform, developed with advanced information technologies for serving information to the users at the finger tips, regardless of physical location whether the member is in the library or at a remote location. It brings the library online try presenting bibliographic data in a read only manner. Following are some of the library services that can be made available through web OPAC.

- Library catalogue
- Search facility on entire database.
- New Arrivals, current awareness services
- Selective dissemination of information
- Journals
- Online Journals
- Latest issue of Journals
- Place reservation

Library Blogs: Blog is website, usually maintained by an individual, contains chronologically the brief entries of commentary, descriptions of events, or other materials like audio, video graphics, etc. Blogs can be very effective tools for reaching online audiences.

DISTRIBUTORS OF INFORMATION

Information generation/production is a continuous process. On the other hand, the information gets accumulated at such a fast pace that the extraction of relevant information becomes difficult for the users to go through all of them. For this, proper distribution channels are necessary to fulfill the specific needs of the users. Traditionally, libraries and information centers functioned as the facilitators. Some of the facilitators are:

1. Documentation and Information Centers: The purpose of these centers is to accelerate the information retrieval and dissemination process, e.g., National Institute of Science, Communication and Information Resources (NISCAIR), New Delhi and National Social Science Documentation Centre (NASSDOC), New Delhi, etc.
2. Information Analysis Centre: It is a type of organisation whose key activities are analysis, interpretation, synthesis, evaluation and repackaging of information or numerical data.
3. Referral Centers: This function as a sort of 'information desk', which do not provide inquires directly with the information they need, but suggest sources (organisations or individuals) likely to satisfy the clients.

The purpose of marketing information services is to make such services more responsive to user needs and wants to improve people's satisfaction.

CONCLUSION

The modern library is now generally called an *information market* and the library user is a *consumer of information. Information* is a vital resource for research and development of any nation. Marketing is essential in making the proper planning, designing and use of such services and products for the better and optimal use of information. The library should give priority to provide excellent customer service enhancing its image as *information provider* in the information era. The library and information services should be user (customer) oriented in order to satisfy their *information needs* effectively. Marketing of library and information services includes customer (users) priorities, expectations, individuality, responsiveness, relationship, quality of services, professional skills and competencies, value-added services, etc. The ultimate aim of marketing here is *to provide the right information to the right user at the right time.*

REFERENCES

Ashcroft, L. (2002). The marketing and management of electronic journals in academic libraries: A need for change. *Education and research for marketing and quality management in libraries.* (Savard, R., ed). Munich, K. G Saur, pp. 173-89.

Bateson, J.E.G. (1995). *Managing services marketing: Texts and readings* (3rd edition). Dryden Press.

Besant, L. (2002). Relationship marketing of services-perspectives from 1983 and 2000. *Journal of Relationship Marketing*, 1, pp. 59-77.

Booms, B.H., & Bitner, M.J. (1981). Marketing strategies and organisation structures for service firms. *Marketing of services.* American Marketing Association.

Clague, L. (1991). Charging for information services: Is there a best way for internal and exteral cost recoveries? I. *New Zealand Libraries*, 46 (9), pp. 12-14.

Coote, Helen (1994). *How to market your library service effectively.* The Aslib Know How Series, Ed. S.P. Webb, The Association for Information Management, 1994.

Dibb, S., Simkin, L., Pride, W.M., & Ferrell, O.C. (1994). *Marketing Concepts and Strategies*, 2nd European edition. Boston and London: Houghton Mifflin.

Hernon, P., & Dugan, R. (2002). *An action plan for outcomes assessment in your library.* Chicago: American Library Association.

Hoadley, I.B. (1995). Customer service? Not really. *College and Research Libraries News*, 56(3), pp. 175-76.

Jambhekar, A., et al. (Eds.) (1995). *Marketing of information products and services.* Ahmedabad: Indian Institute of Management.

Keiser, B.E., & Galvin, C.K. (1995). *Marketing library services: A nuts-and-bolts approach.* The Hague: FID.

Kotler, P. (1994). *Marketing management: Analysis, planning, implementation, and control.* 8th ed. New Jersey, Englewood Cliffs: Prentice-Hall.

Kotler, P. (1995). *Marketing for nonprofit organisations* (2nd ed.). New Delhi: Prentice-Hall of India.

Kotler, P. (1988). *Marketing management: Analysis, planning, implementation, and control* (6th edition). New Jersey, Englewood Cliffs: Prentice-Hall.

Kotler, P., & Armsrong, G. (1999). *Principles of marketing* (8th edition). Upper Saddle River, New Jersey: Prentice-Hall.

Kuronen, T., & Pekkarinen, P. (1996). Ranganathan's five laws of library science revisited: The challenge of the virtual library. *Herald of Library Science*, 35 (1-2), pp. 3-17.

Levitt, T. (1983). The globalisation of markets. *Harvard Business Review*, 61(3), pp. 92-102.

Morgan, E.L. (1998). Marketing future libraries. *Computers in libraries*, 18 (8), pp. 50-51.

7

E-resources in Library Management: An Overview

— *Rachana*

INTRODUCTION

The need for e-learning and electronic information resource and various advantages of e-learning and electronic resource. It further discusses that can be rendered through electronic resource. E- Resource is becoming more popular, easy to use and reliable. Searching relevant information in a time frame is significant for both the researchers and the information professionals. Resource are getting popularity due to its easy and fast accessibility. This paper focuses on various forms of electronic resource, and also creating awareness regarding the utility of resource

WHAT ARE E-RESOURCES?

Electronic resources are sources, which provide on time information in electronics format, the information is available at any time as per need of users. Electronic resources are enabled by technical capability to create, search, and use enormous amount of information. Electronic Resources are e-book, e-journals, e-newspaper, database, bibliographic database etc.

FEATURES OF E-RESOURCE

- Multi-access
- Speed
- Functionality

- Content
- Re-use
- Management
- Storage
- Timeliness

ADVANTAGES OF E-RESOURCE

Information access can be made without wasting any time.\ Desired information can be retrieved within few minutes at the learning desk.

Vast collection of information may be stored in a small place. Resource sharing at the desired level among the libraries and information centers. Copy with open mouth problem of space and budget etc. in libraries and information centers etc.

TYPES OF E-RESOURCES

Electronics resource include electronics book, electronics journals, electronics database, CD-ROMs, Internet resource resources etc. The different types of e-resource are described as follows:

E-JOURNALS

E-journals are the simple electronics representation of a journal. The library at the university of **Glasgow** provides the following definition.

> "Any Journal that is available over the internet can be called an electronic journal. In case, not. Some electronics journals (e–journals) are freely available; other has changing mechanism of different types. Established publishers issue some"
>
> - other are products from an individual academic's office. As by means of relevance of e-journals, the quality and relevance of e-journals can vary considerably. In other words, e-journals are one, which is available electronically to be used with the

help of computer and other communication technologies. Journals available on internet are also referred to as Internet journals are networked journals. They include newsletters, magazines, periodicals and discussion lists. The Full Text e-resource is:

- ACM Digital Library

  ASCE Journals

  ASME Journals

  IEL online

  Springer's Link

  ASTP (Applied Science and Technology Plus)

Electronics journals can be grouped under the following three broad categories.

(i) **Online Journals:** These are paid journals that are available on 'pay-as-you-go or cost –per-access based via online database, such as EBSCO information services. The user or the organisation has to bear the cost of subscription.

(ii) **CD-ROMs:** These are journals published on CD-ROM, may be bibliographical or full-text. They vary in frequency and are distributed along with search software to access and print.

(iii) **Networked e-journals:** Networked e-journals are electronic available over networks, such as Internet or many other commercial networks. Many of the networked e-journals are based on mailing list software, such as listserv, majordomo etc. and are distributed in one of the following two ways.

The central computer holds a list of subscribers and sends them content pages and abstracts by e-mail when a new issue is published. Subscribers can then retrieve articles through file transfer (FTP) and have these delivered to their mailboxes.

Subscribers are automatically sent the full-text of each issue by e-mail.

E-Books

An e book is an electronic representation of a book, usually a parallel publication of a print copy, but occasionally born digital.

The new concise oxford English dictionary (2001) defines e-book as: 'an electronic version of a printed book which can be read for this purpose.'

According to **Ormes** (2009)

"The term e-book is used specifically to describe a text, which requires the use of e-book software or hardware to read."

The term book includes here audio, video, electronic books or e-books. E-books are made on cassette, compact disc, floppy disc, CD-ROM, or downloadable program.

Electronic books are portable computerised devices that allow readers to download text and then read and mark it. E-Book is also referred as paperless book read with a specially designed device such as personal digital assistant (PAD), or a desktop or laptop computer. There are two types of e-books.

- Those, which represent an e-version of a whole book (Print).
- Those, which are effectively database of linked materials.

E- DATABASES

Electronic database are the organised set of data stored in a computer and can be searched automatically. Database contains usable raw data or description of the sources where data can be found. Database generally refers to machine readable file or bibliography records but may be used more specifically to refer to a shared collection of structured data managed by a set of special software.

According to Jennifer Rowley, "Database that might be available to information users in the public arena, and which might be accessed either remotely via an online search service or more locally on CD-ROM can be categorised as follows."

- Bibliographic database: In bibliographic database, all those database are counted in which the information related with documents such as books, periodicals, encyclopedias etc. is contained and users use them for the access of information.
- Full text database: This category contains not only full text of the documents but tells source also; hence one can get primary information along with the full.
- Numeric Database: Numeric Database are those that contain numeric, statistical or survey type information to give answers of numeric queries.

CD-ROM

Today CD-ROM has become a popular e-media for archival, retrieval and distribution of information. Now every possible title on commercial and technology products, entertainment, database, education and business applications are available on CD-ROMs .The rising demand for multimedia applications, due to easy accessibility of PCs is also fuelling its growth.

FEATURES OF CD-ROMS

The Success of CD/DVD-ROMs over traditional removable media such as floppy disk, tapes can be attributed to the following key factors:

- Cross-Platform standard
- Capacity
- Durability
- Portability
- Inexpensive
- Random access

DVDS

DVD-digital video disc or Digital Versatile disc for the computer industry is the next generation to compact Disc in optical disc storage technology. A DVD looks just like a CD (Both 120 MM. Diameter), but has higher data storage capacity like a CD data is recorded on DVD in a spiral trail of tiny pits, and the discs are read using beam. The larger capacity of DVD is archived by making the pits smaller and spiral tighter, and by recording the data in as many as four layers, two on each side of the disc.

The main feature of DVD is the compression technology and storing data on the multi-layer sides. A single-sided layer DVD holds 4.7 GB and two-sided layers DVD can hold 8.5 GB of data.

INTERNET RESOURCES

Internet has been defined as a **"networks of networks".** It opened new vistas for information seekers during 1990. During the period, the internet transformed into a widespread, popular and commercial means of communication, accessible by a large number of people, organisation and libraries of all kinds. Individuals/institutions on Internet as key information server tool, the World Wide Web (**WWW**), set up most amount of Information. Many journals, reports papers and reference sources are available free on Internet and they even constitute many of the sites on the web.

INDEST

The Ministry of Human Resource Development (**MHRD**) has set up the "Indian National Digital Library in Engineering Science and Technology (**INDEST**) Consortium" on the recommendation made by export Group appointed by the minister under the chairmanship of Prof. N. Balakrishnan.

The ministry provides funds required for subscription to electronic resource for (47) Institutions including **IISc., IITs., NITs., IIMs.** And a few other centrally funded Government institutions through the consortium headquarters set up at the IIT Delhi. Government or Government added engineering colleges and technical deportment of universities have joined the consortium, as an open-ended proposition, welcomes other institutions to join it on their own for sharing benefits it offers in terms of highly discommended rates of subscription and better terms of agreement with the publishers. All electronic resources being subscribed are available from the publisher's website. The consortium has an active mailing list, a web site hosted at the IIT Delhi.

E-Resource INDEST-AICTE Consortium

The INDEST-AICTE Consortium subscribes the following resources for various categories of institutions. All electronic resources subscribed are available from the publisher's web site. Local hosting of resource has been considered at this stage: Full –Text E-Resource

UGC-INFONET

The UGC-Infonet Digital Library Consortium was formally launched in December, 2003 by Honorable **Dr. A. P. J. Abdul Kalam,** the then President of India soon after providing the Internet connectivity to the universities in the year 2003 under the UGC Infonet programme. The Consortium proved to be a recipe to university libraries which have been discontinuing subscription of scholarly journals because of "Serials Crisis". The term "serials crisis" refers to exponential and continuing increase in subscription cost of scholarly journals. The crisis is a result of rise in cost of journals much faster than the rate of inflation, increase in number of journals and the paucity of funds available to the libraries.

The Consortium provides current as well as archival access to more than 5000 core and peer-reviewed journals and nine bibliographic databases from 23 publishers and aggregators in different disciplines. The programme has been implemented in phased manner. In the first phase that began in 2004, access to e-resources was provided to 50 universities who had Internet connectivity under the **UGC-Infonet** Connectivity programme of the UGC. In the second phase, 50 more universities were added to the programme in the year 2005. So far **153** Universities out of **171** that come under the purview of **UGC** have been provided differential access to subscribed e-resources. These e-resources cover almost all subject disciplines including arts, humanities, social sciences, physical sciences, chemical sciences, life sciences, computer sciences, mathematics and statistics, etc. The programme is wholly funded by the UGC and executed by the INFLIBNET (Information and Library Network) Centre, Ahmedabad.

UGC-INFO NET DIGITAL LIBRARY CONSORTIUM

The UGC Infonet Digital Library Consortium subscribes to the following resources for its member institutions.

FULL-TEXT E-RESOURCES

- American Chemical Society http://www.pubs.acs.org/
- American Institute of Physics http://scittation.aip.org/publications/mybrowsepub.jsp#ASP
- Annual Reviews http://arjournals.annualreviews.org/
- Blackwell Publishing http://www3interscience.wiley.com
- Cambridge University Press http://journal.combridge.org
- Oxford University Press http://www.oxfordjournals.org
- Royal Society of Chemical http://www.rsc.org/publishing/journals

OPEN ACCESS RESOURCE

- About Open Assess Oaersources.html
- Open Access E-Journals Oaeresources.html#ejournals
- IRs@ member Institutions Oaeresources.html#IRs
- Open Access Directories Oasersources.html#directories

CONCLUSION

Library have faced and surmounted the challenges post by new formats of materials, from print to microfilms, audio-visual materials, CD-ROMs, computer software, and machine-readable data files. Beginning in the mid 1990s, electronic journal's access through the internet has made librarianship more challenging. Even though major issues inherent in electronic access management have been raised, not all have been resolved. Librarians are continuing to seek way to make access for users as easy as possible. While they are confused with the challenging aspect of hunting for creative solutions,

REFERENCES

ARMSTRONG (E.Alan) al. Electronic resource accessed; Issues and resolutions in two academic libraries. Emerald accessed from Internet through www.du.ac.in. on 12 April 2007.

http//www.libsuite.com/webopac.htm.

http://inflibnet.ac.in/Accessed on 10th Sept.2009.

Mounissamy (P) Kaliammal (A) amd RANI .users attitude towards electronic journals.IASLIC Bulletin.50, 2; 2005; pp. 91-95.

Ramvir Singh and Kulshreshitha,S. K. Electronic information resource: An Introduction.op.cit.p-45.

Ramvir singh and kulshreshitha,S.K. (2005) Journal of library and information technology.1,2; pp. 42-45.

Singh, S.P. and Krishna Kumar, Special libraries in electronic environment. op cit. pp. 113-19.

Thapa et al(2002).E-Publishing: Beginning of a new era of e-journals.IASLIC Bulletin.47,4; pp. 216-21.

Vijay Kumar and Das C.D. (2000).Rom to DVD-Rom: A new era in electronic publishing of database and multimedia reference source. IASLIC Bulletin.45, 2; pp. 49-54.

8

Total Quality Management in Libraries

— *Manju Devi*

ABSTRACT

In this paper evolution of quality management can be traced back to the days of the industrial revolution. Total quality management (TQM) is the integration of all efforts of the organisation towards customer satisfaction at economical levels and products. This paper discusses the significance of TQM, its benefits and barriers. Thereafter the paper concludes with the potential challenges.

Keywords: *Quality management, customer satisfaction.*

INTRODUCTION

All organisation, big or small, has the four common elements: Purpose – this is what drives the organisation. It could consist of one or more of the followings: vision and mission, commercial considerations and societal objectives. People – it is the people at various levels who convert the vision of an organisation into reality. People operate at various levels: conceptual, directional, and functional. Processes – these are the means available to "people" to convert thought into action. They could be: intellectual, technological and financial.

Products – these are the end results of effort put in by the people in an organisation. They could be concepts, physical entities and services. The evolution of quality management and can be traced back to the days of industrial revolution. Initially, all "productions" were limited in scale, and complexity. The responsibility of ensuring the quality of the product was vested with the producer. With workers beginning to become more conscious of their rights and privileges, the trade unions movement began to gather strength. It, therefore, becomes imperative for "management" to learn how to relate with the representatives of trade unions, giving rise to the need of "industrial relations". The latter half of the twentieth century saw a paradigm shift in the approach of enterprises towards quality, while inspection merely separated products into "acceptable" and "not acceptable"; quality Assurance provided evidence that quality was indeed being controlled.

NEED OF TOTAL QUALITY MANAGEMENT (TQM)

The following are some of the reasons for which TQM is necessary to any organisation, whether profit oriented or non-profit oriented, like libraries:

- Increasing competition
- Demanding customer
- Reduction of wastes inherent in the system
- Change of perceptions of stakeholders
- Empower employees
- Mere survival

OBJECTIVES OF TOTAL QUALITY MANAGEMENT (TQM)

To develop a conceptual understanding of the basic principles and methods associated with TQM;

To develop an understanding of how these principles and methods have been put into effect in a variety of organisations;

To develop an understanding of the relationship between TQM principles and the theories and models studied in traditional management;

To do the right things, right for the first time, for every time.

BENEFITS OF TQM

While applying TQM in any organisation, the organisation will reap the following benefits:

- Greatly improved product or service
- Major decrease in wasted resources
- Sustained competitive advantage
- Increased market share
- Enhanced returns on investment
- Motivated workforce

BARRIERS TO TQM

Some of the barriers may exist while implementing the TQM in organisations. These are:

- Lack of management commitment
- Lack of vision and planning
- Satisfaction with quick fix
- Bureaucratic approach
- Noninvolvement of participants
- Immeasurable

TQM IN LIBRARIES

TQM is now practised in business as well as in government, military, education, and in non-profit organisations including libraries (Jurow & Barnard, 1993). The practice of quality management in libraries existed since the evolution of the subject itself. But the terminology used for these varied widely. Performance indicators: performance evolution; evaluation of reference sources using check-list of criteria; evolution of information Retrieval system using precision and Recall ratios; user surveys electing opinions on library services – all these studies are parts and parcel of quality studies using different mechanisms of assessment and methodologies.

Quality studies in LIS sector are mostly isolated and are made on different aspects of library management, services, user-studies, etc. The evidence produced by some TQM cases in the LIS sector indicates that TQM is a highly relevant management theory for information sector (Saroja and Sujatha).

Library should focus on providing the best services possible, and be willing to change to serve its customers. The administrator might ask the following questions:

- What are our niche makers?
- What do the customers come for?
- How can I enhance the efficiency of my library?
- How do we serve the current customers?

Sirkin suggests some ways a library might use the principles of TQM to enhance library services. These are:

- Create service brochures and information kits
- Conduct a user survey about library services
- Improve signage
- Change hours of operation
- Provide a more convenient material return
- Simplify checkout of materials
- Use flexibility in staff assignments
- Cooperate with local government
- Ask vendors to give product demonstrations
- Give new staff a thorough orientation by creating interdepartmental Library advisory groups
- Improve the physical layout of the library
- Track complaints
- Open satellite offices
- Develop user and staff training materials

- Target services to specific groups
- Offer electronic document delivery
- Follow the mission statement
- Serve with a smile

PURPOSE

The main functions of a library are: acquisition, organisation and dissemination. The said functions should be based on vision and mission statement of the parent institution (Library or information center is considered as subordinate body) and societal objectives. For example, clearly defined policies for collection development: processing; stacking, lending, weeding out of books will help to achieve total quality control to certain extent.

People

In a library, people are working at various levels to convert the vision of an organisation into reality. As far as the library and information centre is concerned the people are staff of different levels and categories. The possible groups include top level managers (librarian /information officer / director), middle level managers (assistant librarian / information assistant), skilled employees, and unskilled employees.

Process

These are the means available to "people" to convert thought into action. The intellectual processes could be acquisition of information materials/resources, classification, cataloguing or metadata harvesting, delivering various technical services, etc. The technological processes include design and creation of databases, portal, preparation for automated personalised services, selective dissemination of information, etc. Preparation of information products for marketing, planning, drafting and maintaining of budget and balance sheet, etc. are some of the financial processes.

Product

These are the end results of efforts put in by the people in an organisation. These could be concepts, physical entities and services. Products decide the services required to meet the changing needs of the clients. New conceptual ideas can be evolved based on system which can be added to the discipline. The physical entities such as information consolidation and repackaged products, such as, bibliographies, indexing and abstracting periodicals, bulletins, etc., are the outputs. The new services can be introduced using available resources with the help of information and communication technology. Evaluation of services in terms of accuracy of information, relevance to the purpose and cost of providing service is necessary.

Potential Challenges of TQM

While TQM clearly has positive aspects, implementing it can have potential challenges as well. Jurow and Barnard (1993) identify four barriers to the adoption of TQM in libraries:

(1) Vocabulary: Objections to terms such as "total," "quality" and "management" which simplify those high standards are not already being met;

(2) Commitment: TQM takes several years to implement and requires a long–term commitment by library managers;

(3) Process: Our culture tends to be impatient and we try to solve problems quickly, contrary to TQM's careful process analysis; and

(4) Professionalisation: Professional staff can resist to the turning over their practices and services to what they perceive as the "uninformed whims of the customer." Sirkin (1993) also notes that it is not possible to satisfy everyone's demands; choices will need to be made.

CONCLUSION

Libraries are ideal places to implement TQM's are service.

Libraries organisations dedicated to their customers, the patrons. By formulating a strategic plan and following with a commitment to continuous quality improvement, library managers can transform and improve their organisations. Riggs (1992) summary the notable principles of TQM:

(1) Manage by fact: make library decisions after careful analysis of data gathered with tools such as check sheets, histograms, and Pareto charts:

(2) Eliminate rework: library work is often labour intensive – simplify it and make sure it is done properly the first time;

(3) Respect people and ideas: the library staff act responsibly. They should be given the appropriate authority to make decisions that can improve the quality of work they do.

- Quality Assurance of library and information system should be part of the quality Assurance of parent institution's TQM project;
- Need to develop standards / norms for assessing quality of information services with particular reference to libraries and information centers;
- Need to evolve methodologies and mechanisms for the improvement of quality information services;
- More funds to be allocated for studying the quality of information services on project base;
- Training of staff members in providing quality information services

Finally, remember that TQM is not a "quick fix". It needs to be implemented gradually over a period of time.

REFERENCES

Ashher, M. (1996) Managing Quality in the services sector. Kogan Page, London.

Jablonski, J. (1992). Implementing TQM; Competing in the Nineties through Total Quality Management, 2nd. ed., San Diege.

Jurow, S. and Barnard, S.B. (Eds.) (1993).Integrating Total Quality Management in a Liibrary Setting. Birghamton NY: Hawworth Press.

Libraries Blumberg, B, and others (2005). Business Research Methods, 1st ed.

Oakland, J.S.(1989), Total Quality Management, 1st ed. Oxford, Butterworth-Heinemann.

Riggs, D.E. (1993). Managing Quality: TQM in Libraries. Library Administration & Management, 7(2), pp.73-78.

Saroja, G. and Sujatha , G. Application of Total Quality Management to library and Information Services in Indian open Universities. Available at http:/www.google.com/Saroja pdf (Accessed on 05 December 2010).

Sirkin, A. F. (1993). Customer Services: Another side of TQM. Journal of Library Administration, 18(1/2), pp. 71-83.

9

Knowledge Management for Modern Public Library in Digital Era

— *Dinesh Kumar*
— *Arjun*

ABSTRACT

Knowledge Management is a form of application of sound management practices to human resources as a whole which are the carrying vectors of Knowledge in a sense. Knowledge Management System will be the desktop from which the user can search for and display file folder information, loose paper information, electronic documents, images, e-mail, faxes, sound files, video files, etc. Our knowledge management system sits over' all physical and electronic information, whatever the form or location, and builds a virtual model of an organisation's scattered and varied information resources as if they were a neatly ordered, homogeneous collection. Knowledge management will be the major requirement of all successful organisations over the next few years.

Knowledge management (KM) is an emerging field, much tooted or hyped since late 1990s. However, due to the complicated nature of knowledge per se and its consequent management, it is often difficult to estimate or demonstrate the value of knowledge management. Public libraries, with limited budget and human resources, may hesitate to follow the business sector and plunge into the uncharted sea of knowledge management. This paper suggests a pragmatic approach to the implementation of Knowledge Management for Modern Public Library in Digital Era: utilising the existing staffing, technology, and management structure.

Keywords: *Modern Public Library, Digital Era, Knowledge Management.*

INTRODUCTION

Knowledge plays an important role in the modern world of organisation. The term Knowledge Management was First introduced in the keynote address to a European Management Conferences held in 1986. Knowledge Management, before the term was coined, used to be simply the transfer of knowledge from one person to another, the result of which enabled the recipient to advantage from the collected wisdom of the more experienced members of organisation or group. Knowledge management (KM), a new discipline that promotes an integral approach to identify, capture, retrieve share and evaluate. An enterprise's knowledge asset is the driver of productivity and growth of any organisation. It is a strategy of systematic and constructive management of vital knowledge and its associated processes of creating, gathering, organising, diffusing, usage and exploitation.

The most important aim of knowledge management is to provide the right knowledge at the right time to the right persons. For the success of the organisation knowledge management is very essential as it not only helps in discovering the resources, but also helps in evolving new business rules and models. In the Present Information age, the increasing demand of new technology has forced the librarians to take the advantages of emerging advanced information communication technology for providing Public library services in digital form. Librarians have been giving new shapes to library services by automating the Public libraries. Making use of barcode, radio frequency identification, digital library Internet, databases, making consortia arrangement for subscribing electronic books and journals. Knowledge Management in Public libraries should be focused on effective research and development of knowledge, creation of knowledge bases, exchange and sharing of knowledge between library staff users, trainers, researchers etc. In electronic age, the library professionals should play an essential role in speeding up explicit processing of the implicit knowledge and realising the importance of its sharing. So with the wide array of solutions available today, how come knowledge management efforts still fail so often? Although many reasons have been postulated, few are as important as making sure that you understand how knowledge is used and created in your organisation, and making sure that you have a balanced knowledge system portfolio that not only captures, stores, and disseminates your corporate knowledge, but also allows opportunity for the creation of knowledge. Why do current Knowledge Management (KM) systems find it so hard to achieve solid Return-On-Investment (ROI)? And why is it that so many KM success stories revolve around the unplanned, unofficial applications of technology by informal Communities of Practice? In order to take a fully balanced approach to building a comprehensive and successful KM system, you have to take several factors into account. What is the knowledge that you're trying to collect? What form is it in? What are you trying to do with the knowledge?

WHAT IS KNOWLEDGE MANAGEMENT?

Knowledge is commonly distinguished form data and information. Data represent observations or facts out of context and therefore not directing meaningful. Information results from placing data within some meaningful context often in the form of message. Knowledge is defined as what we know: knowledge involves the mental processes of comprehension, understanding and learning that act on the mind and only in the mind, however much they involve interaction with others. Knowledge is not just an explicit tangible thing, like information, but information combined with experience, context interpretation and reflection. Knowledge involves the full person, integrating the elements of both thinking and feeling. Knowledge is invisible, closely related to action and decision, different in processing spiritual product, identified with existing environment, transferable learning and not duplicate.

In a preliminary way, let it suggests that knowledge management is the systematic:

- Underpinning
- Observation
- Instrumentation and
- Optimisation of the firm's knowledge economies.

These activities – or perhaps process areas – are sequential. That is to say, it is not possible to optimise a firm's knowledge economies until they are instrumented; instrumentation is selective measurement based on empirical observation and observation for-the-most-part underground knowledge economies within the firm requires that these economies be brought out into the light of day, made official, and formally underpinned with technology, process and policy that makes construction, embodiment, dissemination and use of knowledge officially-sanctioned and formally-valued activities within the firm.

FIVE ELEMENTS ESSENTIAL FOR EFFECTIVE KNOWLEDGE MANAGEMENT

Effective knowledge management has the potential of creating characteristic competencies, unique market positioning and sustained growth. For an effective knowledge management, the following elements are required.

- Acceptance of effective KM solutions.
- Appraisal of knowledge requirements for new jobs.
- Better HRM policies for proper identification and reward for knowledge workers.

- Good communication and information sharing.
- Top management support.

PUBLIC LIBRARY

Public libraries are recognised as an essential ingredient in civilised society for the individual and social progress and prosperity in all human activities. They play an important role in serving the society through their extension services. Thus there is an immediate need to study their existing conditions, positions, operations and services to identify their strength and weakness. This will help them in providing better services in the changing social, political and digital environment. The public libraries in the states covered under study have been established long back when education was at the developing stage. Today, the society is moving towards an electronic age. The Public library is practical demonstration of democracy's faith in universal education as a continuing and life long process, in the appreciation of the achievement of humanity in knowledge and culture. The public libraries provide access to recorded man's thoughts and ideas, and are made freely available to all. A public library is an organisation established, supported and funded by the community, either through local, regional or national government or through some other form of community organisation. It provides access to knowledge, information and works of the imagination through a range of resources and services and equally available to all members of the community regardless of race, nationality, age, gender, religion, language, disability, economic and employment status and educational attainment." The public library is the local center of information making all kinds of knowledge and information readily available to its users. The services of the public library are provided on the basis of equality of access for all, regardless of age, race, sex, religion, nationality, languages or social status. Specific services and materials must be provided for those users who cannot, for whatever reason, use the regular services and materials for example linguistic materials, people with disabilities or people in hospital or prison. A Public library is a temple of learning. Public library system is an important organ of the state entrusted with the responsibility of maintains and organizes collection of documents in the services of storage and retrieval is a gigantic problem of today's public libraries. A public library is essentially a free library financed by public funds providing impartial service to all the members of a local community and which serves as an auxiliary educational institution. It is a democratic institution providing information, education and culture to each according to his needs.

Public libraries are information centers established in support of the mission of their parent institutions to generate knowledge, and people equipped with knowledge in order to serve the society and advance the well-being of mankind. In the digital age, Public libraries face challenges from both within (academia) and without (the business sector). Public departments, or even faculty and students, may purchase or build their own portals to meet their Public and/or research needs. Will that marginalise the services provided by Public libraries? Commercial companies have entered the field of information services. Will that influence upon or wear away into the territory of Public libraries?

KNOWLEDGE MANAGEMENT IN PUBLIC LIBRARIES

Knowledge Management has been tooted and hyped since late 1990s, (DiMattia, 1997) first in the business sector, and then in higher education and now in library management. The impetus for embracing Knowledge Management in Public libraries is mainly from a combination of library budget shortfall and higher user expectations. Rather than adopting an often trumpeted high-tech approach, it is more practical to utilise the existing staffing, technology and management structure for Public libraries.

WHY IMPLEMENTING KNOWLEDGE MANAGEMENT IN PUBLIC LIBRARIES

Public Libraries are pinched on both sides: reduced budget and increased demand from faculty and students. To implement Knowledge Management in Public libraries is mainly driven by its mission rather than by the competition from Internet-based reference services or electronic books.

MOVEMENT OF PUBLIC LIBRARY

Where there is a new phenomenon emerged, there must be an impetus. In Knowledge Management, the driving force is the necessity to survive in the business sector in the face of fierce competition with rival firms or other competitors. The goal of Knowledge Management is to make full use of the knowledge existing in a corporation to increase the productivity and/or operational efficiency so as to build an edge in the competition. What's the driving force for Public libraries? Budget shortfall is a primary driving force for the implementation of Knowledge Management in Public libraries. In the recent years, budgets in Public libraries are stagnant at best and declining in general.

OPERATION OF PUBLIC LIBRARY

Public Libraries depend more on the support from their parent institution and immediate user constituents. To survive or thrive, libraries should constantly gauge and cater to users' needs. Moreover, libraries should be more proactive in marketing their services and values to their user constituents. We should change our mindset and tradition of just waiting for users to come to the Public library.

HOW TO APPLY KNOWLEDGE MANAGEMENT IN PUBLIC LIBRARIES

Most researchers consent that Knowledge Management consists of two components: human factor and technology. And most proponents of Knowledge Management advocate a top-down approach under a Chief Knowledge Officer (CKO).

While a top down approach is preferable, a bottom-up approach might be more practical in many instances.

HUMAN FACTOR

Knowledge Management is a new paradigm in Public libraries in the sense that concerted efforts need to be exerted to manage knowledge systematically. (Ahmed, Lim, & Loh, 2002) Instead of establishing a new network of Knowledge Management managers under a Knowledge Management or CKO (Chief Knowledge Officer), it is more practical to utilise the current management structure. Managers at all levels shall be charged to implement Knowledge Management in their respective units so that a network of Knowledge Management managers is in place. In addition to managing staff and workflow in their units, each manager is responsible for managing knowledge pertaining to their unit's goals and operations.

TECHNOLOGY AND KNOWLEDGE MANAGEMENT

The new emerging communication and technology has been playing a very important role in the field of information storage and retrieval and now it has shown its impact on knowledge management. For the creation of knowledge from any new events or activity on a continual basis, new infrastructure is required. The new tools and techniques are the most important component of any organisation and are essentials for the creation of new knowledge. An effective infrastructure is a repository of knowledge and distribution systems to distribute the knowledge to the members of parent organisation and is helpful in the creation of new knowledge. Information technology is very helpful in enhancing quality and standardisation if automation is implemented in the organisation. Web technology has provided a common technological infrastructure to support the collective knowledge management. Earlier also Zhang and Chen stated that Web-based technology uses standard transmission-control protocol/internet protocol (TCP/IP), which is mature and is supported by almost every vendor. Information can be collected, retrieved, and shared through popular browsers like Netscape, Navigator and Internet Explorer. A home page can be quickly developed, and shared.

There are languages specially developed for web based applications, such as java or VB script. Java applets can be embedded in web home pages. The Applets are executed on client's PC and make it possible to develop interactive home pages with instant user responses and with multimedia features. With web technologies, an organisation enjoys platform independence or cross-platform operation. Java applets do not have to be rewritten to work with PC browsers, Macintosh browsers and UNIX browsers.

Now how to record knowledge pertaining to library operations? What is more: How to retrieve such knowledge when needed? Many advocators of Knowledge Management stress the importance of using advanced technology to store and retrieve knowledge. And some others advocate for a centralised turnkey Knowledge Management software product or system.

MANAGEMENT OF DIGITAL LIBRARIES

Difficulties or challenges arise in managing the digital libraries, in five areas:

- Planning,
- Organising
- Staffing
- Directing
- Controlling

Planning

The main problem in the planning processor for the manager of the digital library is the creation of long-range plans and establishment of evaluation standards. Long-range plans must be made without direct reference to rapidly evolving technology in order to be applicable over time. As most technologies have a life of three years, a five year plan can be difficult to follow beyond the third year. In the creation plans, library mangers must "differentiate between short-term survival and long-term evolution". Therefore, successful long-term range plans will be flexible enough to encompass new information technologies, which are needed by the digital libraries.

Organising

Organisational problem center around the merging of roles traditionally filled by public and technical services. These difficulties stem from the changing technologies and resulting changes in capabilities of the systems and the support then needed. According to Wahlda and Schiller "Mew organisational structure will be needed if libraries are going to be successful in an electronic, networked environment. Libraries will need structures which allow for increased flexibility and innovation and which are more responsive to change than at present." As virtual users will require on-line help which may involve technical details along with more traditional reference questions, technical and public services can not be considered separate entities. A group of technically minded staff members who are trained in public services will be needed to bridge the gap between the service groups. Another solution is to break up the task based departments and reorganise the staff into teams by subject.

Staffing

Challenges in staffing involve changes in physical staff, virtual staff and a new emphasis on training and development. The evolving technologies required to run a digital library require personnel with expertise, time and access to constant training to keep up with changes. Managers may build a dependency on out-of-house consultants or the local computer center. Another possibility is that this dependency for the daily operation of the digital library may exist around one or two on-staff computer experts. Managers must work with these experts to prepare contingency plans and training in case of an emergency. Managers of a digital library and their superiors must believe that staff development is highly important, and commit funding and time for this increased level of training. This training, therefore, must be a continuing process that can be easily changed and expanded to reflect the new technologies.

Directing

Managers may have to adopt new directing skills to help calm staff fears about the technology. Some librarians have the concern that by furthering the digital or virtual library, they are putting themselves out of a job. It seems, therefore, that until such time as computer are able of matching human intelligence and until such time as all the information required by a user is delivered at his/ her desktop at an affordable price, the role of librarian in the process of managing and imparting knowledge will remain central. Managers can prepare their staff for these changes by developing a 'trusting team environment built on organisational flexibility and deep staff understanding of the digitised information world. "Training, development and enthusiastic leadership will help those that are afraid of the new technologies."

Controlling

The final area of management that is affected by the digital library is controlling. This includes computer security, increased budgetary needs, and copyright issues. Security plays a very different role in a digital library. In traditional library, physical materials can be protected through electronic devices and security guards. However, an electronic material has weaknesses that print does not. A user could conceivably copy all of the materials in a very little time and the digital library would not notice anything. That user could then publish the information for profit, having the source material provided free by their local library.

TOP-DOWN OR BOTTOM-UP

Depending on the priority of the library administration or the library structure, Knowledge Management can be started from either bottom-up or top-down (Quintas, 2003) or in the middle. A top-down strategy has the advantage of the support and direction from the library administration.

WHAT TO CULTIVATE IN KNOWLEDGE MANAGEMENT IMPLEMENTATION

Unlike the private or business sector, Public libraries typically do not have extra financial resources to reward staffs who have contributed their knowledge. Again, I'd like to advocate that we incorporate such an incentive or reward system within the current management structure.

KNOWLEDGE MANAGEMENT AS REFLECTED IN LIBRARY LITERATURE

A cursory review of library literature on Knowledge Management reveals the following trends:

- Of all types of libraries, special libraries, especially business and corporate libraries, are taking the lead on Knowledge Management research; and
- Of Public libraries, public services and digital libraries are in the limelight.

TREND IN LIBRARIES: BUSINESS/CORPORATE LIBRARIES TAKING THE LEAD

In the realm of Knowledge Management in libraries, Townley (2001) concludes, "Special libraries have taken the lead, but some applications now are taking place in other libraries." Trend in Public Libraries:

The literature review also reveals that within Public libraries, public services are taking the lead in the research and implementation of Knowledge Management. Jantz (2001) examined important issues of knowledge management within Public libraries and how reference librarians can become more effective as information intermediaries.

MISSING PIECE: HOW TO IMPROVE THE EFFICIENCY OF LIBRARY OPERATIONS

Such research has deviated from the original intent of Knowledge Management. The concept of Knowledge Management originated in the business sector, the purpose of which is to maximise the utilisation of the corporate knowledge so as to run a company more efficiently and make the company more competitive in the market. The current trend in library literature on Knowledge Management is a twist of the original intent of Knowledge Management.

BENEFITS OF KNOWLEDGE MANAGEMENT IN PUBLIC LIBRARIES

The following benefits of Knowledge management in libraries may be observed:

- Best selection, collection, processing, storage, retrieval and dissemination of information in the area of interest of the parent organisation.
- Enhance responsiveness and communicative capabilities.
- Improve status credibility of the library as well as of organisation.
- Improve the efficiency of the library in terms of saving of time and enhancing overall quality of library services.
- Promotes innovation.
- Promotion of scientific research in the field of parent organisation.
- Reduce employee's turnover.
- Strengthening knowledge flow among libraries in order to share and enhance the resources.

PUBLIC LIBRARIES AND LIBRARIANS' ROLE IN KNOWLEDGE MANAGEMENT

Libraries are a crucial element in the chain of knowledge

generation process. Knowledge innovation is the center of the knowledge society. Librarians provide a base to research by collection, processing, storage and distribution of knowledge and information. Libraries make a link between information and the information seeker. Knowledge dissemination is another area where libraries can work. Obviously the creator who creates the knowledge does not have time to disseminate it. The libraries can take initiatives to obtain knowledge from the creator and make it accessible to the users. Librarians can play an effectual role as a member of the knowledge management system.

- Acquisition of documents from external sources.
- Categorise the knowledge located inside or outside the organisation for easy retrieval.
- Creating knowledge maps to find out when: and what is available.
- Extract success story and technical anecdotes from resource persons and diffusing them over a corporate network
- Generation of knowledge vocabulary for standardisation of terms and retrieval.

ADVANTAGES OF FOR DIGITAL PUBLIC LIBRARY

The advantages of Digital Public libraries are to:

- Access through the campus 'CAN'.
- Bring for New edition.
- Downloading and printing.
- Everybody can use because of simple operations.
- High speed communication.
- One master copy of the documents will be viewed by many numbers of users at a time.
- Provide multiple accesses.
- Provided access to more information.

- Reliability and quality of data seeking.
- Save space.
- Save the manpower.
- Save time.
- The digital library would allow learner to use resources from anywhere in the world.

DISADVANTAGES OF DIGITAL PUBLIC LIBRARY

The Disadvantages of Digital libraries are:

- It necessitates for huge budget which is not possible for small libraries.
- Failure of current and telecommunication resist the use of the digital library.
- Continuous use of digital library creates stress on eyes and brain of the user.
- Computer virus is a growing threat and if permanent solution is not found then it can destroy the digital library.
- Elimination of physical space for study etc.

PUBLIC LIBRARY SERVICE IN DIGITAL ENVIRONMENT TODAY

India has to be in the information highway as a sea of information is knocking at its doors. India has the expertise to meet the challenge and to set up digital Public libraries in the country. We are at the threshold of breaking into cyberspace and navigate through internet and World Wide Web. Through internet it has now become possible to be a part of 'global village' and exchange information instantly. WWW is the most advanced browsing and searching system deployed on internet based on hypertext paradigm. WWW allows one to explore an unlimited world wide digital "WEB" of human knowledge. With all these facilities it is possible to access hundreds of databases and make the information available to the user community in the country. Availability of CDROM databases accessible through LAN and WAN are added advantages.

The public library service is not noted for attracting publicity. However, two recent episodes will have been welcomed by those who believe that "there is no such thing as bad publicity".

Within the service itself there is some recognition that all is not well. The diagnosis contains a number of elements:

- Libraries are low on the list of government priorities, and receive insufficient funding, especially for the renewal of buildings and the modernisation of services.
- There are problems within the management of the service itself, and particularly some doubts about the strength of the senior management cadre.
- There is a degree of fatalism about changing social trends.
- There is a failure to recognise some of libraries' important strengths, e.g. their role as community spaces and to build on this.
- There is a failure to recognise the existence and performance of competitor services.
- There is a lack of the most useful performance data, for example about who does and does not use libraries.
- There is an ageing customer base.
- There is complacency among staff, a failure to recognise and adapt to changing trends, and an aversion to risk.

There is a poor understanding of the social changes which are having an effect on libraries' operating environment.

CONCLUSION

Knowledge management has become a powerful tool for promoting innovation and realising and recognising the various walks of life. Knowledge management in libraries should help effective research and development of knowledge, creation of knowledge bases, exchanges and sharing of knowledge between libraries and users. We can conclude the Knowledge Management is the management of the organisation towards the continuous renewal of the organisational knowledge base. Knowledge Management is not owned by anyone group in an organisation, nor by anyone profession or industry. Knowledge Management requires a holistic and a multidisciplinary approach to management process and an understanding of the dimension of knowledge work. It is an evolution of good management practice sensibly and purposely applied. But librarians and information specialists, it they want to be key players in the emerging Knowledge Management phenomenon, have to understand the multiple perspectives of the other players. Knowledge Management occupies a very outstanding position in the creation of the knowledge innovation system of a country. It has become a powerful tool for promoting innovation and realising re-engineering the various walks of life. It is an altogether a new concept for libraries in India. It is bound to gain prominence with the passage of time. That is where the role of knowledge managers comes into play. KM is a buzzword turned business phenomenon, in the library world, there is a lesson to be learned from the business world. For any library to succeed in implementing knowledge management will require a strong leadership and vision from the top administration. Information technology and systems can provide effective support in implementing knowledge management. Libraries should work together with Information Technology Professionals and others to develop the appropriate Knowledge management systems. Libraries, with limited budget and human resources, should utilise the current management structure and technology to implement KM, either bottom-up or top-down. With an effort, KM will help to increase libraries' operational efficiency and later to the ever-increasing needs of our clientele.

REFERENCES

Babu & Singh. Knowledge management: A Genesis NCDDP.2008, New Delhi.

Bansal A (2000). Knowledge management: A Review. DESIDOC Bulletin of Inf. Technol. 20(4): pp. 3-9.

Bansal A (2000). Knowledge management: A Review. DESIDOC Bulletin of Inf. Technol. 20(4): pp. 3-9.

Davenport, T. and Prosaic, L. Working Knowledge. Cambridge, MA: Howard Business School Press, Collis, DJ. and Montgomery, C. A. "Competing on Resources: Strategy in the I990s". Harvard Business Review (1995): pp. 118-28.

Denning S. (2001). The Strategy of Knowledge. http://wwwstevedenning .com /staegy knowledge-sharing.html

Ghosh M. (2003). Knowledge management in the digital age:Challenges and opprtunities in India. In International Conference (Asia-Pacific):

Grant, R. M. "The Resource-Based Theory of Competitive Advantage: Implications for Strategy Formulation." California Management Review (1991): pp. 114-35.

Haridasan S. (1998). Knowledge management: A new challenge for library professionals. Iaslic Bulletin, 43 (4), pp. 145-47

http://www.insmkt.com/kmwhite.htm

http://www.kit.nl/frameset.asp?/specials/html/km_knowledge_management.asp&frnr=1&

M.Ramshirish and Aparajita Suman, Knowledge management for community at large, Information Studies, Vol 14, No.3, July 2008.

Mandalia, Knowledge management in libraries NCDDP.2008, New Delhi.

Nandhan & Grish Kumar, Manning Knowledge for Knowledge Society. ESS ESS .New Delhi. 2008.

Shanmugam, C G. "The Need for Knowledge Management in Special-Libraries." In Proceedings of the National Conference on Information management in e-libraries held at Kharagpur, 26-27 February, 2002. New Delhi: Allied Publishers, 2002. pp. 43-52.

Stratigos, A (2001). Knowledge management meets future information users. Online.

Subramaniam SR, Gokulakrishnan J. (2002). Knowledge management at Infosys. IEEE Software, pp.53-55.

Waltz, Edward. Knowledge management in the intelligence enterprise.

Weill, P. and Broadbent, M. (1998). Leveraging the new infrastructure. Cambridge: Harvard Business School Press. .

10

Knowledge Management use in Library in Modern Era

— *Vinay Shanker Mahajan*
— *Mohd. Asif*
— *Mustafa Khan*
— *Syed Misham Abbas Abidy and Vipin Kumar*

ABSTRACTS

This paper discusses how knowledge is created, the types of knowledge, why knowledge management, Characteristics, Objectives, Modules, Scope, Life Cycle of Knowledge management. Knowledge Management in library information centers and its need for LIS professionals. Later if tells about digital library being a suitable solution for managing knowledge.

Keywords: *Knowledge management; Knowledge management in Library*

INTRODUCTION

One time the important characteristic of time and space is their un-detachable association with change, which in turn impacts on the creation and utilisation of knowledge. Knowledge management as a concept appears to have many definitions, the reason being its multi-disciplinary nature. It has been defined almost in every discipline that deals with information as an input or as a product. One of the definitions describes Knowledge management as the process of capturing and sharing people's collective expertise to fulfill its mission. The very idea of Knowledge management came to ensure that the right information gets to the right people at the right time to make the right decisions. For information professionals, Knowledge management has evolved as a process that imbibes almost all the five laws of Dr. S. R. Ranganathatn, the only difference being the replacement of books by the replacement of books by information.

KNOWLEDGE

Knowledge is the awareness of what one knows through study, reasoning express of association, or through various other types of learning. It is Acquaintance with or understanding of a science, art or technique. The Oxford English Dictionary presents the word "Knowledge" as meaning "acknowledging, Recognising, inquiring, being aware, understanding, cognizance, intelligence information acquired through study and learning".

TYPES OF KNOWLEDGE

Tacit Knowledge

Tacit knowledge is implicit and is not necessarily or easily articulated in formal documents. The owners of this knowledge are aware that they have it and it is gained over a period of time from experiences and includes insights, emotions and the concept of 'how things are done around here'. People build up tacit knowledge during time spent in a role or within an organisation. New employees begin to build up tacit knowledge when they join a new organisation. It is often hard to share with others.

Explicit Knowledge

Explicit knowledge is a knowledge that an individual knows and can easily write down. This type of knowledge often comes through learning by observation, reading or group discussion. Often this type of knowledge can be made into print or electronic guides or stored on an intranet or database. For example, the exact sequence of steps that needs to be taken to check the receipt of journals within your information service.

Cultural Knowledge

B. B. Chand describes cultural knowledge as knowledge which includes assumption and beliefs. It is used to understand, describe and explain the reality as well as conventions. It is also useful to form the frame work among organisational members, recognise the new information and evaluate alternative interpretations and actions.

KNOWLEDGE MANAGEMENT

Knowledge management is not just like a data management and information management. Organisation Knowledge management has been characterised as consisting of three overlapping progresses; knowledge creation, knowledge codification and knowledge application. Knowledge creation refers to the development of new knowledge through the inter play of tacit and explicit knowledge at different ontological levels. Most knowledge creation occurs within the system such as problem solving groups and project teams. Some new knowledge is explicated and formalised during the knowledge codification phase. Codification of complex knowledge frequently relies on information technology. Expert system, decision support system, document system, and relation database tools represents some of the technological solutions development primarily to support to this phase of knowledge management.

KNOWLEDGE MANAGEMENT IN LIBRARY INFORMATION CENTERS AND ITS NEED FOR LIS PROFESSIONALS

As a learning organisation, libraries should provide a strong leadership in knowledge management. Libraries should improve their knowledge management in all the key areas of library services. To cope with the exponential growth in human knowledge, libraries need to develop their resources, access and sharing strategies from printed to electronic and digital resources. Limited by funding, technology, staff and space libraries must carefully analyse the needs of their users and seek to develop cooperative acquisition plans to meet the needs of users. Libraries should be developed and maintained an integrated online public access catalogue (OPAC) with both internal and external resources as well as printed and other formats of knowledge. Useful websites and knowledge sources should be regularly searched and selected from the internet and included in OPACs. In the current digital and networked knowledge age, the size of information sources on the web is growing exponentially. No one really knows exactly how many web pages are on the internet, because new web pages are added every second. Universities and research organisations are knowledge reservoirs. These highly valued intellectual assets, regardless of whether they are explicit or tacit, should be inventoried, archived, indexed, frequently updated and made accessible in digital form. Libraries should use the new approach to capture web information by cooperative efforts such as Dublin core metadata and the cooperative online resources catalogue (CORC).

WHY KNOWLEDGE MANAGEMENT

- Faster delivery of information to users.
- Effective organisation of information/information.
- Sharing Knowledge.
- Special Information Services to users.
- Ease of access across/ different platforms.

CHARACTERISTICS OF KNOWLEDGE MANAGEMENT

The role of Knowledge management in libraries will become more and more important along with the development of knowledge economy because knowledge is renewable and reusable. Some more characteristics of knowledge management are:

- It is created to enhance decision power at a time or moment.
- It is circulated to communities in many ways.
- It is more effective than charts and models.
- It is easy to use.
- It is a time saver.
- It makes information retrieval easy.

OBJECTIVES OF KNOWLEDGE MANAGEMENT

- Knowledge data information: Data are input that creates the information, which becomes knowledge when an individual processes it.
- State of mind: Knowledge is a state of knowing and understanding. It also provides access to sources of knowledge.
- Object: Knowledge is an object to be stored and manipulated. It also helps gather, store and transfer knowledge.
- Process: Knowledge is the process of applying expertise; it provides links among sources of knowledge to increase the depth and breadth of knowledge flows.
- Access to information: Knowledge is a condition of access to information. It provides search and retrieval mechanic for locating relevant information.
- Capability: Knowledge is the potential to influence action, it supports development of individual and organisation competencies.

MODULES OF KNOWLEDGE MANAGEMENT

- Information: the most important bezel, is an instant access to update and customise information.

- Knowledge capture: initial identification and capturing of knowledge in its explicit and tacit forms.
- Expertise: Expertise lancets in seal time experts in an organisation to members who earn assistance even the tacit knowledge can be made explicit.
- Enabling communities: Identifying, promoting and supporting knowledge based community working across and between libraries.
- Collaboration; Collaboration plays an important role to facilitate online brain storming session and reserves information.
- Supporting a knowledge culture: To develop and embed the necessary cultural change and knowledge environment, to embed knowledge management activities.
- Team: Teams ensures efficient and systematic management for sharing skills.
- Learning: Learning abridges skill gap with the help of online sessions.
- Knowledge transfer: the effective transfer of knowledge among its various sources and between its various forms. Knowledge transfer is a structured electronic form according to William Saffody.
- Machine-readable data files.
- Various online database and CD-ROM information products.
- Computer storage devices in which information resides in the shape of optical disks, magnetic tape and computerised network system.
- Knowledge mapping; Knowledge mapping identifies the body of knowledge within.

- The organisation which is primarily concerned with mute knowledge base and make a repository of all skills and expertise in the organisation.

KNOWLEDGE MANAGEMENT FOR DIGITAL LIBRARY

Digital library concept tells us that it has some means of digital object collection. There is no sensible definition for digital libraries. Digital libraries are still in mid-stage but rapidly developing to serve the user community in a better way. Digital libraries are in one type, a solution for the Knowledge Management, provided that a digital library is built for serving the Knowledge Society and capable of handling and managing knowledge. Today's digital libraries mostly do not support multiform access too. In knowledge society the quality and the services offered by the service provider is expected in full, that is, a user may need an information source to be opened on a personal computer (eg: PDF or Word) and if he likes to carry it with him, he may ask for the same source to be made compatible over his mobile phone or PDA for accessing with e-book or any other software that his device support. In such cover the library must be always ready to satisfy the needs of the patrons.

CLOSURE

The Knowledge management is a growing demand of modern organisation and is perceived as an opportunity to create competitive advantage. Knowledge Management is understanding of dimensions of knowledge work. Knowledge management has become a powerful tool for promoting innovation and realising and recognising the various walks of life. Knowledge management in libraries should help effective research and development of knowledge, creation of knowledge bases, exchanges and sharing of knowledge between libraries and users.

REFERENCES

Waltz, Edward. Knowledge management in the intelligence enterprise.

CGLA 1st conference proceedings , Mussoorie.

Second International CALIBER 2004 Proceedings, New Delhi.

Sudharma Haridarshan: A new challenge for Library Proessionals,Isalic Bulletin, Vol 43 No.4 .1998.

Mandalia, Knowledge management in libraries NCDDP.2008, New Delhi.

Babu & Singh. Knowledge management: A Genesis NCDDP.2008, New Delhi.

M.Ramshirish and Aparajita Suman. Knowledge management for community at large, Information Studies, Vol 14, No.3 July 2008.

Nandhan & Grish Kumar, Manning Knowledge for Knowledge Society. ESS ESS . New Delhi. 2008.

Bansal A (2000). Knowledge management: A Review. DESIDOC Bulletin of Inf. Technol. 20(4): pp. 3-9.

Cheng G (2001). The shifting information landscape: re-inventing the wheel or a whole new frontier for librarians. New Library World. 102(1160/1161): pp. 26-33.

http://www.ics.heacademy.ac.uk/resources/rlos/wakefield/km/html/page

11

Tools for Knowledge Management in Academic Libraries

— *Divya Sharma*

ABSTRACT

Well established library is essential for academic institution. As focal point for teaching, learning and research, it is expected to provide standard information resources. Evolution of information and knowledge has impacted all organisations, including academic libraries. Knowledge management has drawn the attention of LIS Professionals for the past decade. Knowledge management is the powerful tool for any organisational competitiveness knowledge is the heart of the organisation. Later it started a role in academic libraries too. This paper deals with the need of knowledge management in libraries, knowledge explosion or generation, process and management, various component or tool for knowledge management.

INTRODUCTION

Knowledge has become more dynamic which instantly changes its direction and dimensions. We are living in an era of information and knowledge explosion. The unprecedented growth of knowledge and information has impacted all organisations including libraries. As library is the heart of any organisation, libraries has moved from depository or warehouses to knowledge centers, which preserve, classify, and disseminate knowledge from the creator to the knowledge seeking community irrespective of location and distance. The success of libraries and information centers (LICs) depend on their ability to utilise information knowledge of its staff to serve the user community. There is an important issue of Knowledge Management within Academic Libraries. The Knowledge management system is developing rapidly in the present era in the form of collection of data or knowledge information. Knowledge management is the systematic process of creating, maintaining and nurturing an organisation to optimise the use of judgment in the attainment of mission and goals. Knowledge management provides an opportunity for achieving sustainable saving, signified improvement in human performance, and enhanced competitiveness. Knowledge management is multidisciplinary by nature and integrates concepts used in strategic management, organisation theory and information system management. Knowledge management stresses a formalised, integrated approach to managing an enterprise's intangible information assets; Major enablers of KM include organisational mechanisms, information technologies and software for libraries.

ACADEMIC LIBRARIES

Well established library is essential for academic institution. As focal point for teaching, learning and research, it is expected to provide standard information resources. Academic libraries are information centers established in support of the mission of their parent institutions to generate knowledge, equip people with knowledge in order to serve the society and advance the well being of mankind. The primary objective of academic institutions of higher education is advancement of learning and acquisition of knowledge. Academic libraries are parts of the institution and its organisational culture. Whatever affects institute also has an impact on their libraries too. As a result the role of institution libraries is changing to provide the competitive advantage for the institution. In the age of information, libraries are changed into information centers or learning resources centers in which the library professionals perform as information professionals. Today librarians are connected to a vast ocean of network based services. Academic libraries are the nerve centers of academic institutions and are mandated to support teaching, research and other academic programs.

KNOWLEDGE MANAGEMENT

Knowledge can be divided into two types: explicit and implicit. Explicit knowledge includes printed materials, like book and periodicals, audio-visual materials, like CDs, films and videos and electronic formats like data software, website etc. Implicit (or tacit) knowledge is invisible and often confined to mind of a person. It is hard to codify and therefore, difficult to communicate to others. The externalisation of implicit knowledge is the transformation of knowledge from the implicit to the explicit. It can be eternalised only by the owner of the knowledge. The explicit knowledge is the main source to form new implicit knowledge after combining with research, information, content and experiences; this is internalisation of external knowledge. The explicit and implicit knowledge accomplish the knowledge circulation systems.

Definition of Knowledge Management

Knowledge Management is the management of knowledge resources and embodied knowledge. Knowledge is the totality of all existing information that is known; every piece of information that is recovered in logical and systematic manner creates knowledge.

- "Knowledge is organised information available to problem solving." –Webster's New World Dictionary.
- "Knowledge is reasoning about information and data to actively enable performance, problem solving, decision making, learning and teaching." – By Beckman T.

- "Knowledge Management is getting the right knowledge, to the right people, at the right time."- By Petrash. This seems to be similar to the Five Laws of Library Science formulated by S.R Ranganathan.

NEED OF KNOWLEDGE MANAGEMENT IN LIBRARIES

The objective of knowledge management in libraries is to promote knowledge innovation. Knowledge innovation is the core of the knowledge economy society. As foundation for collection, processing, storage and distribution of knowledge and information, libraries represent an indispensable link in the scientific system chain, an important link in the knowledge innovation. Libraries take part in scientific research process directly. Library work is a component of knowledge innovation. Libraries must pay attention to diffusion and conversion of Knowledge. They act as bridges for turning the results of knowledge innovation into realistic productive forces.

The aim of Knowledge management in libraries is to promote relationship in and between libraries, between library and user, to strengthen knowledge internet working and to quicken the knowledge flow. In the knowledge economy era, libraries are entrusted with an important job of carrying out researches on development and application of information resources, construction of virtual libraries, protection of intellectual property right in electronic era, etc., and paving the way for knowledge innovation.

COMPONENTS OF KNOWLEDGE MANAGEMENT

The Knowledge Management environment centered round three components. These are:

I. Human Factor	:	Technology experts, knowledge professionals, knowledge managers.
II. Process	:	Creation, Capturing, Storing, Sharing, application.
III. Technology	:	Hardware and software packages.

I. *Human Factor*: Knowledge Management in their respective units is that a network of knowledge management managers is in place. In addition to managing staff and workflow in their units, each manager is responsible for managing knowledge pertaining to their unit's goals and operations. This calls for not only gathering knowledge existing currently in their units but also knowledge relevant to their operations from other units/departments and even other libraries or professions.

- *Technology Expert:* are those concerned with design and development of tools and services for knowledge discovery.
- *Knowledge Professionals:* are the individuals in the organisation who have the skills, Training and know-how to organise information/knowledge into systems and structures that facilitate effective use of knowledge resources.
- *Knowledge Managers:* They are the groups of people, who focus on the achievement of organisational goals.

II. *Process*: Knowledge management process consists to several stages:

- *Environmental Creation:* People working in the organisation have to change their mindset to share their tacit(Implicit) knowledge, nurture it, and learn more about the system, users of the system, identify and integrate people and process and technology.
- *Knowledge Capturing:* Knowledge in public domain is explicit and published. In a personal domain it is tacit. Knowledge is human capital. Identifying new knowledge and creating new knowledge and adding value and vision to the new knowledge and its application is the essence of knowledge Management.
- *Knowledge Organisation:* The traditional and the current KM oriented organisation have a common orientation i.e. establishing semantic relationship, providing syntax, hyper linking, etc.

- *Knowledge Distribution:* In Knowledge Management distribution deals with creating a value for the intangible assets.
- *Knowledge Application:* The intrinsic value of knowledge created lies in its application in an appropriate situation. Application may be started from top-down to bottom-up and even in the middle. Each strategy has its own merits and risks.

Knowledge Management is comprehensive activity that manages information and knowledge under the environment that supports knowledge creation, acquisition, organisation, storage and distribution and utilisation accompanying information and communication technology (ICT).

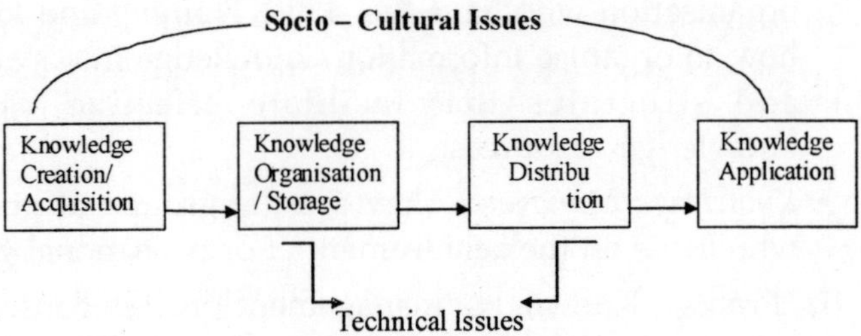

Fig. 11.1 : Knowledge Management Process

III. ***Technologies:*** Technologies needed for processing, storing and retrieval within and outside internet and a variety of Knowledge Management solution software packages are available from vendors. All the gadgets (Hardware and Software) requires interconnecting individual, i.e. Intranet. We are making use of existing technology to store and retrieve knowledge for promoting Knowledge Management in library operations.

In addition to Microsoft Office Suite, discussion lists, online help desk, virtual reference desk, web portal, etc. can all be employed to implement Knowledge Management in Academic Libraries. The beauty of digital age is that all documents are created in a digital format, which can be later ported to other storage and retrieval media/carrier.

INFRASTRUCTURE OF KNOWLEDGE MANAGEMENT

With the Knowledge management in libraries, many libraries incorporated Information Communication Technology (ICT) with internet and intranet facilities for rapid information access. KM is a useful resource. Qualified and dedicated personnel are required for a successful KM effort, as a supporting technology. The infra structure required for effective KM are:

- *Technical Skills*: Information management, information technology skills.
- *Business Knowledge*: Industry, markets, customer, competitors and general business context.
- *Interpersonal Skills*: Networking, listening, interpreting, challenging, teamwork, communication.
- *Management Skills*: Motivating, coaching, facilitating, influencing.
- *Organisation Knowledge*: Knowledge of precedures and culture.
- *Personal Characteristics*: Integrity, confidence, openness, trust, supportive, honesty, willingness to learn.

INTRANET: A KNOWLEDGE MANAGEMENT TOOL

An Intranet as a means of exploiting Internet Technologies within organisation based computer environment to aid the progression towards the seamless navigation of both internet based and in-house generated learning materials. Intranets have emerged as one of the most effective ways of sharing information and knowledge in most of the organisations. They act as circulation systems for supporting the flow of information. Therefore, it is necessary here to mention the importance of Intranet as a Knowledge Management tool.

Intranet as a private computing network, internal to an organisation allowing access only to authorised users.

Advantage of Intranet

- *User-friendly Interface*: Intranet application uses an interface that is conducive to point and click navigation. Users can easily get to the information they need and it is easy to learn.
- *Simplicity*: It can be created and maintained with a minimum of performing expertise.
- *Inexpensive updating*: One can easily and inexpensively update online publications. This can be done as frequently as necessary.
- *Consistency*: Knowledge existing on intranet can be viewed by all always as long as the network is online.
- *Interactivity*: One can create discussion groups, and other two-way communication tools.
- *Centralisation*: Users can access information from a central database at any time and in a number of geographical locations.
- *Flexibility*: Provides one access point to the organisation database from all corners of the organisation, as if it is available in one's own office.
- *Simplicity*: It can be created and maintained with a minimum of programming expertise.
- *Reduces paper work*: Intranet is closer to a paperless working environment, because the more the intranet progresses, the less paper will be used.
- *Currency*: The intranet contains the most current information knowledge in a format that can be searched.
- *Accuracy and timeliness*: Information and data are as accurate as supplied by people and will not change between requests and barring technical problems, messages will be delivered on time.
- *Faster and improved services*: Intranet improves the way in which services are rendered easily and quickly.

SIGNIFICANCE OF KNOWLEDGE MANAGEMENT IN ACADEMIC LIBRARIES

Knowledge Management is an emerging field, much tooted or hyped since late 1990s. Utilise the current management structure and technology to implement Knowledge Management, either bottom-up or top-down. With a concerted effort, Knowledge Management will help to increase libraries' operational efficiency and cater to the ever-increasing needs of our clientele. Knowledge Management as a discipline that promote as integrated approach to identifying, capturing, evaluating, retrieving and sharing all the information assets of organisation. Knowledge management is a process of identifying, acquiring, organising and sharing of information packages among the user groups.

CONCLUSION

Library acts as the major storehouse of human knowledge. With the implementation of modern technology with computers, telecommunication and net working, librarian acts as a knowledge manager who classifies, preserves and disseminates knowledge from the creator to knowledge seeking community irrespective of location and distance. Through Knowledge Management so far a corporate feature, the environment in which the academic libraries operate is changing. Academic libraries have not yet fully realised the potential of knowledge management. It is not individualistic but teamwork. They have the knowledge of information organisation along with certain amount of expertise is ICT application too. But they are poor in integration of work and individual skills. This is very essential as knowledge is considered as serviceable good and insures continued viability of libraries in ever changing knowledge.

REFERENCES

Jantz, R.C. (2001): Knowledge management in academic libraries: special tools and processes to support information professionals. *Reference Services Review, 29*(1): p. 33.

Branin, J.J (2003): Knowledge Management on Academic Libraries. *Journal of Library Administration,39(4)*, pp. 1-56.

Robinson,H.(1999), "The development of an intranet as a Knowledge Management tool". The law of Librarian, Vol. 30, No. 2, pp. 95-7.

Graterner Group: "Knowledge Management" available at:www.stevedenning.com/what_is_knowledge_management.html

http://en.wikipedia.org/wiki/five_laws_of_library_science

12

Knowledge Management: Value Added Functioning

— Noushia Parveen

ABSTRACT

Knowledge Management is a form of application of sound management practices as a whole which are the carrying factors of knowledge. Knowledge Management is the process through which organisation generate value added functioning from their intellectual and knowledge based asset. Knowledge considered as an intellectual capital as it results in productive usage. Intellectual capital means the property which is created by virtue of one's creation; it may be his/her idea, thought, design or any skill. Knowledge is presenting as a sign of power and prosperity. It has economic and fundamental value also, but beside this there are few issues as the society is suffering from knowledge explosion and inadequate information. People are lacking technical skills to explore their hidden talent. The paper examines the tools of Knowledge Management and role of a librarian as knowledge manager in Knowledge Management system and suggest the librarian in the present digital age to participate in the process of Knowledge Management.

Key words: *Information Management, Knowledge Explosion, Intellectual Capital, Knowledge Management Process, Knowledge Management Tools*

INTRODUCTION

Knowledge Management means the management of knowledge which resides in our brain as a result of observation. It deals not only with the information content of documents but also information present in employee's brain. It depends on the use of our knowledge which is dividing the world between fast moving economics that makes effective use of information and slow moving economics that do not use it. The significance of knowledge paved the ways for development of any country as well as of individual in the world.

Knowledge Management is concerned with the challenge that lies in tapping the tacit knowledge, which can not be easily codified and created in an environment that would facilitate creation of new knowledge and sharing it for organisation development.

The age in which we are living today is the age of information and knowledge that is presently driving all our human activities. It is indispensable raw material for right decision making from personal level to the social level. Knowledge is considering essential ingredient due to its multidimensional usage. No area of the society is untouched to the knowledge management. One can see its impact every where. The foundation of Knowledge Management is the power of learning. No organisation can improve without learning something new.

Definitions

"...a discipline that promotes an integrated approach to identifying, managing and sharing all of an enterprise's information assets. These information assets may include databases, documents, policies and procedures, as well as previously unarticulated expertise and experience residing in individual workers." **(Gartner Group Inc, October 1998)**

"Knowledge Management is the explicit and systematic management of vital knowledge and its associated processes of creating, gathering, organising, diffusing, using and exploiting. It requires turning personal knowledge into corporate knowledge that can be widely shared throughout an organisation and appropriately applied."

"Knowledge Management is the process of capturing, distributing and effectively using knowledge".-**Davenport**

"Knowledge Management is newly emerging interdisciplinary business model dealing with all aspects of knowledge within the context of the firm including knowledge creation, codification, sharing learning and innovation."

Ruggles.R.

What emerges from the above observations is that in this era of information and knowledge, knowledge is considered as an asset which includes documentary sources as patent, standard or database, policies and procedures as well as expertise. Knowledge Management comprises the process of creation, organisation, storage and dissemination for value added functioning of an organisation. Knowledge Management raises from personal to social level for developmental purpose. It emphasizes here that how personal knowledge converts into organisational for sharing and defusing among all for development.

KNOWLEDGE MANAGEMENT FEATURES

- **Intellectual Capital:** Knowledge is considered as an intellectual capital. Intellectual capital is the capital which is created by virtue of one's talent that is his ideas, design, and invention etc. Like other material knowledge, also can be purchased, sold and shared.
- **Sign of Power:** Knowledge is considered as a sign of power and prosperity. The development of an individual as well as of organisation depends on how their scholar or scientist are concerned regarding the use of knowledge into most productive effort.

- **Economic Value:** Knowledge Management consists of economic value in transforming all natural sources into finished products. Management of knowledge becomes tradable commodity which can be produced, sold and consumed like other essential commodities.
- **Fundamental Value:** The development of any individual as well as of nations depends on how its scholars or knowledge managers are enthusiastic towards managing the knowledge inside or outside. Standard of living of the people is depending on how in a better ways they utilise their knowledge. Knowledge Management establishes the knowledge profile of individuals and groups.
- **Decision Making:** Information professionals could provide consultation, advice about the selection of information sources, design of information search strategies and the evaluation of information. They could participate in decision-making activities. The outcome of knowledge based decision-making process results positively.
- **Value-Added:** It draws upon pooled expertise, relationships, and alliances. Organisations can further the two-way exchange of ideas by bringing in experts from the field to advise or educate managers on the recent trends and developments.

KNOWLEDGE MANAGEMENT TOOLS

Computing Tools	To enhance Tacit knowledge transfer within the organisation
Knowledge Server	Knowledge repositories, to search and access resources from many sources such as the internet, database etc.
Electronic Document Management	Content management system

Enterprise Knowledge Portals	Gateway of knowledge management system, supports web browser, database management system etc.
Knowledge Harvesting Tools	Capturing knowledge, maintain a directory of expertise and offers ways to content expert
Search Engines	Locating and retrieving vast collective accumulated in repositories.

KNOWLEDGE MANAGEMENT PROCESS

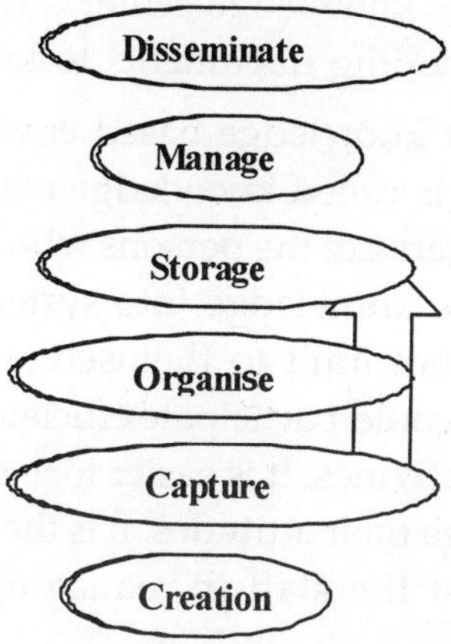

Fig. 12.1 : Knowledge Management Process

Creation: Generating new knowledge by virtue of ones ideas, thought and design etc.

Capture: Collection of resources to represent the generated knowledge.

Organise: Organise the created knowledge in format which is easy to use.

Store: Store the organised knowledge for further usage.

Manage: Stored knowledge is refined to transfer existing knowledge around the organisation.

Disseminate: Disseminate the filtered knowledge to mass.

KNOWLEDGE MANAGEMENT IN LIBRARIES

Knowledge Management in libraries is to prompt knowledge innovation. Knowledge Management is a discipline that promotes an integrated approach to creation, capturing organisation, accessing and using of a library's information asset. Libraries are considered warehouse of information and knowledge. Knowledge Management in libraries should be emphasised on the activities of research and development, to develop technical skills in the staff and the concept of how to best utilise the information and knowledge recitation in employee's brain to the most productive usage. Libraries are being reinvented as knowledge centers. The role of library is changed from providing documents to knowledge.

In the present knowledge based environment, the duty of a librarian who is called knowledge manager is increased. Knowledge managers are the persons who have the potentials of how to organise knowledge into system in a better way. Librarian should not limit to themselves as gatekeepers of information. They could participate efficiently in planning and decision making activities. It is easier to teach people technical skills than to change their attitudes. It is the duty of knowledge managers to assist the staff in managing and distributing knowledge.

KNOWLEDGE MANAGEMENT IN DIGITAL ERA

Libraries are grown to digital with the passage of time to meet the rapid changes in the information and communication technologies. Libraries are developing their resource access and sharing from print to digital format to provide easy and fast accessing of information to right user at least time. Digital Library efforts to strengthen the information resources, add and enhance resources to supply information and knowledge on demand as well as in anticipation. Knowledge Management is applicable to new information contexts, such as the management of metadata, the design and application of search engines or the creation of organisational structure.

Digital library is making a library undergo a change in the paradigm of its role of creating, organising and diffusing information resources. Digital Library needs user interfaces, networks, information networking for knowledge developing programs.

In the present scenario all the communications are electronic and process such as telecommunication, teleconferencing, substitute the person to person interaction. The ways, in which information is producing and disseminating also varies. In the current digital and networking knowledge age, the size of information resources on the Web is growing exponentially. Several Web pages are created in every second. A huge number of information is available on Internet.

KNOWLEDGE MANAGEMENT ISSUES

- **Knowledge Explosion:** Today people are suffering from the problem of knowledge explosion. Information is publishing in so many forms that it has become impossible to trace which part is usable and which is not. The tremendous growth in the knowledge available online as well as offline makes it difficult to get the desired one. It makes difficult to manage the knowledge.
- **Inadequate Information**: Beside the huge publication of information, information is publishing in incomplete format. Incomplete information unable to transmit the knowledge and it creates confusions. When one wants to get the desired information, he finds huge amount of information in an uncompleted format.
- **Vocational Training of Staff:** Talent is the key factor in the Knowledge Management. It becomes the focus of competition in the knowledge economy era. In the

knowledge economy of staff to raise their knowledge level and ability acquiring and innovative knowledge era organizations will have to attach importance to vocational training and life-long education.

- **Lack of Resources:** The earmarked plan and non plan fund allotted to the organisation are insufficient. Lapses in the management of fund allotted to the organisation can be seen from time to time.
- **Lack of Measure of Evaluation:** There is no system able to evaluate how and what knowledge one has created and disseminated and what is its effectiveness.

CONCLUSION

The value of Knowledge Management relates to the effectiveness of an organisation to organise past experiences, to deal with today's competitive situation and develop their future. Essence of Knowledge Management is to connect mass to mass to create and share knowledge for the development of an individual as well as of organisations. It is practical and action oriented. Its objective is to create value and to leverage, improve, and refine the competences and knowledge assets to meet organisational goals and targets. Information technology and systems can provide effective support in implementing knowledge Management. In this Knowledge Management society libraries can act as bridges for turning the results of knowledge innovation into realistic productive forces.

Knowledge is information that has been understood, interpreted and validated in the context of application. As such, knowledge represents a recognised platform for action. Knowledge Management is a very complex and highly dynamic activity. Although efforts are underway to make knowledge Management related approaches more practical and measurable. As globalisation trends increase pressures to adopt world class standards of performance and innovation, Knowledge Management becomes the predominant approach for optimising value creation.

REFERENCES

Chopra.H.S. Digital Library. Shree. 2006. pp. 6-13.

Davonport, T.H. Real success knowledge management project. Saloan Manage.Rev.,1998,39 (1), pp. 43-57.

Hubert Saint-Onge. How Knowledge Management adds critical value to distributed channel management. Journal of Systemic Knowledge Management, January 1998.The Mutual Group.

Hwa-Wei Lee. Knowledge Management and the Role of Libraries. Asian Division, Library of Congress. Wshington. DC. USA. hlee@lc.gov

Michael Egan. News That Stays News: Knowledge Management and the News Organization Model. Journal of Systemic Knowledge Management, January. 1998.

National conference on Digitisation and Digital Preservation, 11-12 December 2008, pp. 450-58 ©2008, DESIDOC.

Pandey, B.N et al. Knowledge Management software and tools for global libraries.Desidoc.2008, pp.430-37.

Ruggles, R. The state of the nation: Knowledge Management in practice. California Manage. Rev., 1998,40 (Spring), pp. 80-89.

Skyrme, D. Knowledge management: making sense of an oxymoron. 1997 (Management Insight, 2nd series, no (2) Web page ref http://www.skyrme.com/insights/22km.htm.

Upadhaya. J.L. Information Retrieval and Digital Libraries.Shree2004, pp. 42-68.

www.about-goal-setting.com/KM- **Library.**

13

Knowledge Management Issue, Concept and Challenges for LIS Professionals: In Modern Information Technology Age

— *Sunil Tyagi*

ABSTRACT

The paper discusses various facets of knowledge management, knowledge management technologies and tools and implementation and challenges in electronic age. It presents the role of knowledge management in business, learning and research organisations. It is the need of the hour to big, medium, and small and all kinds of organisations to cope with the challenges of knowledge management in the new century. Most extant knowledge management systems are constrained by their overly rational, static and a contextual view of knowledge. Effectiveness of such systems is constrained by the rapid and discontinuous change that characterises new organisational environments. The prevailing knowledge management paradigm limits itself by its emphasis on convergence and consensus-oriented processing of information. Strategy experts have underscored that the focus of organisational knowledge management should shift from 'prediction of future' [that cannot be computed] to 'anticipation of surprise.' Such systems may be enabled by leveraging the divergent interpretations of information based upon the meaning-making capability of human beings. By underscoring the need for synergy between innovation and creativity of humans and the advanced capabilities of new information technologies, this article advances current thinking about the knowledge management. Knowledge management is a strategy and shows a path how to face the global challenges in the most accelerated information technology world. It gives a message—"if they don't they won't survive".

Key Words: *Knowledge Management, KM Models, Intranet, Data mining Tools, Data warehousing Tools, Hi-Tech.*

INTRODUCTION

The exponential growth of information irrespective of the fields in the midst of information technology era created havoc for the availability of pin-pointed, authentic and timely information in a structured form which paved the way to establish the multidimensional, multidisciplinary, and versatile information in an organised form. The management of the increased complexities of prolix information due to technology's revolution, causing technological advancement thereby, intensive research and development, varied tastes of information of user communities, and more pertinently the information explosion in the 21st century created much impact upon the information managers and the decision making authorities to obtain, store, process, retrieve, and dissemination of the same in an organised form. The optimum use of the products and resources as well, from the Computer Technology Systems in an edifice and consolidated form and accumulated pool of information generated from the brains of Stalwarts in the field precipitated to establishment of Knowledge Management.

The Knowledge Management is the upshot of intensified research of scientists to contrive the overwhelming growth of information in an efficacious way with the help of the modern technological devices and is thus, an indispensable path in the highly competitive service oriented business environment which require more responsive, innovative, and competitive and efficiency. Knowledge Management is more of an art by which a skilled Knowledge Management practitioner makes an intelligent use of Information Technology systems and the pool of knowledge in an organisation to succor further its core competency. Information congregated form various sources and its compilation through electronically operated devices has become a powerful knowledge tool to meet the challenging and constant growing demands of the clientele in an effective way. Knowledge Management is a revolutionary method by which, the dispersed knowledge available from diversified sources is captured, assimilated and converted into a powerful competitive intelligence through various electronic stratagems such as CD-ROM, Floppy, Hard Disks, and Software etc.

KNOWLEDGE MANAGEMENT

Knowledge Management caters to the critical issues of organisational adaptation, survival, and competence in the face of increasingly discontinuous environmental change..... Essentially, it embodies organisational processes that seek synergistic combination of data and information processing capacity of information technologies, and the creative and innovative capacity of human beings.

Knowledge Management involves binding a company's internal and external information and turning it into actionable knowledge through technology. Knowledge Management principles recognised that it is important for institutions to "Know they know". All institutions inherently state, access, and deliver knowledge in some manner. The question is what value is added to the products and services they deliver by the effective use of that knowledge capital.

KM involves the "discovery and capture of knowledge, the filtering and arrangement of this knowledge, and the value derived from sharing and using this knowledge throughout the organisation". It is this "organisation complexity" of collaborative work to share and use information across all aspects of an institution which marks the effective use of knowledge. Knowledge Management is an integrated, systematic approach to identifying, managing, and sharing all of an enterprise's assets, including databases, documents, policies of procedures, as well as previously unarticulated expertise and experience held by individual workers.

Knowledge Management describes the way in which organisations are attempting to capture, enhance and utilise the knowledge necessary for their survival. It encompasses the spectrum of management concerns from knowledge creation to knowledge exploitation. It embraces the rapid developments in information technology and their effective use for the benefit of organisation.

Thus Knowledge Management is the process of capturing organisational collective expertise wherever it resides in databases, on paper, or in people's head and distributing it to wherever it can help produce the biggest payoff. "Knowledge Management is getting right knowledge to the right people at the right time so they can make the best decision."

Knowledge Management has many definitions, but is generally acknowledged to be the next "age" or revolution, in business and organisations, and is seen as a discipline. The concept behind Knowledge Management is applying an environment of management to the most valuable: asset of an organisation, i.e. its knowledge. The research proposed will pursue Knowledge Management as previously defined, that is, as an integrated approach to information assets. These may include databases, documents, policies, procedures, tacit expertise and experience, as well as content management.

Expected benefits from knowledge management: Process of Creation and Management of Knowledge

To capture the knowledge as assets of the company

- Expertise of the potential employees must be tapped and coded.

- Output resulting from research must be stored and processed.
- Output resulting from individual and group decision-making must be coded and stored.

Managing Intellectual Assets

- Components of Intellectual Capital have to be defined and framed.
- Methods have to be developed to identify and account for intellectual capital.
- Intellectual assets that qualify for legal or commercial protections e.g. patents trademarks, copyrights, trade secrets, etc must be maintained.

Continuous Improvement of Service delivery

- Planning and initiating a knowledge measurement programme.
- Installation of Performance Measurement Systems.

The Re-Learning of on-going service skills and competencies

- The full utilisation of organisation's knowledge base, coupled with the potential of individual skills, competencies, thoughts, innovations and ideas will enable a company to compete more effectively in the future.

Global sharing and teamwork

- Access to a worldwide network of knowledge specialists and facilitators with changed management skills.
- Virtual team working using videoconferencing or any other relevant platform will speed up the solution of critical operations' problems.

Knowledge management function

While every organisation's objectives and requirements are

different, basic knowledge management functions—including abstracting, making meaning explicit and deconstructing information into nodes and relationships to represent knowledge—are common to all business environments.

These functions can be categorised in the following way:

- **Finding, mapping, gathering, and filtering information:** They facilitate the collection, recording, organisation, filtering, analysis, retrieval, and dissemination of explicit knowledge *(consisting of all documents, accounting records, and data stored in computer memories. This information must be widely and easily available for an organisation to run smoothly)* and implicit or tacit knowledge (consisting of informal and unrecorded procedures, practices, and skills).
- **Developing new knowledge:** Creating and developing new knowledge is a crucial step. It is the essence of the knowledge management process. Developing repositories and knowledge teams, identification of potential and reliable new sources will help in the creation and development of knowledge.
- **Converting personal knowledge into shared knowledge resources:** As knowledge is personalised and it resides with the user, it must be coded and stored and shared among all knowledge seekers.
- **Understanding and learning:** Acquiring or extracting knowledge value.
- **Adding value to information to create knowledge:** The value of knowledge is pervasively influenced by the context of its use. Capabilities should be provided for flexibly arranging, selecting, for this Hyper processing of information must be done thoroughly.
- **Enabling action through knowledge:** Performance and management.
- **Processing shared knowledge resources:** Consistent improvement in knowledge sharing mechanisms and processing of the same is required to be done.

- **Delivering (transferring) knowledge:** Making implicit knowledge more explicit and putting it to use through improved mechanism can be widely shared throughout an organisation and appropriately applied.
- **Building a technical infrastructure:** A sound and well-integrated technical architecture has to be developed that is appropriate to the processing needs of the organisation. There is a need for seamless integration of the various tools in the areas of database management, communication and messaging, and browsing and retrieval of processed information.

CHALLENGES TO IMPLEMENTING KNOWLEDGE MANAGEMENT

An Institution, which has decided to implement Knowledge Management, will have to take up various challenges. These include employee participation, identification of relevant knowledge, managing dynamics of knowledge, and identifying the right person for seeing the project through.

Every educational institution across the country is wrestling with how to get the most out of its information systems. Certainly, there is no single road map for those colleges interested in using more informed decision-making to improve performance. But there are important signposts along the way: what organisational challenges are other colleges facing as they move towards more informed decision making? How is information shared and by whom? Who provides and interprets information? How is information used to resolve conflict? Are people rewarded for sharing information?

There are obvious challenges to the implementation of Knowledge Management. The Knowledge Management Magazine/IDC survey documents the following:

- Employee has no time for Knowledge Management.
- Current culture does not encourage sharing.
- Lack of understanding of Knowledge Management and benefits.

- Inability to measure financial benefits of Knowledge Management.
- Lack of skill in knowledge management techniques.
- Organisation's processes are not designed for knowledge management.
- Lack of funding for knowledge management.
- Lack of incentives, rewards to share.
- Have not yet begun implementing knowledge management.
- Lack of appropriate technology.
- Lack of commitment from senior management.
- No challenge encountered.

Obstacles in implementation of Knowledge Management

Implementation of knowledge management is more than a project. Much more effort has to be put in operation and management of knowledge. There are many obstacles and barriers on the individual, organisation levels which are constituted in a knowledge-oriented corporate culture. Some of the most common obstacles are:

- Introversion-afraid to learn from outsiders or expose internal operations to customers.
- Lack of balance between knowledge giver and knowledge receiver.
- Lack of trust among themselves.
- Lack of common terminology and shared understanding of key ideas inhibit a reasoned discourse among the practitioners and theorists of knowledge management.
- Diverse cultures, language habits.
- Lack of acceptance of knowledge: Statements of colleagues with low status are often ignored even if

they were the best and most practical. Employees in low status may also show reluctance in accepting senior's ideas and advices due to imperfections and egoistic state of mind.

- Business managers reluctant to adopt knowledge management solutions of any kind, no matter how well conceived.
- The poor local value of knowledge in the organisation (the local value of knowledge in the company is poor because of less productive work, gossiping in official hours, lack of commitments and seriousness etc.).
- Organised recognition and reward systems usually do not sufficiently recognise knowledge contributions. They are linked to traditional financial measures.
- Intolerance against mistakes and lack of help when there is a need.
- Unorganised information: Information, which is not organised/updated as per requirements, soon becomes outdated.
- Lack of systematic approach in dealing with information.
- Poor network infrastructure.

For successful implementation and management of knowledge, there is a need to develop a systematic approach, which enables you to perform in a better way at every stage of knowledge management process, which ultimately helps to achieve competitive advantages.

Creating competitive advantage by effectively implementing/managing knowledge

The successful implementation of knowledge management requires foresight and planning. It also requires perseverance on the part of both employees and managers, as well as an understanding of how the new process will affect corporate culture.

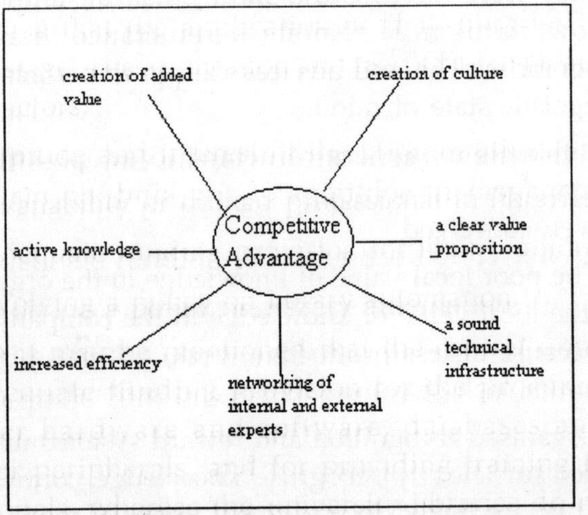

Fig. 13.1 : Efficient implementation of Knowledge Management leads to competitive advantage

- Creation of added value in the organisation by intensive usage of knowledge of all the employees and partners.
- Creation of a culture that supports innovation, learning and knowledge sharing.
- Increasing efficiency through repeated use and further developing best practice descriptions.
- A clear value proposition-identification of the link between knowledge and the bottom line business benefit; new measures of performance and appropriate rewards.
- Activating the knowledge of all managers at functional and strategic levels, customers, suppliers, and stakeholders by integrating their knowledge to have knowledge pool.
- Networking of internal and external experts in order to have the right knowledge at the right time at the right location or find it as quickly as possible.

- A technical infrastructure that supports knowledge work from simple knowledge support tools to intranets and ultimately more sophisticated groupware and decision support.

Implementing successful knowledge management requires a systematic change and project management approach. Over time, knowledge management changes the way that people work so that their individual knowledge is more effectively harnessed for the benefit of all.

Organisational/staffing implications

- Implementing knowledge management requires a change in behaviour and mindset of the people working in the organisation.
- A well-coordinated approach with clear accountability for overall implementation is a key to success.
- Each department, office and unit should decide how much staff time would be devoted to knowledge management-related activities.

Knowledge Management is resource intensive and its impact on productivity takes time to start. So staff at all levels will need to progressively invest time in training and to acquire the skills to operate new systems for processing knowledge.

New organisational environments & changing knowledge needs

The organisational environments are changing — at an ever-increasing rate, and toward ever increasing complexity. More recently, increased significance of environmental change for organisation's knowledge creation needs is apparent in the suggested need for more flexible and adaptive organisations. Organisational change is generally described as a response to the increasing environmental complexity and environmental turbulence. While environmental complexity is a function of the luminosity, diversity and interdependence of other entities in the organisation's environment, environmental turbulence is a consequence of the decreasing cycle-time of the individual events [such as new product introduction, customer response, etc.]. It has been suggested that the levels of both environmental complexity and turbulence, as well as their absolute rates of growth will be significantly greater in the future than in the past. Hence, future environmental change is expected to be more rapid and more discontinuous in nature.

Increasing complexity and turbulence of the external environment impose upon the organisation greater demand for processing information and making quick decisions. Within this scenario, organisational response to environmental change is the crucial determinant of its effectiveness. Radically changing organisational environments that demand ever-faster rate of information-processing, information-renewal and knowledge creation have motivated contemporary managers' interest in retrieving, archiving, storing and disseminating their organisation's information by using advanced information technologies. Organisations are devising means to accumulate employees' knowledge in electronic databases to use them as repositories of the shared, firm-wide "structural intellectual capital".

However, for most post-industrial organisations characterised by dynamically complex and uncertain environment, more and more knowledge *utilisation* as well as knowledge *creation* is *needed* at the interface of the organisation and the environment. The information-processing model of knowledge management is overwhelmed by the intense information flows required for:

(a) Keeping the centralised knowledge base and its custodians (managers) *continuously* current with the *discontinuously changing* external environment.

(b) Continually updating the employees on the latest changes in their outputs (goals) and changes in procedures to achieve those outputs.

Furthermore, increasing hyper turbulence and discontinuous change are not conducive for the sustained role of managers as the custodians of organisational knowledge:

> "...control is a function of knowledge [of managers], and in uncertain environments, knowledge [of managers] often does not exist." Within such environments, it is more efficient to handle complexity wherever and whenever it first enters the organisation – efficient operations in the new environment require a more equitable distribution of knowledge and authority. Such environments impose the need for *anticipating the future* based on multiple interpretations instead of predicting the 'right forecast'. Members of such organisations would need to be "effective anticipators" who can carry out the mandate of a faster cycle of knowledge-creation and action based on new knowledge. However, the prevailing information-processing view of knowledge management that is tuned to optimisation-based efficiency is unable to provide the organisational agility and adaptability that is necessary for radically changing environments.

'HI-TECH HIDE BOUND' KNOWLEDGE MANAGEMENT

The current thrust of organisational knowledge management efforts is on archiving 'best practices' for later reference by other employees. It is a popular belief that archival and subsequent observance of such practices would facilitate efficient problem-solving and prevent unnecessary allocation of sources to inefficient search processes. Incidentally, in due course, archived 'best practices' tend to define the 'dominant logic' or the 'company way'. Knowledge management *solutions* characterised by memorisation of best practices tend to define the assumptions that are embedded not only in information databases, but also in the organisation's strategy, reward systems and resource allocation systems. However, most such solutions represent "a temporary event, specific to a context, developed through the relationship of persons and circumstances". Such *recipes* for specific problem based situations [with the implicit assumption of *ceteris paribus*] may turn out to be recipes for disaster when future solutions need to be either thought afresh or in discontinuation from the past solutions.

The 'dominant logic' often persists even after the underlying assumptions have changed fundamentally. Hardwiring of underlying assumptions in organisational knowledge bases may lead to "perceptual insensitivity" of the organisation to the changing environment. Due to the changing business environment, such organisations may find themselves doing "more of the same" better and better, however, with diminishing marginal returns. The locked-in behaviour patterns lead to decreasing sensitiveness to the obsolescence of yesterday's 'best practices' archived in knowledge repositories. Just like the 'boiling frog' that is unable to sense the gradual change in temperature and ultimately boils to death, the cycle of doing "more of the same" leads to the organisational "death spiral". Yesterday's core capabilities embedded into information technologies could become tomorrow's core rigidities. Institutionalisation of the 'best practices' by embedding them into information technology might facilitate efficient handling of routine, 'linear,' and predictable situations during stable or incrementally changing environments. However, when change is radical and discontinuous, there is a persistent need for continual renewal of the basic premises underlying the practices archived in the knowledge repositories. Often, effective knowledge management in such environment may need "imaginative suggestions more than it does concrete, documented answers".

Unfortunately, the information-processing paradigm of knowledge management is devoid of capabilities that are essential for continuous learning *and* unlearning processes mandated by radical and discontinuous change. To ensure that yesterday's 'core capabilities' do not become tomorrow's 'core rigidities' organisations' capacity to *unlearn* ineffective 'best practices' assumes increased significance. However, the mechanistic and rigid nature of the routines embedded into information-processing based knowledge management is incapable of keeping pace with dynamic knowledge-creation needs for wicked environments.

TECHNOLOGIES FOR ENABLING KNOWLEDGE MANAGEMENT

Vendors of information-oriented products are rushing to introduce new knowledge management products and their reliable existing products as knowledge management products in an effort to quickly gain mindshare and market share in a potentially enormous market. But computer applications have addressed aspects of knowledge management for years.

No single technology fills all the criteria required of a knowledge management system, because knowledge management is not solely about technology. It is a multi-disciplinary field that draws on aspects of information science, interpersonal communication, organisational learning, cognitive science, motivation, training, publishing and business process analysis. The following sections look at the roles specific technologies play in an enterprise-wide knowledge management environment.

Intranets

Intranets have sprung up across corporations at a rate that challenges any previous introduction of new technology. They are ideal environments for sharing information that is both dynamic and richly linked. However, most large organisations quickly reach a point where much information exists on the intranet that it begins to suffer the same problems that exist on the www; no one knows where everything is, so no one can quickly find what he or she is looking for.

Document management systems

Document management systems are repositories of important corporate documents and are, therefore, important stores of explicit knowledge. They are also valuable tools for creating and processing complex documents, such as new drug applications in pharmaceutical companies. Document management systems excel at controlling the process of document creation, processing and review. Document management systems are important knowledge silos that must be integrated into the corporate knowledge infrastructure, but are not used by most organisations as the basis for a complete knowledge management system.

Information retrieval engines

Information retrieval technology, whether it is in the form of corporate text repositories or intranet search facilities, exists in many organisations as a knowledge silo containing legacy information. Information retrieval vendors continue to be concerned with satisfying the needs of information seekers and have added features such as relevancy ranking, natural language querying, summarisation and others that have increased the speed and precision of finding information.

Electronic publishing systems

With the advent of the internet, intranets, extranets, CD-ROM/DVD-ROM and other new delivery systems, the management and distribution of corporate knowledge has become much more complex. Leading organisations are integrating enterprise-level electronic publishing systems with their knowledge silos and will likely do so in the future with their knowledge management systems allowing users to present information in a consistent format regardless of its source, author or location.

Groupware and workflow systems

Organisations use groupware systems when users in workgroups or departments need to communicate and collaborate. Groupware allows formal and ad hoc conversations in cases when the participants can not communicate in real time. This makes groupware an important technology for enhancing the exchange of tacit information. However, like other applications, groupware databases become knowledge silos that must be integrated into enterprise knowledge architecture.

Push technologies and agents

Technologies that automate the transfer of information to end users have received considerable attention recently. Although e-mail served this purpose for over a decade, new web-based technologies have added better presentation, real-time updates and the ability to push applications as well as content. Content push is a dynamic form of electronic publishing and is, therefore, an important feature of a knowledge management system.

Help-desk applications

Many organisations use help-desk technology to respond to both internal and external requests for information. However, knowledge accumulated in help-desk systems can have much broader applications than answering specific questions. For example, service request logs are valuable tools to assist in product design and improving services.

Brainstorming applications

Brainstorming tools help inspire creative thinking and convert tacit knowledge into an explicit one. These end user applications help categorise, organise and identify knowledge resources and are, therefore, useful knowledge creation tools. While it should not try to replicate their functionality, an organisation's knowledge management system must provide an easy way for users or these applications to identify, capture and share the results of these activities with others across the enterprise.

Data warehouses and data mining tools

Organisations are creating data warehouses and arming their business managers with data mining tools to optimise existing relationships and discover new ones among the customers, suppliers and internal processes. Used primarily by business managers, leading organisations are now broadening their use since everyone in a knowledge-based organisation needs to make decisions based on increasingly complex sets of data. Knowledge management systems must provide meaningful access to data warehouses by supporting standard protocols such as Open Database Connectivity (ODBC) and Structured Query Language (SQL). Knowledge management systems also need to provide a way to describe and provide access to common reports so that users not intimately familiar with data mining tools and techniques can find and access current reports on subject areas they are investigating.

THE ROLE OF TECHNOLOGIES IN KNOWLEDGE MANAGEMENT

Two distinct factions exist in the knowledge management world. Those, who maintain that organisational behaviour and individual socialisation determine how much knowledge passes between individuals, generally believe that technology is not the answer. Rather, they see technology as merely a distraction from issues such as change management, culture and leadership. Information technology evangelists, who focus on technology as the solution to knowledge management question, occupy the other end of the spectrum.

Most case studies to date, however, have shown that a successful knowledge management program requires a change in organisational behaviour and in technology infrastructure. Technology is not the solution to an organisation's knowledge management needs; however, it is required to enable the organisation's knowledge management processes.

CHALLENGES FACED BY THE LIBRARIANS AND INFORMATION PROFESSIONALS: SERVICE PARADIGM SHIFTS

Knowledge Management is the collection of processes that govern the creation, dissemination and utilisation of knowledge to fulfill organisational objectives. Librarians and information professionals who work as integral members of business team will face new challenges calling for refinement in service paradigm. Obviously, the use of new technologies within libraries will bring more exciting possibilities for the development of new approaches to knowledge management. The approaches may be summarised as:

Knowledge Sharing: Most work described in the information profession as knowledge management is concerned with the development of computer-based information systems for knowledge sharing. The aim is to build networked 'Knowledge Management Systems' that provide access to the knowledge of organisational members regardless of geographical location of the persons who hold knowledge.

Knowledge Transfer: Knowledge may be acquired through research and development, organisational learning, and knowledge transfer. Knowledge transfer includes both the sharing of existing organisational knowledge and the acquisition of knowledge from external sources.

Library as a switching centre: The library of the future may not be having any collection of its own, but it would be a mere switching centre, referring users to potentially appropriate points in the vast network of resources accessible through Internet and world wide web.

Library as access provider: Library must develop its own collection of some high demand items by downloading from the national network to the campus network; it should also facilitate access to the resources available on national and international networks on demand.

The Library as Filter: An important role of the library is to 'feed' the personal database of its users in a dynamic way (through some form of profile matching), the most obvious criterion would relate to the frequency with which an individual needs to go beyond personal and institutional resources to satisfy a particular need.

CONCLUSION

Knowledge Management has been identified as the major and important management initiative that will help organisations, institutions, libraries and information centre to utilise the very fruit of information technology in fulfilling the objectives of parent organisation. The availability of new IT offshoot technologies, particularly Internet and WWW, has been instrumental in catalysing the Knowledge Management. It is equally important that if, the ICT tools and techniques are well resourced and effectively implemented, they will certainly provide a comprehensive knowledge platform for speedy, pin-pointed, exhaustively accessed, interactive delivery of the requisite contents to users. In the technological environment that is constantly changing, and especially one in which library services can be expected to become increasingly 'digital', it is extremely important for librarians to keep themselves well informed concerning new products and new developments of the type referred in the preceding sections. This is needed not only because librarians may be in good position to bring the relevant new technologies to the attention of others.

Organisational knowledge goes beyond mere documents, URLs and other explicit forms. Finding 'who knows what' in an organisation has always been a time-intensive process. Knowledge Management Solution must include a knowledge directory of peoples' skills and areas of expertise, so employee can quickly find the experts they are looking for. As global competitive pressures continue to increase, organisations that effectively manage their knowledge assets and continuously improve their knowledge transfer processes will gain substantial competitive advantage. Knowledge Management Practices, enabled by effective technologies, can add to both the top and bottom lines through reduced cycle times, greater efficiency and greater use of superior solutions across the enterprise.

REFERENCES

Applegate, L., Cash, J. & Mills D.Q (1988). "Information Technology and Tomorrow's Manager," In McGowan, W.G. (Ed.), *Revolution in Real Time: Managing Information Technology in the 1990s*, pp. 33-48, Boston, MA, Harvard Business School Press.

Bartlett, C.A. & Ghoshal, S (1995). "Changing the Role of the Top Management: Beyond Systems to People," *Harvard Business Review*, pp. 132-42.

Dubey, Yogendra P (2003). New Challenges in Information Management and E-Learning. *Library Herald*. 41(2): pp. 81-89.

http://www.emeraldinsight.com [Accessed on 26 Dec 2010]

http://www.iupindia.org [Accessed on 26 Dec 2010]

Mishra, Rabinarayan (2005). Strategies of Knowledge Management in Information Technology Age. *Library Herald*. 43(2): pp. 36-42.

Offsey, Steve (1997). Knowledge Management: Linking people to knowledge for bottom line results. *Journal of Knowledge Management*. 1(2): pp. 113-22.

Singh, K P (2005). Knowledge Management and Challenges to LIS Professionals. *Library Herald*. 43(2): pp. 115-23.

Srivastava, Kiran (2006). Knowledge Management and Higher Education. *University News*. 44(47): pp. 12-21.

Thakur, D S (2003). Knowledge Management: A Growing Discipline. *Library Herald*. 41(4): pp. 259-73.

14

Knowledge Management of Libraries in Digital Environment Era

— *Lata Patil*

ABSTRACT

This article will evaluate the development of knowledge management in the libraries in Electronic era. It will also examine the role of library professionals/libraries in knowledge management and suggests that library professionals/ libraries in the digital and knowledge age should be in charge of knowledge management in their respective organisations. Knowledge Management is the systematic process of creating, maintaining and nurturing an organisation to optimise the use of judgment in the attainment of mission and goals. Knowledge management provides an opportunity for achieving sustainable saving; signified improvement in human performance, and enhanced competitiveness. Knowledge management is multidisciplinary by nature and integrates concepts used in strategic management, organisation theory and information systems management.

Knowledge management stresses a formalised, integrated approach to managing an enterprise's intangible information assets.

INTRODUCTION

"People and ideas interact in both the real and virtual environments to expand learning and facilitate the creation of new knowledge."

Gartner Group defines Knowledge Management as:

"A discipline that promotes an integrated approach to identifying, capturing, evaluating, retrieving and sharing all of an enterprise's information assets."

The digital and knowledge management development in 21st century has become the key concern for library professionals. Today we live in a highly competitive world, everything is knowledge-based. E-libraries, E-news, E-information, E-Publishing and E-everything. The management of information has long been regarded as the domain of library professionals/libraries. Librarians and information professionals are trained to be experts in information searching, selecting, acquiring, organising, preserving and making them available to users.

The utmost goal of KM is to provide users with a variety of quality services in order to improve the communication, use and creation of knowledge. The services need to be tailored to the interest and needs of each user.

In the business world, knowledge management has been regarded as strategically important for organisations to gain a competitive advantage over their competitors, to add value to their products, and to win greater satisfaction from their customers.

In the library world, Knowledge management is as important for libraries as for the businesses minus the competitive, proprietary, and moneymaking concerns. In fact, libraries have had a long and rich experience in the management of information. Many of such knowledge and skills of librarianship can be applied to knowledge management.

For any library to succeed in implementing knowledge management will require a strong leadership and vision from the top administration, which can influence the organisation's knowledge sharing efforts in a positive way.

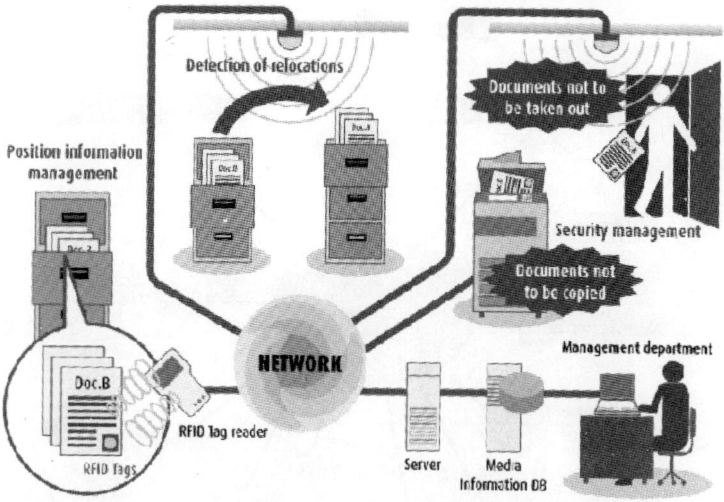

The Advanced Process of Knowledge Management

KNOWLEDGE MANAGEMENT IN LIBRARIES

While the business world is changing in the new knowledge economy and digital age, libraries of all types are undergoing drastic changes also. The new role of libraries in the 21st century needs to be as a learning and knowledge center for their users as well as the intellectual commons for their respective communities.

WHAT IS KM (KNOWLEDGE MANAGEMENT)

It's a combination of 3 elements - **Data * Information * Knowledge**

- Data: Raw Images; numbers, words, sounds, etc, which results from observations or measurement.
- Information: Data arranged or organised into meaningful patterns.
- Knowledge: Means to analyse/understand information/data; belief about casualty of events/ actions, and provides the basis to guide meaningful action and thought.

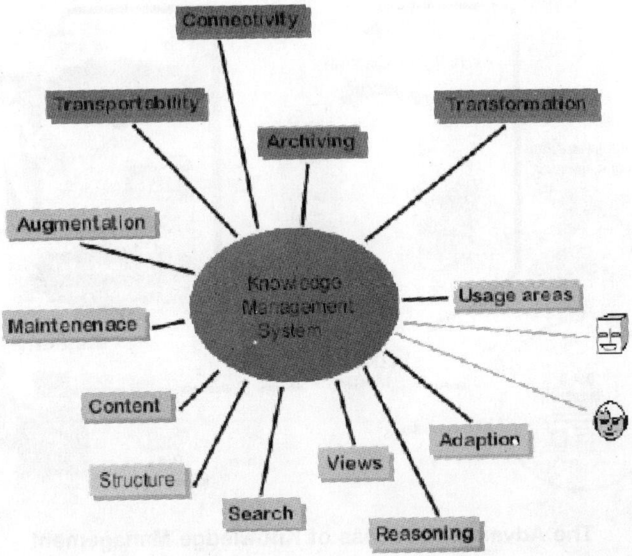

The Rotational process of Knowledge Management System

The common way that data, information and knowledge are interrelated is in a hierarchical structure, where the relationship is primarily unidirectional, with data supporting the generation of information, which is in turn used to generate knowledge. However, the interrelationship between these elements is much more complicated. While data and information can provide building blocks of knowledge, equally knowledge can be used to generate data and information. Therefore, the relationship between them is dynamic and interactive, rather than simply unidirectional.

Because of the exponential growth in human knowledge in a variety of formats, libraries need to develop their resources access and sharing strategies from printed to electronic and digital forms in concert with their mission and charges.

Universities and research organisations are themselves knowledge reservoirs. These highly valued intellectual assets, regardless of whether they are explicit or tacit, should be inventoried, archived, indexed, frequently updated, and made accessible in digital form.

Knowledge and technology are at present playing a major role in transforming into a Knowledge-Based Economy. The shift from industrial society to knowledge society is increasingly recognising knowledge as a crucial organisational resource.

The knowledge worker and knowledge management have, therefore, emerged as key elements for organisations to increase their efficiencies. In this context , various facets such as potential of knowledge sharing, creation of Knowledge Sharing Culture fostering Communities of Practice (CoP), role of KM in organisation learning and the need for KM education are extensively discussed, understood and practised.

BENEFITS OF KNOWLEDGE MANAGEMENT

- Can prevent Knowledge Walk Outs.
- If a person is shifted from one department to another, one can virtually walk away with almost all the knowledge with him.
- And if a person leaves the organisation, the knowledge is lost forever.
- Enhances the ability to know at an organisational level.
- Many things are known only at an individual level; so person sitting next to each other may not know the knowledge available with other (e.g. Past experience with a Vendor).
- Reduces the communication gap between an EXPERT & a NOVICE in an organisation.
- Due to geographical locations, hierarchy in an organisation, experts and novices hardly get any chance to interact and share knowledge.

- Improves the interaction between the design, production, service, maintenance and other varied departments.
- Any modern corporation's viability will depend only upon the ability to remain flexible to the demands as the service and products are converging in the modern world.
- Helps to avoid repetition of past mistakes.
- Successful organisation avoids repeating past mistakes.

CHALLENGES IN KNOWLEDGE MANAGEMENT

- Knowledge Management varies from organisation to organisation.
- Defining a knowledge framework is a complex operation.
- Controlling the correctness of knowledge is very essential.
- Accessibility of knowledge in wrong hands can have disastrous effects.
- People have the tendency of keeping the knowledge to themselves.

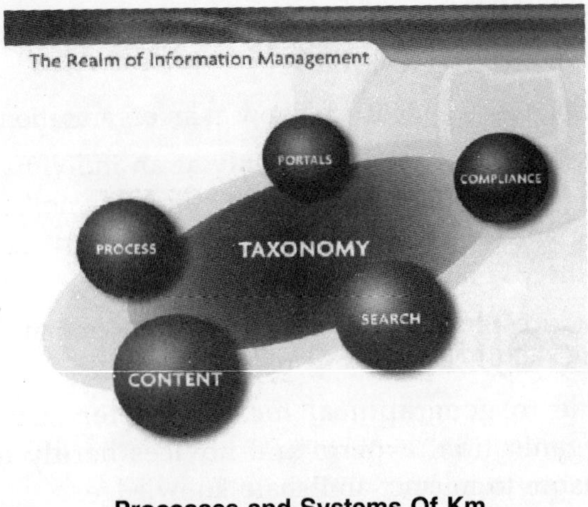

Processes and Systems Of Km

Knowledge Framework

- Understand, define and design various projects or work areas.
- Understand the members, departments and designations.
- Create Special Interest Groups.
- Identify and define the functional experts.
- Compile the various types of documents produced.
- Decide publishers for controlling correctness of information.

Roles of Individual in KM

K- Seek & K-Submit

- Every individual in an organisation has two roles in a knowledge community.
- Individual can submit knowledge.
- Individual would like to seek knowledge.

The apparent legion of difficulties can be distilled down to just four areas:

- **Objectives**: well defined, communicated, understood, and committed to
- **Demand**: commensurate with the level of capacity of the organisation
- **Capacity**: adequate to meet the current and projected demands
- **Effectiveness**: extent to which the organisation promotes demand, and manages capacity to respond to the demand on its journey toward its objectives.

Repository

- Prepare minimum information like title, author etc. about a document.
- Upload the document on the server through proper way based on software used and its retrieval process.

- Need functional experts to check the correctness of information for publishing module.
- Define the accessibility of the document on the basis of Confidential, Private and Public.
- Handle revisions & edition of the documents.

Seek Knowledge

Search the knowledge for a specific term & get the

- Documents
- Functional Experts
- FAQ Sessions
- Minute of the meetings.
- Poll
- Any knowledge snippet on that topic.

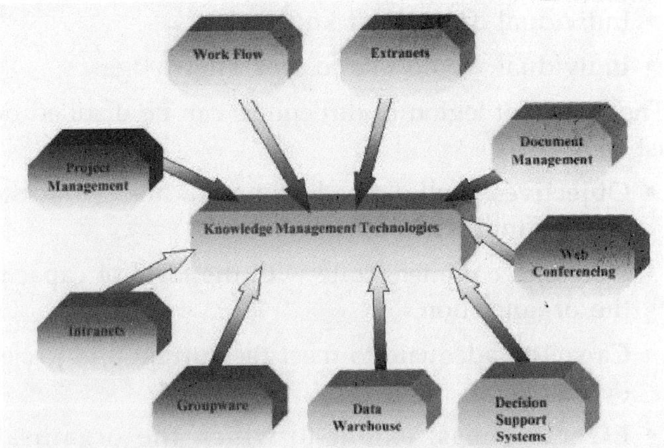

Diagram represents the main technologies that presently support knowledge management systems.

Software will provide any piece of knowledge based on:

- Latest Uploads – Knowledge added lately.
- Suggested Docs – An expert can suggest a doc for reference to all the juniors.

- Popular Docs – Give your vote on the popularity of the document.
- S.D.I. – Selective Dissemination of Information provides you the knowledge based on your subject profile.

KNOWLEDGE MOBILISATION

- Whenever one view any piece of knowledge, they can share the tacit knowledge which is called a Knowledge Snippet.
- One can add new keywords and make the document more searchable.
- One can even comment on the knowledge snippet already entered in the past into the system.

Efficiency of Software

The knowledge base of any organisation can get created and managed by KM which in turn protects the Intellectual Property.

- It is a 100 % web enabled solution and hence anyone can log in from any terminal and hence the access is very easy.
- Suggesting a document or answering to a question posted to an expert can be handled very easily.
- Dissemination of knowledge is very fast because it is Web enabled.
- Intellectual Property is the most important asset; any organisation can create in the modern world.
- Knowledge Management is the first step towards creating and protecting this asset.
- Knowledge Management is a journey and not a destination!
- Software –KM is a vehicle to make this journey comfortable.

ROI Analysis (Return On Investment)

- Observation had clarified that every WORD document is copied on a machine at least 5 to 10 times! – **Document Repository can eliminate these duplications and result in a cost saving.**
- An employee walks away with almost 90 % of knowledge when they leave the organisation – **Tacit knowledge mobilisation helps in retaining if not 100%, at least some percentage of the tacit knowledge.**
- A major portion of every meeting is taking the review of earlier meeting. – **Since the action taken on every meeting point is available online, there is a tremendous cost saving on meetings.**
- Interaction between functional experts and members takes place through expensive seminars and conferences. – **A constant dialogue can be maintained between the experts and members resulting in cost savings.**
- Repetition of mistakes takes place because of the communication gap between employees. – **KM also allows sharing experiences, which are searchable helping in avoiding repetition of mistakes.**

CONCLUSION

The article deals with (the integration of) methods, techniques, and tools to support users to structure documents and data of multiple formats, and to query knowledge and information from multiple views.

The focus of knowledge management is connecting people, processes and technology for the purpose of leveraging organisation knowledge. The database professionals of today are the Knowledge Managers of the future, and they will play an integral role in making these Connections possible.

Organisations are realising that intellectual capital or institutional knowledge is a valuable asset that can be managed as effectively as physical assets in order to improve performance.

REFERENCES

Hislop, Donald "Knowledge Management in Organisations" - 2007.

Krishnan, Jaya (Ed.) "Knowledge Management Practices and Experiences" - 2006.

Koganurmath, Muttayya (Ed.) "Knowledge for All" – Roll of Libraries and Information Centres - 2008.

Jim Bair, "Knowledge management is about cooperation and context." Gartner Advisory Services Research Note. May, 14, 1999.

http://www.bestpicturesof.com

15

Role of Total Quality Management as a Knowledge Facilitator

— *Harmanpreet Singh*

— *Harpreet Kaur Rana*

ABSTRACT

Purpose *– The purpose of this paper is to investigate the role of total quality management (TQM) as a knowledge facilitator in the creation and exploitation of organisational knowledge.*

Design/methodology/approach *– This qualitative investigation adopts a case-study methodology to analyse the role of TQM in knowledge creation in few prominent ûrms, utilising an investigation framework based on the "socialisation", "externalisation," "combination," and "internalisation" model of knowledge generation.*

Findings *– TQM is shown to be an effective facilitator of knowledge generation. TQM provides policies and tools (such as general involvement of all employees, teamwork, feedback mechanisms, and widespread communication) that are inherently useful as enablers of knowledge creation and dissemination.*

Research limitations/implications *– Future studies should investigate the speciûc causal nexus between TQM and product innovation.*

Practical implications *– TQM can be utilised to support an organisation's utilisation of corporate knowledge as a real source of competitive advantage.*

Originality/value *– Empirical research on knowledge and quality management is scanty. This paper addresses the gap by empirically examining the relationship between TQM and knowledge creation.*

KEYWORDS: Total quality management, Knowledge management, Knowledge creation, Learning.

INTRODUCTION

Firms have become increasingly interested in making effective use of the knowledge that continuously develops within their organisations. The capacity to organise and manage processes in a manner that facilitates the creation and sharing of knowledge within the organisation has become a signiûcant competitive asset. The important role played by intangible resources (such as knowledge) in gaining a sustained competitive advantage has been emphasized by various authors who have adopted a resource based view. Against this background, the notion of "knowledge enablers" has received increasing attention from several authors (Ichijo et al., 1998; von Krogh et al., 2000). Knowledge enablers are organisational mechanisms that facilitate both the random occurrence and the systematic development of knowledge within an organisation. Five such knowledge enablers have been identiûed in the literature (Ichijo et al., 1998; von Krogh et al., 2000):

(1) Instilling a knowledge vision;

(2) Developing and managing an "organisational conversation";

(3) Creating the right context by developing an organisational structure that facilitates knowledge creation;

(4) Managing caring relationships; and

(5) Disseminating local knowledge across several organisational levels.

Such enablers are especially significant in facilitating knowledge sharing and interaction among the members of the organisation, thereby transforming individual knowledge into organisational knowledge (Ichijo et al., 1998). In the view of von Krogh et al. (2000), knowledge creation requires an enabling context.

Several authors have adopted such a knowledge-based view of total quality management (TQM) and its potential to facilitate knowledge creation and sharing (Grant et al., 1994; Zairi and Yousef, 1995; Thiagarajan and Zairi, 1997; Sitkin et al., 1994; Shiba et al., 1990; Graham and Shiba, 1993). In this regard, it has been noted that the implementation of quality systems is inherently linked to organisational learning. The adoption of quality principles and methodologies throughout an organisation is recognised as a necessary pre-condition for the development of a modern and successful enterprise. Similarly, it is acknowledged that a primary source of competitive advantage is constituted by a continuous process of knowledge creation (Nonaka and Takeuchi, 1995; Mele, 2003). TQM would thus seem to have the potential to satisfy some fundamental organisational needs by facilitating the attainment of advanced levels of knowledge that exceed actual operational needs and that can be translated into continuous improvement processes and innovative solutions.

Despite the apparent affinity that exists between TQM and enhanced organisational knowledge, empirical studies of the link between quality systems and knowledge creation are scanty. The objective of this study is, therefore, to investigate whether TQM really is a knowledge enabler in practice. More specifically, the study aims to discover whether TQM facilitates knowledge creation in terms of new product and process development.

LITERATURE REVIEW

Researchers have often noted the role played by knowledge in various quality practices, but only recently have academics speciûcally related knowledge creation and learning to quality management (Linderman et al., 2004). In this regard, Fine (1986) studied learning in terms of conformity and failure costs (that is, the impact of learning on quality levels); Tapiero (1987) analysed the effect of learning on quality control; and Sitkin et al. (1994) attributed an important role to knowledge within TQM in advocating the need for a "total quality learning system" in parallel to a "total quality control system". Until the latter half of the 1990s, studies of quality and knowledge in the academic literature were primarily focused on explicit knowledge – that is, knowledge that is easily shared and imitated (Linderman et al., 2004). It was only relatively recently that noted that any consideration of TQM and knowledge must consider both tacit knowledge and explicit knowledge.

Several researchers have noted that a comprehensive theory of knowledge creation is required to develop an integrated perspective of the dynamic relationship between explicit knowledge and implicit knowledge (Colurcio, 2001; Linderman et al., 2004; Ichijo et al., 1998). In this regard, Nonaka's (1994) four-step model of "socialisation," "externalisation," "combination," and "internalisation" (SECI) proposed four modes of knowledge conversion from the tacit level to the explicit level (and vice versa).

According to the SECI model (Nonaka, 1994; Nonaka and Takeuchi, 1995), organisational knowledge creation takes place in a dynamic way within an organisation when:

(1) Feelings, experiences, and mental models are shared (that is, tacit to tacit via "socialisation").

(2) Tacit knowledge is exploited in a wider and more conscious way than in its original ambit and becomes conceptual knowledge (that is, tacit to explicit via "externalisation").

(3) Explicit knowledge of different types interacts (that is, explicit to explicit via "combination").

(4) Explicit knowledge that is already "socialised", "externalised", and "combined" is again transferred into the tacit dimension as experience (that is, explicit to tacit via "internalisation").

More recently, Linderman et al. (2004) integrated the quality dimensions proposed by Sitkin et al. (1994) and the knowledge-creation process proposed by Nonaka (1994) to develop a theoretical framework that links knowledge and quality. This integrated framework is shown in Table I.

RESEARCH METHODOLOGY

Figure: 1 illustrates the framework adopted for this empirical study. The framework, which is based on the SECI model (Nonaka, 1994; Nonaka and Takeuchi, 1995), is focused on an organisational knowledge-creation process. As shown in Figure 1, the socialisation phase is examined by identifying organisational actions that aim to promote interactive teamwork among individuals with a view to pre-existing tacit knowledge being shared. To analyse the evolution from tacit group knowledge to explicit knowledge (that is, the externalisation phase, followed by the combination phase), the framework focuses on the formalisation of knowledge by the organisation and on internal communication actions that foster knowledge explication by each organisation member. Finally, to investigate the internalisation phase, the framework

	Tacit knowledge to	*Explicit knowledge*
Tacit Knowledge To *Explicit Knowledge*	Team Work (Socialisation)	Organisational formalisation (externalisation)
	Feedback mechanisms and procedures (internalisation)	All employees involvement and sharing objective (combination)

Fig. 1 : The investigation framework

Table 1. Integration of knowledge and quality management

Quality	Knowledge			
Customer Satisfaction	Socialisation Tacit → tacit Extent of interactions between organisational members and customers	Externalisation Tacit → explicit Extent that customer needs are articulated or conceptualized	Combination Explicit → explicit Extent of information analysis conducted on customer data	Internalisation Explicit → tacit Extent of monitoring and providing feedback of customer information
Continuous improvement	Extent of interactions between organisational members in improvement activities	Extent that improvement ideas are articulated in the form of theories, concepts, or cause-and-effect reasoning	Extent of information analysis conducted on problem understanding and diagnosis	Extent of ongoing process monitoring and control
System view	Extent of interactions between heterogeneous organisational member	Extent that organisation conceptualizes the purpose and the aim of system	Extent that organisation synthesizes information from heterogeneous source	Extent that organisation consistently acts in conformance with its purpose, aim, and strategy

focuses on feedback mechanisms to assess the effective implementation of elaborated procedures and tools.

RESEARCH DESIGN

The objective of the study was to explore the relationship between the adoption of TQM and the creation of knowledge in large enterprises. To obtain rich and varied data on these qualitative phenomena, the study adopted a case-study methodology (Yin, 1999). The selection of cases for study was restricted to enterprises that had already adopted TQM and that had a reputation for excellence in quality issues through their involvement with the European Foundation for Quality Management. The ûnal sample consisted of 20 large enterprises from a variety of industries, as shown in Table II.

The field study began with interviews with managers on the subjects of:

The ûrm's TQM model;

The ûrm's new product development (NPD) model

Other relevant internal variables (operative procedures, organisational structure); and

Other relevant external variables (competitive positioning, business image)

Table 2 : The research sample

	Firms	Industry
	1	2
1.	Orion Engg works	Agriculture Equipments
2.	Airtel	Telecommunications
3.	Canon	Information Technology
4.	Compaq	Electronic
5.	Hewlett-Packard	Information Technology
6.	WaveTech Electronics	Electronic
7.	IBM	Information Technology

	1	2
8.	BSNL	Telecommunications
9.	Kodak	Optical
10.	Super Impex	Electronic
11.	GE India	Power and Automation
12.	Nestle	Food
13.	Nokia	Telecommunications
14.	Aarkay	Engineering
15.	Rotomac	Automation
16.	JMD Engg works	Automobiles
17.	S&T Microelectronics	Automation
18.	Instronix India	Electronic
19.	Ajanta Chemical Inds.	Chemical
20.	Xerox	Information Technology

This ensured that the study's data were derived from people with first-hand knowledge and experience of the investigated phenomena. Data triangulation (Mari, 1994) was also employed using a variety of tools, such as documentary analysis, direct observation, and informal conversations.

FINDINGS: SOCIALISATION STAGE

The socialisation process enables individuals to share experiences with each other and to share tacit knowledge (such as technical abilities and mental models). In the investigated firms, the key to the development of socialisation was identiûed as a form of on-the-job training, whereby individuals utilised observation and imitation to learn skills and work procedures.

In all of the ûrms studied here, the socialisation stage was dependent on leadership from senior management to engender a commitment to quality and to coordinate resources for the achievement of quality objectives. The research sample of the studied ûrms fostered teamwork to facilitate the sharing of tacit knowledge and to encourage the involvement of employees. In AIRTEL managerial guidelines (entitled "information for managers"), which contain managerial advice on TQM, all subsidiaries are encouraged to "share in house experience". All business units are assessed annually with respect to the implementation of best practice with regard to the sharing of information. The leadership policy deployed by Airtel with respect to TQM and the management of human resources was systematic and effective in promoting teamwork. At Orion Engineering works, teamwork is understood to be a means of assisting employees in their individual careers, as well as being a means of helping employees to gain familiarity with the tools of TQM in their everyday tasks. Teams are trained in both "quality circle" techniques and leadership skills to ensure that TQM tools are shared for problem solving. Within each team, a leader is chosen, and when a particular project has been completed (or the problem that led to the team's formation has been solved), the leadership role passes to another member.

Teamwork also played a prominent role in the socialisation process among organisation members at WaveTech Electronics. About four years ago, the company began an experimental project that aimed to stimulate the involvement of all employees in the sharing of objectives and cultural change. This involved the breaking down of all preconceived notions and mental habits. At the beginning, this project in teamwork and team building involved 80 employees who were chosen from among the youngest people in the organisation. Today, such teams are organised throughout the whole company, and teamwork is considered to be a daily routine by which all of the ûrm's activities are managed.

Teamwork also has a long history at S&T Microelectronics, where it is seen as an effective method for developing competencies, fostering knowledge interaction, and facilitating the development of a homogeneous corporate culture. More speciûcally, teams at S&T consist of six or seven individuals, of whom two-thirds have experience and knowledge of the particular matter under consideration whereas the remainder has absolutely no knowledge of it. This procedure highlights the role of so-called "tacit knowledge bags," which are held by individuals who are not formally involved in speciûc activities and who are not usually inclined to share the experiences (for reasons of individual shyness or poor motivation).

Other methods to encourage knowledge sharing among employees have been trialled by GE India and by Kodak, in which formal meetings have been constituted to stimulate individual knowledge and improve relationships among employees (Choi and Lee, 2000).

Table III presents a summary of the main actions implemented by the investigated ûrms to foster the socialisation process.

EXTERNALISATION STAGE

Formalisation of the knowledge that had been created by sharing and teamwork (in the socialisation stage) was a prominent feature (of the subsequent externalisation stage) in all of the investigated ûrms. Formalisation of concepts, routines, knowledge, and experiences facilitated the evolution of knowledge from the individual (tacit) level to the organisational (explicit) level. In this regard, it is of interest that formalisation is important within many quality systems for:

- Legitimising the principles of the quality system; and
- Overcoming any opposition to their implementation.

Moreover, formalisation is an important element in such regulatory models as ISO 9000, which had been applied in all of the investigated ûrms as a preliminary to the full implementation of TQM systems. According to some of the interviewed managers, such formalisation of created knowledge stimulates access and consultation by everybody, and thus legitimises the crossing-over of functions and the formation of new relationships. Interesting examples of "electronic formalisation" were apparent in Airtel, GE India, and Xerox. With the support of efficient computer technology, formalisation in these ûrms overcame the bureaucratic obstacles that inevitably arise from written documentation. In these ûrms, formalisation through electronic networking ensured "leaner management" of the quality system because it enabled rapid interaction, consultation, and updating.

In other companies, such as S&T and JMD, formalisation of quality policy was promoted by billposting and printed material delivered to employees with their salaries. Some companies (Nestle´, Kodak, Xerox, and Compaq) distributed manuals of company procedure to both managers and employees. This is in accordance with common practice in the deployment of TQM, which, in general terms, is a strategy deûned by corporate headquarters and then deployed throughout the organisation as the principles and action plan of TQM are formalised into speciûc documents, manuals, and quality plans.

Table IV summarises the main actions undertaken by the investigated firms in the externalisation stage.

Table 3 : Actions to foster the socialisation stage

Actions	Level of implementation
Brainstorming	+ +
Formal meetings	+ +
Informal events	+ +
Personalised teamwork	+ + +
Quality circle	+
Structured interfunctional conversation	+ +
Structured conversation	+
Traditional teamwork	+ + +

Table 4 : Actions to foster the externalisation stage

Actions	Level of implementation
Action plans	+ + +
Handbook	+ + +
Information for managers	+
Intranet procedures	+ +
Others	+ +

All of the companies studied here had policies that aimed to ensure the sharing of knowledge and experiences among all members of the organisation. Human-resource training and management emphasised participation, individual knowledge development, teamwork, and interaction among individuals. Some of the companies had developed excellent programs for involvement of the whole organisation and the sharing of objectives, which stimulated the internalisation of a diffuse organisational culture among all employees and managers. Within IBM and Super Impex, senior management had created an enterprise culture based on trust and open dialogue through the "manager interview", which aimed to optimise the collaboration between managers and their subordinates. This is a process of structured interviews during which subordinates inform their direct supervisors about what they have gained from their activities and the possibilities for improvement. The supervisor then uses this feedback from various subordinates to formulate the objectives to be achieved in the forthcoming year. This process supports the team-building process and enhances understanding between supervisors and dependants – thus optimising collaboration and the attainment of reciprocal trust.

In HP and Aarkay, some programs were identiûed which, originating within the ûrm's TQM system, explicitly recognised the value of cooperation and the results obtained by teamwork. In these programs, the authority to undertake actions is given to the employees. This empowerment moves decision making to parts of the organisation where it can effectively add value to the customer; however, this requires investment in training and communication. Similarly, empowerment was a TQM factor that had been enthusiastically adopted by Kodak – a company that consciously sets out to stimulate employees' creativity, encourages the development of quality teams, and promotes effective teamwork in pursuit of quality. A key element of management practice and philosophy in this company was open communication; formal and informal communication mechanisms have been deployed to stimulate an environment of open conversation, disseminated knowledge, and reciprocal trust. Various other mechanisms for knowledge sharing and the transformation of individual knowledge to the organisational level were noted in GE India, Airtel, Nestle´, and Nokia. These included such initiatives as:

- The promotion of individual ideas through the use of a suggestion box; and
- The design of a software program that enables all organisational members to express anonymous opinions freely through the company's intranet.

All of the investigated companies promoted the involvement of employees in organisational sharing, with particular reference to quality targets. Appropriate training and education programs were apparent in all the ûrms.

Table V summarises the actions developed by the investigated ûrms to improve the involvement of employees.

INTERNALISATION STAGE

Within their own TQM systems, the case companies developed appropriate feedback mechanisms regarding the degree of human resources involvement in employees' perceptions of the company environment. Almost all of the companies conducted "climate surveys" to ascertain whether work procedures and routines had been transformed effectively. Such analysis enabled the ûrms to identify gaps in critical areas for which corrective actions were required to achieve desired organisational targets. In such "climate surveys," all employees were required to complete an anonymous questionnaire about their opinions and perceptions of the current status of the organisation.

Table 5 : Actions to foster the combination stage

Macro Actions	Specific Actions	Level of Implementation
Employees training	Focus groups	+ +
	Open-door policies	+ +
	Teamwork	+ + +
Empowerment	Departmental meetings	+
	Climate interviews	+ + +
Employee satisfaction	Teamwork	+ + +
	Project team	+ +
Knowledge sharing	Wide and diffused communication	+ +
	Intranet	+ +

In Kodak, the implementation of enterprise resource planning has been used as launching platform for information-monitoring mechanisms. Texas Instruments has instituted an "attitude survey," together with informal and formal staff meetings. At these meetings, which often originate at the request of employees, information is gathered through focus groups and question-and-answer sessions.

Table VI summarises the feedback mechanisms identiûed in the investigated ûrms.

To avoid unnecessary repetition, some of the mechanisms identiûed in earlier stages have been omitted from this table.

DISCUSSION

The study has demonstrated that there is a relationship between the implementation of TQM systems and principles and the capacity for knowledge creation within a company. The application of the SECI model (Nonaka and Takeuchi, 1995; Nonaka et al., 2000) in the present study has shown that the fundamental values and procedures of TQM stimulate the development of mechanisms that facilitate the conversion of tacit knowledge into explicit knowledge (and vice versa). Table VII summarises the knowledge-creation process in the ûrms investigated in this study. The widespread application of teamwork appeared to be especially effective in exploiting the so-called "tacit knowledge bags" that exist within all organisations.

Table 6 : Actions to foster the internalisation stage

Actions	Level of Implementation
Employee motivation and satisfaction survey	+ + +
Attitude surveys (gathering perceptions)	+ + +
Climate interviews	+ +

Through inter-functional sharing in a participatory organisational climate, individuals were encouraged to make their tacit knowledge explicit. Moreover, by sharing their knowledge with others, individual employees have become appreciated as thinking who are capable of making a valuable personal contribution to the improvement of their organisations. There is no doubt that, in the companies studied here, the fostering of teamwork and the encouragement of individual initiative and innovative ideas has meant that the socialisation phase has stimulated the effective sharing of tacit knowledge.

With respect to the externalisation phase, TQM was again shown to have a synergistic role in knowledge creation. This was in accordance with common practice in the deployment of TQM, which is typically disseminated throughout organisations in documents and manuals that specify the principles and action plans of TQM. These practices contributed to the creation of explicit knowledge and the sharing of that knowledge within groups.

With regard to the combination phase, various intra-organisational programs to encourage internal communication and job enrichment were identiûed in the studied companies. These programs facilitated the development of a common knowledge platform within an organisational culture of trust and open dialogue. It has been noted by Warglien (1990) that organisational knowledge does not exist in itself; rather, it results from the dynamic interaction of the knowledge of various individuals. In this regard, it is apparent that TQM stimulated the sharing of individual knowledge through the involvement of all organisational members, thus combining their knowledge to form a valuable company asset. Moreover, the strongly formulaic nature of TQM appeared to act as a legitimising factor in facilitating the explication and combination of individual knowledge. With regard to the most delicate phase, the internalisation of knowledge created by all members of the organisation, it emerged that the feedback mechanisms of TQM were eminently suitable for assessing the knowledge of individual employees and for identifying any required corrective actions for improvement.

CONCLUSIONS AND IMPLICATIONS

TQM can be understood as a systematic and global approach to enterprise management, based on the logic of management by process, with the aim of continuous improvement in an enterprise's performances (especially with respect to the utilisation of human resources) in order to satisfy the explicit or implicit expectations of customers and other stakeholders (Shiba et al., 1990; Dean and Bowen, 1994; Grant et al., 1994). On the basis of this study, it is apparent that TQM (as deûned above) can be a potent knowledge enabler within an organisation.

Customer satisfaction is at the heart of the whole TQM apparatus, and its dynamic and continuous nature has an inherent capacity to generate creative innovation and knowledge creation. Moreover, TQM's emphasis is on the involvement of all employees.

Table 7 : The knowledge-creation process in the investigated firms

Actions	Level of Implementation
Socialisation	+ + +
Externalisation	+ + +
Combination	+ +
Internalisation	+ +

The knowledge-creation process in the investigated ûrms open communication, and the sharing of objectives stimulates individual ideas and empowerment.

In terms of managerial implications, the study clearly identiûed the fundamental role played by senior leadership in generating new organisational knowledge. An empowering and open-minded leadership, based on organisational values of sharing and trust, therefore, represents an indispensable pre-condition to the generation of effective knowledge-creation mechanisms.

REFERENCES

Barney, J.B. (1997), Gaining and Sustaining Competitive Advantage, Addison Wesley, Reading, MA.

Choi, B. and Lee, H. (2002), "Knowledge management strategy and its link to knowledge creation process", Expert Systems With Application, Vol. 23, pp. 173-87.

Colurcio, M. (2001), "Investigation of the relationship between TQM and innovation: a research study", Proceedings, EIASM (European Institute for Advanced Studies in Management), 8th International Product Innovation Management Conference, June 9-11, Enschede, The Netherlands.

Colurcio, M. and Mele, C. (2006), "TQM as a route to business excellence and stakeholder value: fundings from a case studies research,"

Journal of Quality and Reliability Management, Vol. 3 No. 5, pp. 464-89.

Dean, J.W. and Bowen, D.E. (1994). "Managing theory and total quality: improving research and practice through theory development," Academy of Management Review, Vol. 19 No. 3, pp. 392-418.

Dooley, K.J. (2001). "The paradigms of quality: evolution and revolution in the history of the discipline," Advances in the Management of Organisational Quality, Vol. 5, pp. 1-28.

Graham, A. and Shiba, S. (1993). "Total quality", The Center of Quality Management Journal, Vol. 2, No. 1, pp. 3-8.

Grant, R.M., Shani, R. and Krishnan, R. (1994). "TQM's challenge to management theory and practise," Sloan Management Review, Winter, Vol. 35. No. 2, pp. 25-35.

Linderman, K.M., Schroeder, R.G., Zaheer, S., Liedtke, C. and Choo, A.S. (2004). "Integrating quality management practices with knowledge creation processes," Journal of Operations.

Nonaka, J., Toyama, R. and Konno, N. (2000). "SECI, ba and leadership: a unified model of dynamic knowledge creation", Long Range Planning, Vol. 33, pp. 3-34.

Probst, G., Bu¨chel, B. and Raub, S. (1998). "Knowledge as a strategic resource", in von Krogh, G.

Roos, J. and Kleine, D. (Eds), Knowing in Firms. Understanding, Managing and Measuring Knowledge, Sage, London.

Scarnati, J.T. and Scarnati, B.J. (2002). "Empowerment: the key to quality", The TQM Magazine, Vol. 14, No. 2, pp. 110-19.

Tapiero, C.S. (1987). "Production learning and quality control", IIE Transactions, Vol. 19 No. 4, pp. 362-70.

Thiagarajan, T. and Zairi, M. (1997), "A review of total quality management in practice: understanding the fundamentals examples of best practice applications – Part II", The TQM Magazine, Vol. 9 No. 6, pp. 414-17.

16

Knowledge: Impact and Implication for Libraries and Information Centers

— Navita Sharma

ABSTRACT

Today, "Knowledge" is the basic need for every human being who wants to be surviving in society. Knowledge is now considered as a capital which has an economic value, Knowledge is a new strategic resource for increasing productivity, Knowledge is a stability factor in a unstable advantage. The present paper is an effort to highlight the growth of Knowledge from traditional to modern times, the impact of knowledge on libraries and information centers, Consolidation of knowledge, Implication of libraries and information centers.

Keywords: *Comprehension, Manuscripts, posterity, Renaissance, Perspective.*

INTRODUCTION

Frances Bacon had earlier said, "Knowledge itself is power." The famous Punjabi writer, late Amrita Pritam, in her novel AKK De Patte observed "Handover to someone before you go." This is probably the raison d'etra of librarian as they exits for organizing knowledge and in other words "Putting knowledge to work." For this librarians need to know:

- The communication process and its role in the transmission of knowledge; and

- Comprehension of human thought patterns so expressed that patterns of recourse to recorded knowledge can be derived from them.

It is here librarians develop an effective mechanism of catalogues, Indexes, abstracts so as to develop a bibliographic connection between the user and the store of recorded knowledge. Only then we will be really "Putting knowledge to work."

IMPACT OF KNOWLEDGE ON LIBRARIES

Libraries are considered as treasure house of knowledge. Libraries are also agencies for communication and distribution of knowledge. Knowledge is the product of human mind as thoughts emerge in men's minds which he wants to share with others. Libraries have helped him in this process.

Age of Manuscripts

More than five hundred years ago when printing was not done by machines, it was the age of manuscripts which used to be stored by the libraries. The number of library users was limited then, and the knowledge contained in the manuscripts was not exposed to the people at large. As a result, the impact of knowledge on libraries was quite limited. The only visible impact was the care and preservation of manuscripts for the posterity.

Age of Printing

With the advancement of printing and printing technology and availability of increased manufacturing facilities of paper, the number of printing books and periodicals started increasing at a pace faster than what was experienced earlier. The greater number of books and periodicals contributed to more and more knowledge contained in them. The impact of the increased knowledge led to the better arrangement of books and periodicals in libraries. Also, the number of readers in libraries started increasing as they were exposed to more knowledge.

Expansion of Education

Meanwhile, education facilities started increasing with the setting up of more number of schools, College and University across the world. The expansion of education gave further impetus to the community of readers. They started visiting the libraries and started maximum utilisation of the available reading materials. On the other hand, the increased number of educated people, particularly those in academic institutes knew knowledge. As a result of the impact of knowledge on libraries, they further started refining their methods and techniques of organising knowledge.

Renaissance and Knowledge

The Renaissance, a period of transition from medieval to modern times was indicative of rebirth or revival of art and learning in Europe. This great movement of revivalism of culture and literature produced many great minds like Leonardo da Vinci, Michel Angelo, Machiavelli, Montague, Marcopolo, Copernicus, Francis Bacon, Shakespeare and the like. It was rightly called the 'Age of Genius'. This entire period of revivalism spread over more than two centuries, was responsible for the growth of knowledge in its various manifestations like art, architecture, literature, humanities and science. It certainly had great impact on the growth and development of libraries of the times.

Industrial Revolution and Knowledge

The socio-economic forces and the discoveries and inventions are dynamic forces that contributed in revolutionising the social, political, cultural structure of the society and changing the outlook of the people. Many great men of this period played a prominent role in bringing the revolution and were responsible for the growth of knowledge. James Watt designed the stream engine thereby quickening the pace of industrial Revolution in the late eighteen and early nineteenth century. There was rapid development of industry through increasing use of machinery supplementing human labour.

Economists like Adam Smith, Malthus, David Ricardo and even Karl Marx studied the serious consequences of industrial Revolution on the society. In this way this new revolution proved a great force in contributing to the growth of knowledge not only on science and technology but also in social sciences, the impact of which were deep on the libraries. The libraries now had to acquire more reading materials and process the same for its dissemination.

CONSOLIDATION AND GROWTH OF KNOWLEDGE IN 20TH CENTURY

It was the 19th century that consolidation and effective utilisation of the knowledge of earlier periods was considered important. Industrially advanced countries made their best efforts to capture markets and wield authority on the under developed countries.

The 20th century has been marked with all-round development. The social development all over the world have been influencing the politics, economics, science policy, research and development, educational policy, future planning, international relation, foreign policy and so on. The pace of development of knowledge has been given a fillip with more and more persons engaged in research using powerful and sophisticated equipments. The most outstanding contribution during the 20th century has been that of Albert, Einstein in physics, Sigmund Freud in psychoanalysis, Berta, Rusell, G.E. Moore etc. The three most important areas where the advances have been made include space, physical sciences and biology.

EVOLUTION OF NEW SUBJECTS

As knowledge grows, there is increasing specialisation in the subjects.

Two processes are involved in this development.

Fission

It is the process of splitting of an existing subject into a number of narrower subjects. For example:

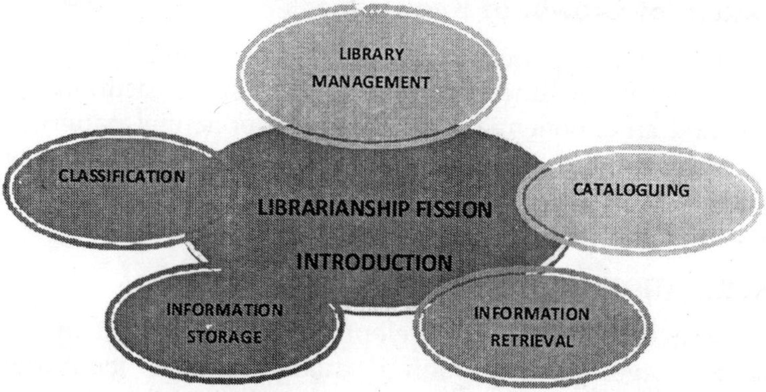

Fusion

It proves that involves the merging of ideas from two or more parent subjects. For Example:

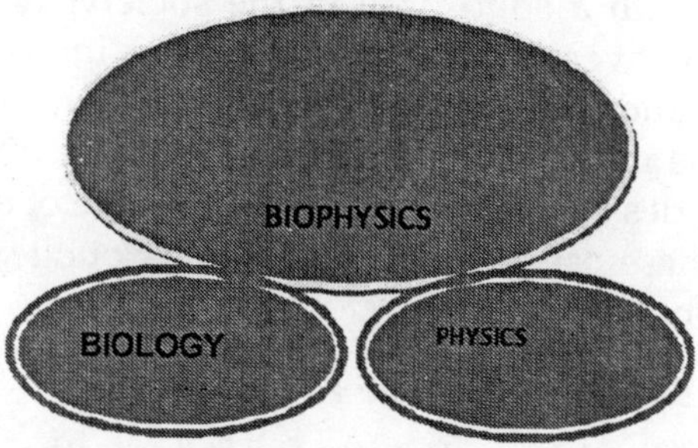

Recorded Knowledge

The ability of man to record knowledge has contributed greatly to make entire social knowledge available for use. Without recording each generation will be able to learn only from previous one generation or two will be able to learn only what that generation (s) knew and remembered. Without recording much knowledge would be lost. Thus recorded knowledge in the form of documents is much more readily available than the particular people. It is, therefore, easily possible to acquire through document, a greater number of ideas than through personal contact.

Pattern of Growth of Knowledge

The general pattern of the growth of knowledge that is quite commonly emerging from the various measurements, is called an exponential growth. The exponential pattern of growth means that it will double not once but frequently. Knowledge also grows by a cumulative process. It implies that new knowledge is gradually accumulated.

IMPLICATIONS FOR LIBRARIES

With the growth and development of knowledge, libraries started developing, through gradually, as social institution of the people, for the people, by the people. Libraries have been functioning to facilitate the communication of social knowledge for such uses as research, education and for environment.

In the twentieth century, the libraries have occupied a key position with a solid base in the society. It spread its wings even to government organisations, in industrial units, in commerce and business sectors, in research institutions, and so on. The modern libraries, as a result are divided into several categories based on the nature and type of documents dealt with. These categories are known as public, academic and special libraries.

IMPLICATIONS OF GROWTH OF KNOWLEDGE:

The growth of knowledge has at least the following implications for libraries.

Storage

One of the important implications of growth of knowledge is the problem of storage, i.e. how and where stack it all. The space in libraries is always inelastic; while the containers of knowledge i.e. documents, always continue to grow, and continue to be acquired in libraries making the storage problems in soluble.

Selection

Selection of document is both more imperative and more

difficult. There is always a larger mass of knowledge, but individual libraries have to make selection of only a small promotion of it as they can neither afford financially nor can store them physically.

Cooperation

As a consequence of the above mentioned two implications, the third implication is the cooperation on the regional, national and international level. In such cooperative activities, the advantage goes in favour of the individual libraries as they no longer are islands in themselves. They have now become part of the larger system. This takes the form of sharing responsibilities of various types including that of sharing the reading materials with the libraries in the system.

Change in Organisation of knowledge

Growth of knowledge being exponential, the amount of change is also big. This change could be even as a result of fusion of two distinct areas of knowledge. This would call for change in the way the material is organised in libraries on such subjects. Even the methods devised for organising knowledge of the libraries considered good, are now likely to be changed to be more helpful in new situations.

Further, it has direct implication for the general classification systems being followed for organising knowledge in libraries. There is every possibility for their frequent revisions to accommodate the growth and change in knowledge or ideas. We already know about the revisions of such classification systems as Dewey Decimal Classification, Universal Classification etc.

Complex and Difficult

The fast growth of knowledge also becomes more and more complex. The implication is that it gives rise to the problem of organising knowledge not in increased quantities but also dealing with a more complex structure as a result of multifaceted growth.

IMPLICATION FOR INFORMATION CENTERS

Today, information is considered of great importance in the lives of all mankind. All our economic and social progress depends on the transfer of scientific and technical information. People in different situations require information on a subject in different forms and with different emphasis and different depths of explanation. Information today is called power, resource, and an asset.

Changing Role

In order to encourage the use of libraries, and increase their participation in teaching and research programmers of the educational institutions, the libraries gradually become the nucleous of intellectual gravity. The library professionals became more aware of the new responsibilities of the active side of information. They change their roles as follows:

- Providing information pinpointed, exhaustively and expeditiously.
- Answering factual and complex reference questions by literature searching.
- Compiling bibliographies, and making annotations.
- Preparing indexing and abstracting services.
- Maintaining of information and other files; and so on.

Now, libraries were faced with the onslaught of intellectual challenges thrown by the explosion and proliferation of knowledge. They started sharpening their techniques of information storage and retrieval for the prompt-dissemination of right information to the right user, at the right time, in the right form and in right amount. The new techniques devised by them included the techniques of documentation, indexing systems, information storage and retrieval, methods of discriminating current awareness services, selective dissemination of information, compiling subject bibliographies, conducting state of the art reviews, preparing the very types of abstracts, preparing technical digests and so on.

Shift from the Traditional Tools

The new libraries are now called information centers established in the research, scientific and technical institutions, where the emphasis shifted from the macro to micro documents. The focus of users as well as of the information professional was information rather than books and periodicals.

From catalogue to OPAC

A catalogue is a list of materials in a library, with entries representing the items arranged in either alphabetical order or classified order. Today many catalogues are held as computer databases, when they are known as Online Public Access Catalogues (OPACs). As an implication on information centre, the shift took place from manual to online searching of the library records. OPACs have provided many facilities to users who can develop a search strategy in one window, call up a thesaurus display in another window, and consult help, or view the results of their searching in yet another window.

From Human Perspective to Machine Perspective

So for information search has been conducted, either known items searching or subject searching, by two methods. Rowley states that the first kind of search is user-conducted where the documents or resources are set out in such a way that users can retrieve information themselves. In the second kind, information professional serves as an intermediary to carry out the search on behalf of the end-user.

From this human perspective, the shift has been to machine perspective where the approach to retrieval of information is in the machine can be used in citation indexing, hypertext links, information filtering, image and sound processing.

From Manual Information Retrieval Systems to Computerise

This is a result of another important implication of the new environment as a consequence of the growth of the knowledge and its organisation by means of information technologies. The result from manual systems to comprised ones has afforded greater accessibility, currency, dynamic information, more access points, and change in search output.

Change in Format of Documents

A document can be defined as a record of knowledge, information or data, or a creative expression. This was true when documents were normally text based. As a result of the impact of the growth of knowledge on the one hand, and increased application of information and communication technology, documents are being produced in new formats where not only optical apparatus like slides, microforms etc. have been with us but electrically readable formats have also reached the libraries and information centers. There has been the growth of electronic documents having their own implications, features and problems.

Library and Information Networks

Libraries have a long history of collaboration in their efforts to organise knowledge. In recent years the application of computers to library and information centers and use of internet has offered infrastructure for information exchange. They have formed networks which comprise user's libraries, national libraries, information centers, publishers and a range of other agencies in the information industry. These networks provide for exchange of, or provision of access to, a range of databases and document type provide like e- journals, CD-ROM documents and so on. The ultimate aim of most networking is to make documents, information or knowledge accessible to the end user. In India some such networks being supported include:

INFLIBNET, DELNET, CALIBNET, BONET, PUNENET, MALIBNET and so on.

Consortia

Consortia are the other ventures of co- operation among

libraries at local, national and international levels. In India INDEST is one of them. The groups of libraries participating in these ventures feel that their users can be benefited by recourse sharing and document delivery.

CONCLUSION

Libraries deal with knowledge created by society and attempt to serve the same to people so that they can use it. Describes the growth of knowledge from manuscript age to present times and identifies various factors responsible for growth stating impact on the growth of developments of libraries. The 20th century saw the consolidation as well as intensification of knowledge along with specialisation and growth of new subjects. Discusses the implications of knowledge for libraries in view of their functions, organisation of recorded knowledge and the library services. Also states the developments of information centers as a result of shift of emphasis from macro documents to micro documents and information. This made these centers to shift from the traditional tools of knowledge organisation to the modern ones to the development of networks and consortia.

REFERRENCES

Aggarwal,D.S.(1985).Lectures on Universe of Knowledge. Delhi : Academic Publications.

Kemp, D.A.(1976). The nature of Knowledge: An introduction for Libraries. London: Cive BiGley,

Kochen,M.(Ed). The Growth of Knowledge, Wiley, New York: 1967.

Machlup,F.(1962).Production and distribution of Knowledge in the United States. Princeton: Princeton University Press.

Ranganathan, S.R.(1967). Prolegomene for Library Classification, 3rd Ed.Bombay:Asia Publishing House.

Rowley, J.E., Farrow, J.(2000).Organizing Knowledge : An Introduction to Managing Access of Information,3rd Ed. Aldershot(Eng).Gower.

Shera, J.H.(1965). Libraries and the Organisation of Knowledge. London: Croasby.

17

Application of Information Technology in Libraries in Delhi: A Study

— *Chiranjilal*

INTRODUCTION

In the present day life, we are experiencing the use of technologies and as such the libraries are not an exception. The single force that has brought revolutionary changes in functioning of the libraries is Information Technology (IT). The application of these modern means have elevated modern day library to a high pedestal improving and altering its image, functions and service to revolutionary extent and with great efficiency and effectiveness. The present century has marked a period of revolution with the new technology. Instead of 'paper', computer terminals, printers and other types of data communicating devices have been used effectively. Telecommunication and computerisation are being increasingly seen as the means to improve efficiency and the quality of "Library Service" has greatly improved with the introduction of computers.

The primary functions of a modern library or scientific library are to acquire information from books and non book materials, process them and to disseminate them to the right person in the right form and at the right time, in other words, quick and fast access to information.

Technological advancements have facilitated the designing of new library software and thereby making the delivery of information quicker, more convenient and highly efficient than ever before.

Information technology is, therefore, a combination of computer and telecom communication techniques which makes possible new systems and products to help people at work, in education, and at home. It is thus, all about the application of a wide variety of electronic technologies to information handling activities that are central to the operation of any organisation. Today we are living in an information society. Information has become the lifeblood of complex industrial societies and is growing importance day by day. Information is obtained from the processing of data i.e. assembling, analysis of summarising of data into a meaningful form. Rapid changes in technology and communication have raised the need for acquiring new skills and knowledge in present day work environment.

The primary benefit of IT as experienced is to have better access to information wherever it is available. This helps management to take right decisions at the most appropriate time. The IT also implies the management to be fair and frank with the employees as they too can have access to information. Thus, it has immense potential for a variety of applications in libraries too and therefore, the most talked subject now a days is the need for application of IT Libraries to meet the growing information requirements of the present day changing society.

INFORMATION TECHNOLOGY

The two words, information and technology, combined together, have acquired a special meaning in the last few years. The technology is signified materials, tools, systems and techniques, although modern definitions of technology vary and to the Greeks technology meant a discourse upon the arts, pure and applied. In popular parlance, information is Libraries, the printing industry, telephone exchanges, television studios, computers etc. all encompassed with some aspects of information technology but in fact, as recently as

1981, a British opinion poll (printed in The Times, 14th Jan.1982) indicated that 80 percent of those interviewed, had not heard of the term information technology.

In the Western industrialised world (i.e. Western Europe, North America and Japan in particular) people have suddenly become aware of this new Information Technology. In some countries, the governments have started recognising Information Technology as an important factor in maintaining and enhancing economic well-being.

In Sweden, a Commission on New Information Technology has been appointed in 1981. Canada and United States have placed high priority in developing Information Technology. They claim that information will be more accessible and that more information at low cost will open opportunities for all, with the greatest gain being to those at present at a disadvantage educationally and 'informationally'. In Western Society, Information technology is now a means of wielding power. In view of these factors it was also vital for us to arrive at some understanding of new information technology and of the benefits it can bring to indifferent fields.

This is a generic term used to denote all activities connected with computer based processing, storage and transfer of information. It includes microprocessors, cable access television, fiber optics, satellites, teletext, word processing, electronic mail, video, robotics and such others. The word 'documentation' and 'information science' are considered synonymous to IT. It includes computers, electronic media, satellite, telecom, communications and reprography. Therefore IT is convergence of computers, telecommunication and information. IT is tools and applications support through which or by means of which information is transferred, recorded, edited, stored, manipulated and disseminated to distances. Thus it is a science of information handling, particularly using computers to support the communication of knowledge in technical, economic and social fields. IT is various means of obtaining, storing and transferring information, using computers, telecommunication and microelectronic objects. It could affect society, organisations and people in ways other than making jobs more interesting in improving productivity, etc.

IT is now regarded as a major economic factor in the development of post-industrial society; the production and sale of IT goods have revitalised some sections of economy and to some extent, replaced some of the losses, brought about by the decline in manufacturing. IT is also an enabling technology.

In brief, IT is the use of computing power, typified by the ability of machines to contain and handle very large amounts of information within comparatively small physical space coupled with ability to extend these reasons apparently indefinitely through a variety of communication devices.

It is believed that in the 21st century, a new information society has to emerge in which electronic information will play the key role. 'The primary technology to support an information society is the information technology, which obviously will move to occupy a centre stage role. Information Technology is the modern science of collecting, storing, manipulating, processing and communicating information. Computer and communication technology are the two main supporting pillars of IT; while information science and management science are the two basic discipliners for proper understanding and utilisation of IT. Librarian's connotation of IT should also include all those technologies, which are used for collection, processing, storage, retrieval and dissemination of recorded information and are operative in library automation, library networking, reprography, technical communication and library administration and management environment.

Indian university libraries are still behind their counterparts in developed countries in the matter of the application of IT because our attitude to modernisation of libraries is not governed by some basic convictions such as :

That information is a resource which has value.

That the utilisation of information resources is dependent upon application of information technology (IT).

- That the value and contribution of information in development is dependent upon the individual capacity to access and utilise information.
- That information gains value with use and it should be made available to the broadest possible audience by managing it as a resource.
- That positive framework of librarianship concentrates on the needs, wants, desires and expectations of the library users and not on bureaucratic rules and regulations.
- That information handling activities shift with technological stage of mankind and every organisation is expected to remain ahead of its customers.
- That convergence of traditional and digital culture enables the libraries to provide internal and external information as a unified transaction.
- Those university libraries are no more sacred cows. They must learn the language of rupees and paisa (i.e. efficiency, effectiveness, economy) in delivering of services, products and consultations. And
- That customer service with ease, convenience, comfort, speed, completeness and excitement has become the norm of the day.

In addition to the above factors, increasing cost of reading material, escalating exchange rates, tight budgetary ceiling, self-sufficient movement and financial crunch have further enhanced the problems of the university libraries. But this situation cannot be allowed to continue indefinitely. The University grants Commission (UGC) and other funding agencies, such as INFLIBNET programme of the UGC came to the rescue of the university libraries in developing modern information infrastructure. Moreover, availability of other information providers in the market, raising expectations of users for fast, up to date, consistent, accurate, reliable, comprehensive and exhaustive information services have forced the university libraries to use computers for housekeeping operations and to access national and international networks. It is in this context that the application of IT to the university libraries is timely and required. The study therefore, is an effort to investigate the existing level of IT application in the University libraries of Jamia Millia Islamia, IGNOU and Jamia Hamdard and to identify the problems and prospects in this regard.

HYPOTHESIS

Majority of academic libraries in Delhi have introduced IT. Among academic libraries, University libraries are in better position in the application of IT. They are using commercially developed software packages, viz., Libsys, VTLS, etc. There is an increasing trend in the provision of IT based services in the academic libraries. The services like acquisition, circulation; CAS, etc have been automated. All the libraries in Delhi have access to the networks like DELNET and INTERNET, etc. Users are making use of computerised services and they are availing of on-line services as well. Factors like budget, training to staff etc. have caused hindrances for the provision of IT in academic libraries.

Most of the operations within library are inter-related, inter dependent and mutually supportive for the overall mission of library. Use of IT applications to interface and integrate each function with the other saves a lot of staff time as the same data used not to be entered at every stage. The IT can be applied in four ways in libraries:

- Library Automation
- Information Storage and Retrieval

- Office Automation
- Resource Sharing Network

RESOURCE SHARING NETWORKS

The libraries are also using computers for resource sharing. It can be a part of local library network or part of large joint program, now widely known as 'Resource Sharing Networks'. Libraries having computerised their working and services can be linked with each other through a suitable telecommunication network system. The system enables the participating library to obtain material from each others' collection in the form of list of books, indexes and abstracts of required article, facsimile copies of required pages or documents, charts, figures, graphs, drawings by using computer terminals attached to a large or very large network system and data bases coupled with visual display units (VDUs) and attached with printing facility. Information can be scanned first on the screen, and if required, relevant information can be obtained in the print out form.

Thus, IT has its use on the time, accuracy, efficiency and effectiveness of the various library and information services. Due to advantages of IT devices, it has become inevitable to adopt such technologies by the L&ICs.

LIMITATION OF THE INFORMATION TECHNOLOGY

While computers can be seen in most large libraries of many small ones, traditional library operations have not been substantially altered. The speed manner and success with which utilising new systems by the libraries are uncertain and depend upon the solutions to operational and philosophical problems. Some of the factors are responsible for lopsided applications of IT such as attitude, financial constaints, user charges and lack of trained staff.

Information technology has played an important role in the work of the society and library and information centers. The success of a library depends to a large extent, on the effective organisation of the house keeping activities.

Automated library system offers convenient, more flexible and comprehensive storage and retrieval of information than manual system. Future libraries need to adopt a more particular structure, as impact of information technology can not be contained within one section of its service. In the years ahead, the quality of library and information service will be largely determined by librarian's skills and imagination bringing into balance the needs, priorities, technology and funding. Growing information could with the changing lifestyles and demands of clienteles offer wide array of challenges to libraries.

The adoption of IT can be attributed to four factors:

(i) attitude and interest of the Library Authority;

(ii) availability of trained professional in libraries; and

(iii) Adequate funding provision for library automation.

(iv) Evolving a policy on library automation.

Adequate flow of fund for the library may give ample opportunity for adoption of IT, which is sufficiently available in libraries of central universities, institutions. Hence the library automation is not suffering from the problem of inadequate finance but the inadequate infrastructure to cope up with the task of adopting IT in their libraries.

Libraries are primarily built upon the contribution and dedication of library professionals. The professional manpower requirement is a basic need in which real growth and development of library occurs.

The impact of new technologies can be seen in almost every human activity. The change in the pattern of collection, storage and transmission of information are some of the major challenges in any library. The basic concept in the use of new technology is to free the librarian and information officer from the routine jobs connected with library operations in acquisition, classification, cataloguing, circulation control, serial control, etc. which can be entrusted to computer.

In this age of information, easy access to information is an essential prerequisite for the development of the country, and hence, the Third World countries like India should make earnest efforts to concentrate more on developing and using new technologies that provide better access to information.

RESEARCH METHODOLOGY

A cursory review of library literature reveals that quality service of the library has some relationship with applications of IT. With this objective, the present study was conducted as a case study on 'Application of Information Technology in University Libraries of Delhi with special reference to JMI, IGNOU and Jamia Hamdard and the problems and prospects of adoption in the stated scope. The questionnaire was also prepared and distributed among University Librarians, Deputy and Assistant Librarians and users of the above mentioned university libraries. Interview and observation methods were also applied as and when required for authentic and detailed information.

The study has designed to reflect the application and updating of information technology and to make comparative study to the problems and prospects in modernising these University Libraries. It also aims to discuss the organisational problems associated with the application of IT and to provide suggestions for future improvement of the IT environment in the said library. The study is also based on the literatures available and written on the subject and appeared in the journals and books of the Library and Information Science. The application of information technology and progress in this regard has also obtained from the libraries.

FINDINGS & DISCUSSION

With rapid use of information Technology every organisation whether big or small, is trying to adopt a computer system in their working set-up and so in Libraries.

Organisations/libraries which can effectively manage to computerise their library and information activities have properly adopted IT. Although, this needs a survey, one can hypothesize that the application of IT in libraries is at the minimal stage. The application and use of IT can be attributed to four factors.

- Attitude and interest of the library authority.
- Availability of trained professional in libraries; and
- Adequate funding provision for library automation.
- Evolving a policy on library automation.

Here it may be mentioned that the central universities have adequate funding provision for the procurement of computer hardware and software, databases and other computer peripherals, and for providing training for their professionals, whereas the university libraries do not have sufficient manpower and interest for the application of IT in their libraries.

Adequate flow of fund for the library gives ample opportunity for adoption of IT, which is sufficiently available in libraries of central university institutions. The university under study has already earmarked sufficient funds under the head of modernisation of the library in the Xth plan for their libraries. Thus, these university Libraries have already made an application of IT but they are encountered with the period of transition.

The library automation is not suffering from the problem of inadequate finance but inadequate infrastructure to cope up with the task of adopting IT, the library is found in the comparative study of the data.

Libraries are primarily built upon the contribution and dedication of library professionals. Hence, professional manpower requirement is a basic need in which real growth and development of library occurs. In respect of library professionals having adequate training in IT, there is no scope and opportunity for such professionals to work in such libraries. The library authorities do not evolve any policy considering the importance of the technical know-how and technical manpower development as observed in the university libraries of Delhi under study. They are neither sponsoring their library staff for training in IT nor creating an environment of IT at the university level for imparting training.

Another significant aspect of development of IT is the right attitude of library authority, which appears to be mostly lacking here in contributing to inadequate application of IT. Although the facility of internet connection is provided on restricted basis in the vicinity of the library, for browsing and searching information either by the users on free or by the library professionals. It appears that lack of adequate attitudinal values given to library is responsible for such a poor plight of the use of information technology in libraries.

It was observed and also seeks opinions about what impact of IT applications has on the library functions. They expressed that the library services, users satisfaction, meeting users' demands and library image improved after the application of information technology but still there are services which is heeded attention for proper application and implementation of IT so that the remaining areas could be ensured its automated service.

CONCLUSION & SUGGESTIONS

The library is the heart and main information resource centre of any institution. It is the part and parcel of education and teaching system. The modern age of information explosion poses stiff challenges in providing right information to right user in right time. In such a situation Information Technology (IT) comes to the rescue of libraries and information centers.

IT, networking, and the expanding information market-place represent a combination of factors affecting librarians and opinion of administrative decision makers about libraries.

Technological advances affect the fundamental library operations, and can possibly even change the basic social role of libraries.

A revolution in IT, however, is generating a convergence in interests and an environment for interesting and necessary collaborations. A less visible, but significant collaboration is the one between librarians and engineers. Engineers and Lancaster predicted that we will soon be entering the era of paperless society, an era in which print on paper will be replaced by electronics. Thus library will not contain any printed material at all. It may become a room containing a computer terminal only.

IT, infect, has potential for a variety of applications in libraries which has helped libraries in creating databases of their collections and making them available for easy access to users inside as well as outside through networks. IT also enables libraries to provide most efficient and specialised information services. It has been fairly established that efficient information support and effective communication in an organisation are closely associated with high performance, productivity and innovation.

Thus IT is a strong force, but not an independent agent. It provides librarians with a range of tools to help in providing efficient and effective services to library users. In future, use of such libraries may go up, but the number of users visiting the library buildings may go down.

The application level of information technology in university libraries of Jamia Millia Islamia, IGNOU and Jamia Hamdard can be measured by a single indicator i.e., an insignificant collection (0.15 per cent) of all the libraries is in non print form, while the rest is in print form. The INFLIBNET Programme of the UGC could be helpful in establishing technological infrastructure and training human resources of the university libraries but its various databases are still beyond the reach of academic community.

REFERENCES

Adams, Roy J (1986). Information technology and Libraries in future for academic libraries, London: Croom Helm. p. 188.

Amudhavalli, A. (1986). Information Technology and access to information : Promises & Problems. In Deverajan (G.) Ed. Progress in Information Technology, New Delhi. Ess Ess Publications.

Augustine, CA, Modernisation of university and college libraries in India : New challenges. *In Devarajan, G and Rahelamma, AV (Ed.)* Library computerisation in India, New Delhi, Esss Ess Publication, pp. 52 – 65.

Banerjee, K. Utpal (1992). Information Technology for a Common man, New Delhi, Computer Society of India.

Barmes. C.I. Petrie, J.H. (1976). Definition of information science. *Info Scientist*, pp. 10, 122 – 24.

Besant, J. et al (1985). and others. Information Technology Futures: Why current forecasting literature says about the social impact of information technology, London: NEDC.

Bhatnagar, S.C., (1988). Computers in developing countries. In Proceedings of IFIP Tc9/Tc7 working conference on the Impact of Information systems on developing countries, New Delhi, 24-26 November, 1988.

Bhattacharyya, G (1978). Information sciences; a unified view through systems approach. Calcutta; *IASLIC*, vol. 23. p.55.

Boaz, M. (1978). The future of library and information science. *Educ. Librarianship*, 18, pp. 315-23.

Boddy, D and Buchanan, D., (1984). Information technology and productivity: myths and realities. *Omega International Journal of Management Science*, 12 (3), pp. 233 – 40.

18

The Application of Web 2.0 Model to the Library Services

— Bharat Kumar M. Chaudhari

ABSTRACT

In this article, I explore the Web 2.0 technologies, and how they can power these next generation library services, plus, I take peek into the future of Library 2.0 phenomenon.

***Keywords:** web 2.0, library 2.0, web technologies, social networking*

"The application and adaptation of the Web 2.0 model to the library environment (both virtual and physical) is a Library 2.0."

—Michael C. Habib

"Library 2.0 is a part of a whole new approach to information organisation and dissemination."

—Gali Halevi

INTRODUCTION

We're living in one of the most exciting and challenging times for the information industry. As library and information professionals, we take our responsibility seriously to deliver services including disseminating information, facilitating access to and sharing of information, providing forums to create and share new knowledge, enabling collaboration, and connecting users. Web 2.0 technologies are enabling us to take such services to a new height and make them more interactive and participatory for library users.

WHAT IS WEB 2.0

Web 2.0 is a new expression coined by O'Reilly Media in 2003[1] (and later popularised by the first Web 2.0 conference in 2004) in reference to a perceived second generation of web-based communities and hosted services — such as social-networking sites, Wikis and Folksonomies which facilitate collaboration and sharing between users. O'Reilly Media titled a series of conferences around the phrase, and it has since become widely adopted.

Although the term suggests a new version of the World Wide Web, it does not refer to an update to Web technical specifications, but to changes in the ways software developers and end-users use the web as a platform. According to Tim O'Reilly, "Web 2.0 is the business revolution in the Computer industry caused by the move to the internet as platform, and an attempt to understand the rules for success on that new platform." Some technology experts, notably Tim Berners-Lee, have questioned whether one can use the term in a meaningful way, since many of the technology components of "Web 2.0" have existed since the early days of the Web.

WEB 2.0 TECHNOLOGIES

Ajax

Ajax is one tool of choice for creating interactive pages with easily changeable components. Some commentators equate Web 2.0 with Ajax while others say that Ajax is only a part of Web 2.0. Its definition is a bit more straightforward than that of Web 2.0, since it is really an acronym for Asynchronous JavaScript and XML, although the acronym in all uppercase is no longer common usage. It also involves more technologies than JavaScript and XML. As defined by the Mozilla Development Center, Ajax is an "approach to using a number of existing technologies together, including: HTML or

XHTML, Cascading Style Sheets, JavaScript, The Document Object Model, XML, XSLT, and the XML Http Request object. When these technologies are combined in the Ajax model, web applications are able to make quick, incremental updates to the user interface without reloading the entire browser page."

For the nonprogrammer, the easiest way to understand Ajax is to see some examples. The way users can drag Google Maps is a classic example of Ajax. For another example, look at Protopage, which offers a free, personalised home page. Each panel or box can be dragged, resized, and made into a bar that drops down when the cursor is placed over it. Protopage's interactivity is all made possible using that combination of technologies in Ajax.[2]

AJAX application model:

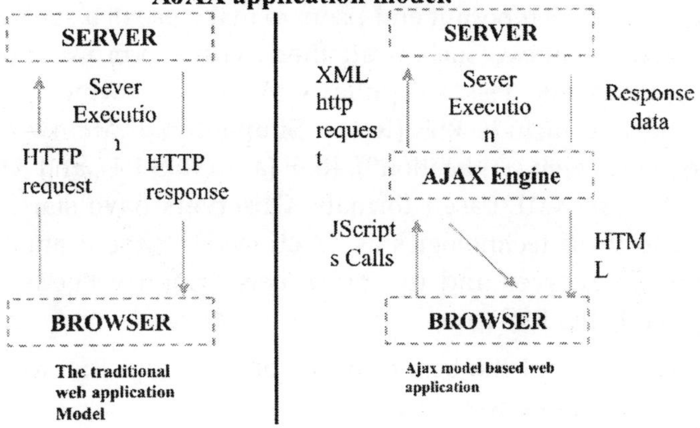

The Dewey Browser uses AJAX technology.[3]

APIs

An Application Programming Interface (API) is used to exchange data with other applications. Even though many commercial software programs carefully guard the secrecy of their APIs, several Internet companies not only publish their APIs but also allow others to use them to incorporate their data. Amazon, eBay, Google, the Internet Archive,

NASA, and Yahoo! all have APIs that let other sites pull content from the source to display on their Web site or use to create new concatenations of data, called mashups.

APIs help designers find ways to mashup data from several sources into a new look, feel, and functionality. Without going into the technical details of APIs, a great way to get a sense on what ones are available and how they are used is to visit Programmable Web [www.programmableweb.com] that lists freely available APIs along with mashup sites that are using various APIs. Linking to over 150 APIs, the mashup list is even larger with 400-plus entries.

XML and RSS

Advocates of Web 2.0 may regard syndication of site content as a Web 2.0 feature, involving as it does standardised protocols, which permit end-users to make use of a site's data in another context (such as another website, a browser plug-in, or a separate desktop application). Protocols which permit syndication include RSS (Really Simple Syndication — also known as "web syndication"), RDF (as in RSS 1.1), and Atom, all of them XML-based formats. Observers have started to refer to these technologies as "Web feed" as the usability of Web 2.0 evolves and the more user-friendly Feeds icon supplants the RSS icon.

We can find the best example of XML and RSS feed on various libraries websites:

1. **IIM- Ahmedabad, Vikram Sarabhai Library website syndication:** http://www.iimahd.ernet.in/library/index.php?option=com_rss&feed=RSS0.91&no_html=1
2. **Harvard Business School, Baker Library notification:** http://www.library.hbs.edu/tools/rss/bakerannouncements.xml
3. **MIT Libraries, Cambridge, MA RSS feeds:** http://news-libraries.mit.edu/blog/rss-feeds/

Wikis

Wikis are, in general, online content repositories that allow others to contribute and modify entries. The name comes from the "wiki wiki" shuttle buses at the Honolulu International Airport. Ward Cunningham is credited with the original WikiWikiWeb.

Wikis are online, collaborative environments that allow anyone to add, edit, or delete pages. Some Wikis require registered membership, and others are private, but many allow anyone with access to the Web to contribute. Wikis use a simplified mark-up syntax that allows users to contribute without special knowledge of HTML. Many Wikis now also offer What-You-See-Is-What-You-Get (WYSIWYG) editing, similar to a word processor, which makes it easier for some users to contribute. However, many experienced Wiki contributors prefer Wiki syntax.

The good example of library wiki is LISWiki.[4] It is established to give the library community a chance to explore the usefulness of Wikis. It is not intended to replace or detract from the Wikipedia library and information science articles (or those in the printed LIS encyclopedias for that matter), but exist as a niche encyclopedia covering library-related issues. (Just as Memory Alpha, for example, exists as an independent Wiki for a specialised audience.)

The field of librarianship has already benefited from adopting innovative publishing and communication models, such as weblogs and open access archives. Wikis are quickly becoming the next big thing in the field of Library and Information.

Blogging

A blog is a website or a platform where entries are commonly displayed in reverse chronological order. "Blog" can also be used as a verb, meaning to maintain or add content to a blog.

Many blogs provide commentary or news on a particular subject; others function as more personal online diaries. A typical blog combines text, images, and links to other blogs, web pages, and other media related to its topic. The ability for readers to leave comments in an interactive format is an important part of many blogs. Most blogs are primarily textual, although some focus on art (artlog), photographs (photoblog), sketchblog, videos (vlog), music

(MP3 blog), audio (podcasting) are part of a wider network of social media. Micro-blogging is another type of blogging which consists of blogs with very short posts.

Librarians have taken to blogs like ducks to water. Take a few minutes to visit some of the blogs at Peter Scott's list of Library Weblogs (http://www.libdex.com/weblogs.html). Here are just a few examples of library blogs to spark your interest:

- The St. Joseph County Public Library Book Blog focuses on upcoming releases in publishing and entertainment. http://homepage.mac.com/nrdtsjcpl/B1732759005/index.html
- Roselle Public Library's Blogger Book Club is an online book discussion group for kids to share their thoughts about books. http://bloggerbookclub.blogspot.com
- LISNews.com focuses on news for information professionals and is a collaborative Weblog. http://www.lisnews.com
- Library News is a Weblog featuring library-related news, events, and resources for Georgia State University. http://www.library.gsu.edu/news/index.asp
- ... h20boro lib blog is Waterboro Public Library's Weblog of literary and library news and resources. http://www.waterborolibrary.org/blog.htm
- Engineering Library Blog features news and events in one column of the library home page. http://library.usask.ca/engin

- Stark County Law Library Blawg serves the legal community of Stark County, Ohio. http://temp.starklawlibrary.org/blog
- Urbana Free Library has one called Construction News featuring photos and updates on the building underway. http://urbanafreelibrary.org/bldgblog.html
- Jenny Levine's Shifted Librarian looks at how to make libraries more portable to serve users better. http://www.theshiftedlibrarian.com
- Peter Scott's Library Blog offers links and news about library resources and libraries around the world. http://blog.xrefer.com [5]

An example of blogging for Job posting website, managed by University of Mysore, MLISc Students 2006 Mysore, Karnataka, India at **http://lis-job-oppertunities.blogspot.com** And **[LIS LINKS] http:// lislinks.ning.com** is now the best social networking portal for Indian library and information professionals

Media Sharing

Flickr is a photo sharing web site and web services, and an online community platform. It was one of the earliest Web 2.0 applications. In addition to being a popular Web site for users to share personal photographs, the service is widely used by bloggers as a photo repository. Its popularity has been fueled by its innovative online community tools that allow photos to be tagged and browsed by folksonomic means. It hosts over 2 billion images.

Library Flickr accounts are given below:

- Charleston County Public Library http://flickr.com/photos/staff_lines/ and http://www.flickr.com/photos/ccplpr/
- Florence County Library System http://www.flickr.com/photos/florencelibrary/

- Lee County Public Library http://www.flickr.com/photos/leecountypubliclibrary/
- SC State Library http://www.flickr.com/photos/scsl/
- Sumter County Library http://www.flickr.com/photos/sumtercountylibrary/
- Chesterfield County Library System http://www.flickr.com/photos/chesterfieldcountylibrary/
- Anderson County Library http://www.flickr.com/photos/andersoncountylibrary/
- School of Library & Information Science, USC http://www.flickr.com/photos/15368932@N04/sets/

Many Librarians and library experts are enjoying **Flickr** [7]

WEB 2.0 + LIBRARY = LIBRARY 2.0

The Library 2.0 Definition

> "L2 is, to me, a service philosophy built upon three things; a willingness to change and try new things; a willingness to constantly reevaluate our service offerings; and finally, a willingness to look outside our own world for solutions, be they technology-driven or not(this is where Web 2.0 fits in)." [8]
>
> —*Michael Casey*

Library 2.0 is based on the Web 2.0 idea, but applied and related to the library environment. It encourages participation and interaction by the user with the library in an internet environment. However, Library 2.0 is fundamentally about a change in how library services are offered to patrons. This report is intended as an information document. **Library 2.0:** Many people are already using Web 2.0 items, like blogs, wikis, RSS feeds and podcasts. What Library 2.0 does is create specific applications (or mold existing Web 2.0 ones) that are related to library resources and services. An example of this could be a library setting up an RSS (automatic information feed) service for the latest news (as the University of Otago Library has done). Offering podcasts of library instruction (or audio-guided tours of the library) could be another example. The selective dissemination of information (SDIs) service that is already available in some integrated library systems could also be considered a Library 2.0 tool.

Some examples of the move from Library 1.0 to Library 2.0 include:

Library 1.0	Library 2.0
Email reference/Q&A pages	Live Chat (Live Refdesk etc.)
Text-based tutorials	Streaming media tutorials with interactive databases
Email or mailing lists, webmasters	Blogs, wikis, RSS feeds
Controlled classification schemes	Tagging coupled with controlled schemes
OPAC	Personalised social network interface
Catalog of largely reliable print and electronic holdings	Catalog of reliable and suspect holdings, web-pages, blogs, wikis, etc.

LIBRARIAN 2.0

Librarian 2.0 is the guru of the information age. Librarian 2.0 strives to

- Understand the power of the Web 2.0 opportunities
- Learn the major tools of Web 2.0 and Library 2.0
- Combine e-resources and print formats and is container and format agnostic
- Is device independent and uses and delivers to everything from laptops to PDAs to iPods
- Develop targeted federated search and adopts the OpenURL standard
- Connect people and technology and information in context

- Doesn't shy away from non-traditional cataloging and classification and chooses tagging tag clouds, folksonomies, and user-driven content descriptions and classifications where appropriate
- Embrace non-textual information and the power of pictures, moving images, sight, and sound
- Understand the "long tail" and leverages the power of old and new content
- See the potential in using content sources like the Open Content Alliance, Google Print, and Open WorldCat
- Connect users to expert discussions, conversations, and communities of practice and participates there as well
- Use the latest tools of communication (such as Skype) to connect content, expertise, information coaching, and people
- Use and develops advanced social networks to enterprise advantage
- Connect with everyone using their communication mode of choice – telephone, Skype, IM, SMS, texting, email, virtual reference, etc.
- Encourage user driven metadata and user developed content and commentary
- Understand the wisdom of crowds and the emerging roles and impacts of the blogosphere, Web syndicasphere and wikisphere.[9]

First and foremost, Librarian 2.0 understands his or her users at a deep level – not just as pointers and clickers. Librarian 2.0 understands end users deeply in terms of their goals and aspirations, workflows, social and content needs, and more. Librarian 2.0 is where the user is, when the user is there. This is an immersion environment that librarians are eminently qualified to contribute to. Aspects of librarian influenced e-learning and distance education as implemented by our institutions and communities should allow us to contribute to the preparation of our users to acquire and improve their skills and competencies.

It is essential that we start preparing to become Librarian 2.0 now. The Web 2.0 movement is laying the groundwork for exponential business growth and another major shift in the way our users live, work, and play. We have the ability, insight, and knowledge to influence the creation of this new dynamic – and guarantee the future of our library profession.

CONCLUSION

Web 2.0 is not about searching, but finding; not about access, but sharing. Library 2.0 recognises that library users do not seek and utilise information as individuals, but as community.

REFERENCES

MANESS, Jack M. 2006. Library 2.0 Theory: Web 2.0 and Its Implications for Libraries. Webology, 3(2), June, 2006.

SHAH, Rahula and KANJNA, Sourangshu:.Web Technology Enter the Next, PCQUEST, August, 2007, pp. 19-24

WINGE, Sara. Controversy about our "Web 2.0" service mark. http://radar.oreilly.com/2006/05/controversy-about-our-web-20-s.html

ABRAM, S. 2005. Web 2.0 — huh?! Library 2.0, librarian 2.0. *Information Outlook*, 9 (12). pp. 44-46.

VIZINE-GOETZ, Diane. A new, color-coded prototype interface speeds searching and discovery. http://www.oclc.org/nextspace/001/research.htm

CASEY, Michael and Laura, Savastinuk. 2006. Library 2.0. Library Journal, September 1, http://www.infotoday.com/mls/nov03/fichter.shtml

www.scla.org/AnnualConference2007/LibraryAndLibrarianFlickr Account

CORMODE, Graham and KRISHNAMURTHY, Balachander. First Monday, Volume 13 Number 6 - 2 June 2008 http://www.uic.edu/htbin/cgiwrap/bin/ojs/index.php/fm/article/viewArticle/2125/1972.

STEPHENS, Michael and CASEY, Michael. Where Do We Begin? A Library 2.0 Conversation http://www.techsource.ala.org/blog/2005/12/where-do-we-begin-a-library-20-conversation-with-michael-casey.html

19

Use of Hybrid Library in the Information Era

— Ramvveer Sagar
— Dr. Satya Parkash

ABSTRACT

In this paper we discuss the role of the OPAC as a hybrid library service and of the catalogue server as a provider element in a hybrid information environment. We identify developments required in the search and retrieval capabilities of the catalogue server to operate effectively in such an environment. We look under the hybrid library bonnet at the functions and metadata needed for management of online and physical collections. Lastly, we look at the architecture needing to be supported by library systems for storage and delivery of digital collections in a hybrid information environment.

Key Words: *Hybrid library, digital library, OPAC*

THE HYBRID LIBRARY

The term 'hybrid' is often used in descriptions of activities or services that combine two established features. For example, the term 'hybrid manager' was in vogue in the 1970s and 1980s for managers in information technology (IT) intensive companies, who combined knowledge of IT with understanding of personnel and other human issues. Garrod and Sidgreaves have argued for the need for hybrid library professionals who combine library and information skills with technical computing skills. Finbarr and Murray have described research into the development of hybrid World Wide Web/ Z39.50 services. The earliest use of the term 'hybrid library' is by Sutton. In his consideration of service models, he identified four types of libraries on a continuum running from the traditional to the digital: traditional, automated, hybrid and digital. He said there has been or will be 'an inevitable shift along the continuum from library as place to library as logical entity'. The traditional library is defined as a specific place with a finite collection of tangible information and it is geographically constrained. Computerisation of serials control, circulation and cataloguing contribute to the automated library and the online public access catalogue (OPAC) is its principal feature. In the automated library, the tools point to non-digital media and the focus remains on the local collection. In the digital library, the notion of place will be left behind. In Sutton's hybrid library, 'the balance of print and digital meta-information leans increasingly toward the digital'. There is coexistence of traditional and digital collections and the possibility for totally unconstrained geographic access to digital resources located elsewhere to which the library provides a network gateway. Sutton suggested staff assist in the cost-effectiveness of his hybrid library by mediating between the users and, primarily, the digital tools. The Joint Information Systems Committee (JISC) 2 Circular 3/97, the circular that led to the eLib hybrid library projects described below, states that 'we have few if any exemplars of good practice for the hybrid library.' This statement does not make it clear whether JISC was aware of any previous use of the term. The circular goes on to state that 'we also lack a useful model of what we should expect.' Law has written that JISC Circular 3/97 introduced the concept of the hybrid library.

THE HYBRID LIBRARY CONCEPT

This is where the concept of the hybrid library comes in. The hybrid library is a library which can provide a "one stop shop" for both hardcopy and electronic resources. Its information systems should provide the end user with a seamless interface that will allow them to locate paper books and journals held locally and at neighboring sites at the same time as being able to find relevant online resources, electronic publications and digitised material. To do this, the user needs to be provided with a front end that can access information in a variety of databases which are widely distributed and can contain a variety of information in different formats.

Like library automation and electronic libraries, the concept of the hybrid library is not a new one. People have talked about providing access to multiple information systems with a single front end for many years. Often library systems vendors would demonstrate technology that allowed users of their OPACs to access a limited range of other databases and services through the same interface. However, now we have the network infrastructure, open standards and available information systems to attempt to build a distributed searching and retrieval system that does not lock people into one vendor's system.

DEFINING A HYBRID LIBRARY

"The key concept underpinning the hybrid library is integration of both the physical and the electronic library. The hybrid library takes the Web as its delivery mechanism and, from this one access point, customers should be able to have direct access to the electronic information they are entitled to and be able to search for and locate relevant physical resources. The hybrid library aims to provide access to local and remote information resources in a range of formats, offering training and guidance at the point of access."

"The hybrid library was designed to bring a range of technologies from different sources together in the context of a working library, and also to begin to explore integrated systems and services in both the electronic and print environments. The hybrid library should integrate access to all the four different kinds of resources identified above (legacy, transition, new, and future), using different technologies from the digital library world, and across different media. The name hybrid library is intended to reflect the transitional state of the library, which today can neither be fully print nor fully digital. As we have seen, in so many cases the results of adding technology piece-meal are unsatisfactory. The hybrid library tries to use the technologies available to bring things together into a library reflecting the best of both worlds."

Rusbridge uses the terms of legacy, transition, new and future to describe the types of resources held within a hybrid library. These resources effectively create additional issues in the aspects of preservation, access, and control for users and institutions. An explanation of each has been provided below:

- legacy - largely non digital resources
- transition - legacy resources which have been or are being digitised
- new - created as digital or simultaneously as digital and print
- future - resources of the future and the implications of preservation and access in a changing technological environment

JISC identifies a hybrid library as;

"The hybrid library draws together the on-line and physical collections to present them to the user in a seamless and integrated manner, supported by middleware that handles aspects such as authentication and cross-searching."

A hybrid library can be viewed as a combination of a physical library, performing traditional roles but those roles have extra consideration in the delivery of services in digital and print format. In some cases the validity of supplying both simultaneously and others only in one format are factors that have to be considered. Therefore, a hybrid library is based within the physical but operates two services—the physical and the digital. Content is also two-fold. A hybrid library tends to grow out of the physical. However a digital library does not need the physical to merit its evolution and can provide services or communication tools and enable storage. While a physical library producing only paper service can in theory still exist, it is unlikely in the changing technological information era to do so for long. A hybrid library provides both printed and electronic information simultaneously; sometimes this information can be kept in both forms, print and electronic.

CONSIDERATIONS ABOUT THE LIBRARY OF THE FUTURE

A simple way of defining the hybrid library is that it is a means of integrating the traditional library with the digital library. Arguably, so far, the digital library elements have served to augment, rather than replace, conventional libraries. The contemporary information user now has to operate in a hybrid environment where electronic and paper-based sources are used alongside each other. The digital library is more than the existence in libraries of electronic sources of information, such as CD-ROMs and online databases. Some commentators would consider a library with these resources to be an electronic library and that the electronic library should not be confused with the digital library, since telecommunication is an added precondition for the digital library. One of the key points to the digital library is that the information accessed can be remote from the point of access in multiple locations. This means that the place where that access takes place need not be the traditional library building: it could be a workstation situated outside the library.

TECHNOLOGIES FOR THE HYBRID LIBRARY

A number of existing technologies are likely to be used in providing the hybrid library. Obviously, the Internet and the

World Wide Web will have to play a large part as they are now becoming the ubiquitous means of electronic information delivery. Many of the existing services that will need to be tied into the hybrid library only exist on the web. The hypermedia nature of the Web allows it to act as both the front end of the hybrid library's search system if necessary and also the means of delivery of any electronic resources that the end user locates.

TECHNICAL ISSUES AND DIRECTIONS

Librarians were right to be anxious about the future of the library catalogue in one area. It is unlikely that the OPAC module of the integrated library management system will predominate as the client software deployed in broker architectures. The Z39.50 server will be as important as the OPAC in enabling the library catalogue to function as a provider element in a hybrid information environment. For this to happen, work is needed to improve the interoperability of current systems. The issue lies not with the Z39.50 standard itself but with the need for a profile defining the levels of

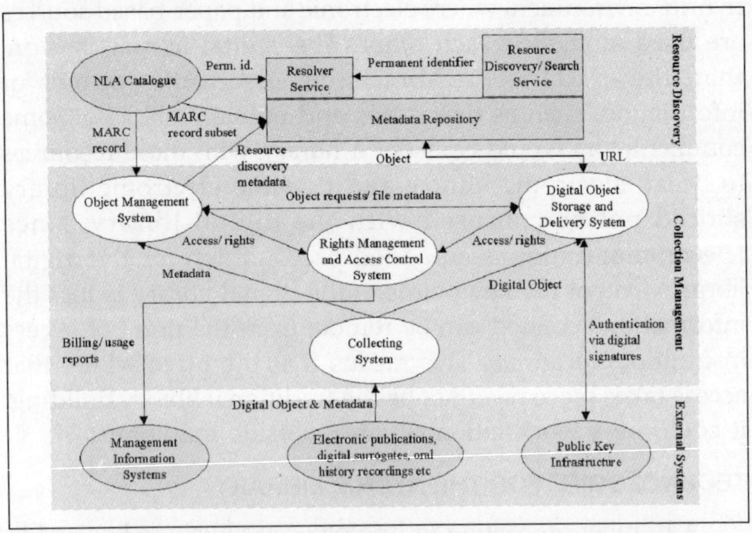

19.1 : NLA's Digital Collection Management System—Logical Systems Architecture

conformance required to ensure interoperability. A profile specifies the use of a particular standard, or group of standards, to support a particular application, function, community *or* environment.

ISSUES IN HYBRID LIBRARY

Some of the issues facing the hybrid libraries are the digital divide, interoperability, and collection development, ownership of electronic resources and preservation of digital media. Any advancement in information technology will be useful only when you know how to use it. The term digital divide is used to describe the gap between those with information technology knowledge and those who do not.

Majority of the libraries these days are hybrid libraries. The libraries own and subscribe to different resources in different formats. Some of the common formats are e-journals, serials, print monographs, CD and DVD. The main components of digital library framework are user interfaces, repository, handles system, and search system. The handle system and search system are the major components that should be designed with interoperability features to search across different repositories owned by different vendors. The user interface should be designed in a generic way that it helps library patrons develop a common knowledge to do advanced searches across all repositories.

COLLECTION DEVELOPMENT

Collection development is another challenge facing the hybrid libraries. The process of collection management in a hybrid library is similar to that of a traditional library. Hybrid libraries follow the same policies and procedures followed in traditional library collection development.

OWNERSHIP OF ELECTRONIC RESOURCES

Ownership of electronic resources is another issue facing the hybrid libraries. Ownership of electronic materials is virtual and not physical. There are no clear policies about the ownership of electronic materials once the subscription is cancelled or expired. Libraries have to pay attention to the legal contracts from the database vendors. If the libraries plan on archiving the electronic resources, then there are legal issues related to it. The most prominent legal issues are intellectual property and authenticity of digital information.

PRESERVATION OF DIGITAL MEDIA

With any new advanced technology related to digital information storage, the main question to be answered is its durability. Digital storage media like disc or tapes deteriorate over time. The main question related to digital preservation is what and how much should be preserved. To make the preservation of digital media cost effective, standardisation of different media format is required. Following are the three possible approaches.

TECHNOLOGY PRESERVATION, EMULATION, AND MIGRATION

In technology preservation, both hardware and software related to digital information are preserved. This may not be cost effective because changes to hardware and different versions of software need to be either maintained or constantly upgraded. In emulation, some emulator software programs will mimic the hardware and software of the original data and display in the original format. In migration, digital information is converted to a standard media with standard format.

CONCLUSION

The integrated library management system has an important role to play in the delivery of hybrid library services. There is an ongoing requirement for development of the catalogue as a provider system. In addition, there is still a role for the OPAC as a means of delivering access to the specialised functions needing to be supported at the local library level. However, there will need to be a shift in development priorities from the OPAC to the Z39.50 server for the catalogue to realise its full potential in a larger hybrid information environment. Efforts to develop the integrated library management system to manage special collections need to be continued and extended to digital collections. Standards in this area are still under development. It will be important to ensure that short-term gains are made recognising the need for convergence with standards as these evolve. Systems designed to support both the discovery of digital objects and their storage and delivery should be developed with recognition that, in a hybrid information environment, digital objects may be linked to from a variety of external resource discovery systems.

REFERENCES

Oppenheim, Charles and Smithson, Daniel (1999). what is the hybrid library? *Journal of Information Science:* 25(97).

Garrod, P and Sidgreaves, (1998). I *Skills for New Information Professionals: The SKIP Project* (Joint Information Systems Committee/Library Information Technology Centre, London.

Finbarr, J and Murray, R(1995) The World Wide Web and Z39.50: which way for libraries? *VINE* 99 38.

Sutton, S (1996). Future service models and the convergence of functions: the reference librarian as technician, author and consultant. In: K. Low (ed.), *The Roles of Reference Librarians, Today and Tomorrow* (Haworth Press, New York, pp. 125–143.)

D. Law, Parlour(1997). Games: the real nature of the Internet, *Serials* 10(2). pp. 195–201.

Andrew Hampson. *The Hybrid Library and Medical Information* Available URL: http://www.icml.org/monday/electronic/ahampson.htm (accessed on (23.12.2010).

Ibid.

Chris Rusbridge, *Towards the Hybrid Library* Available URL: http://www.dlib.org/dlib/july98/rusbridge/07rusbridge.html accessed on (23.12.2010) Ibid.

Stuart Lee and Paul Groves. *On-Line Tutorials and Digital Archives or "Digitising Wilfred"* Available URL: http://www.jtap.ac.uk/reports/htm/jtap-027-5.html accessed on (23.12.2010).

Chris RusbridgeL (1998). "Toward the Hybrid Library", *D-Lib Magazine,* July/August.

Malinconico, S. Michael. (2002) Digital Preservation Technologies and Hybrid Libraries," *Information Services and Use*, 159(74): p. 173

Malinconico, S. Michael. (2002) Digital Preservation Technologies and Hybrid Libraries," *Information Services and Use*, 159(74): p. 162.

Oppenheim, Charles. "Copyright Issues in Digitisation and the Hybrid Library," *Information Services and Use*, 203(7): p. 204

Choemprayong, S.(2006). *Closing Digital Divides: The United States' Policies*,

Arms, W. Y., Blanchi, C., & Overly, E.A. (1997)"An Architecture for Information in Digital Libraries." *D-Lib Magazine*, February

Chowdhury, G. & Chowdhury, S. (2003) *Introduction to Digital Libraries.* London: Facet Publication,

20

Online Book Portal

— Akansha Bhargava

OBJECTIVE AND SCOPE OF PROJECT

This report gives a brief description of the project works on online book portal. This project comes under the B2C e-commerce domain and vertically it is a web-based system.

Project work on this web-based system means focusing on to maintain the quality and features of the product. And for maintaining the quality and features of the system, one has to be very peculiar about the customisation, personalisation and the ease of use of the system. The goal is to provide not just a web based e-business portal that sell books, but also a quality system that have the capability to retain customers by its quality offerings.

Field work gives a clear idea about the functionality of an organisation. Once a student comes in touch with the organisation, he learns the professional behaviour which is very important in today's IT scenario. One should learn how to carry out responsibility in an organisation.

Online books portal is unique web-based practice software. Online book portal is a web based B2C portal that would provide online books. People would now easily search a book of their own choice in seconds and would order it using their credit card. Now they would be able to access their favourite books anywhere & anytime irrespective of their location.

In this system, the customers would select the books from the given choices stored in the database under different categories. Any visitor who visits the site and is interested in a particular book of his/her own choice would first have to register and then have to make the payment with the different options available.

Online book Portal is developed using following technologies:

- Front End: - HTML, Java Script & Internet Explorer.
- Database: - My SQL
- Language: - ASP.NET

DETAILED DESCRIPTION OF WORK

- In this system, any new user who wants to purchase a particular book should first register with the system, then he/she is required to enter the unique username and password for purchase. Next time when the same user wants another book to purchase, he/ she will not have to register again but can use the unique username & password assigned.

For this, the following things have to be done:

1. A database in My Sql has been created with the following attributes. New user will have to enter the details for these fields to register with the system:

- Email
- Password
- Secret Question
- Answer

2. Next codes in asp.net & Html are: login, login check, login validates, password change, password forgets etc. for the module.

Other two modules for online shopping system are:

- Search Module
- Shopping Cart

Now, regarding the shopping Cart, the functionality is as follows: Whenever the user searches for the required books, the details regarding the books such as Name, Author Name, Brief Description, Price, are presented before the user. The coding for this is done in the file product search. Aspx. Next, the user is given the total amount along with the delivery price and is presented with the option: Continue Shopping, Recalculate Order & Continue Shopping. If the user wants to purchase more books, the details are added to the Cart and the amount recalculated.

The code for this functionality is used in cart. aspx

Next, if the user is logged in with the system, then his/her details are asked for, such as:

- Shipping Address,
- Personal Details ,
- Credit Card Number

And if the user is not logged in, then he / she is directed to the *login. aspx page where he/she is asked to give his/her e-mail Id & Password that was provided during the time of registration.

And if the user is new to the system, he has to register with the system in the page *register. aspx.

After the user has provided with all the details, his order is confirmed and a page is displayed citing the details submitted by the user and he/she is asked to print the page for correspondence.

The code for this is: *submitorder.aspx

PAYMENT OPTIONS

Here, in the credit card option, payment can be made using:

- Visa
- Mastercard
- American Express

Here, to check the validity of the card, an algorithm is used in which certain parameters are fixed for each type of card, failing which the order is not accepted and an error is displayed.

The credit card number must start with:

'4 for Visa Cards

'37 for American Express Cards

'5 for MasterCard

The credit card number must be between 13 and 16 digits.

'If the number is less then 13 digits but not more

Than 16 digits then error is displayed.

The following calculation is used checking the card:

'Multiply each digit of the credit card number by the corresponding digit of

'The mask, and sum the results together.

'Loop through each digit

For in Position = 1 To 16

'Parse a digit from a specified position in the number

lnDigit = Mid(lsNumber, lnPosition, 1)

'Determine if we multiply by:

'1 (Even)

'2 (Odd)

'Based on the position that we are reading the digit from

lnMultiplier = 1 + (lnPosition Mod 2)

'Calculate the sum by multiplying the digit and the

Multiplier

lnSum = lnDigit * lnMultiplier

'If the Sum is 10 or more, subtract 9

If lnSum > 9 Then lnSum = lnSum - 9

'Add the sum to the total of all sums

lnTotal = lnTotal + lnSum

Next

'lnPosition

'Once all the results are summed divide

'By 10, if there is no remainder then the credit card number is valid.

And then there is code to check the validity of expiry date.

Here, a Database is designed having the following tables:

The details of the Register table, I had given you in last feedback

Products the attributes for which are:

- ItemID
- ItemProductNumber
- ItemName
- ItemDescription
- ItemPictureFile
- Item Price
- ItemStockQuantity

The attributes for which are:

- OrderID
- OrderDate
- OrderTime
- CustomerName
- CustomerAddress
- CustomerCity
- CustomerState
- CustomerZIP
- CustomerPhone

- OrderAmount
- PaymentMethod
- PaymentAccountExpDate
- Shipped ShipDate
- ShipVia
- ShipInfo
- Order Details

The attributes are:

- Order ID
- Item Product Number
- Quantity
- Price

EXPECTED BENEFITS TO USER ORGANISATION

Some advantages that the online books portal provides are as follows:

A simple, direct and profitable way to sell your items on this B2C Portal. It's advantage is a powerful way for authors, publishers, labels, of all sizes to promote and sell their items on this portal. In the publishing industry, books usually have to reach critical mass before making it into major wholesale channels. This portal is designed to provide the tools and framework to ensure that all titles appear frequently and prominently throughout this web based system. It allows almost anyone to put their products on our virtual shelves. As an independent author or small publisher, it allows you to have a direct and profitable relationship and putting your books in front of millions of qualified customers.

IT'S POWERFUL

Customers don't like to wait—it's that simple. The books are in stock and ready to go. Since we tend to show "In Stock" books first and more frequently, books are more likely to be discovered and purchased by browsing customers.

IT'S SIMPLE

Manage all your business with this web site 24 hours a day, 7 days a week. The titles are listed with immediate availability on online books portal.

IT'S EASY TO JOIN

Methodology used/Implementation detail

First of all I would like to mention the technology used in this project:

Online books Portal is developed using this technologies:

Front End: - HTML, Java Script & Internet Explorer.

Database: - My SQL

Language: - ASP.NET

For Running the Portal the configuration will be:

A Pentium III or Celeron processor 800 MHz or better, 256mb RAM, 20GB Hard Drive, 10/100MB Network Interface Card.

Windows 2000 or Windows XP Professional with the latest service packs and critical updates.

Microsoft Internet Explorer (non-branded) version 6.0 set as default browser and with 128-bit encryption.

The above description gives a brief introduction about technology, then the pictorial presentation of the project along with the steps.

The default page is where the user reaches initially after opening the site.

DEFAULT.ASPX

Here in the home page all the links and options are displayed for the user who visits the website.

All the functions available in the site are presented before the user in a systematic way so as to avoid any sought of ambiguity for the visitor.

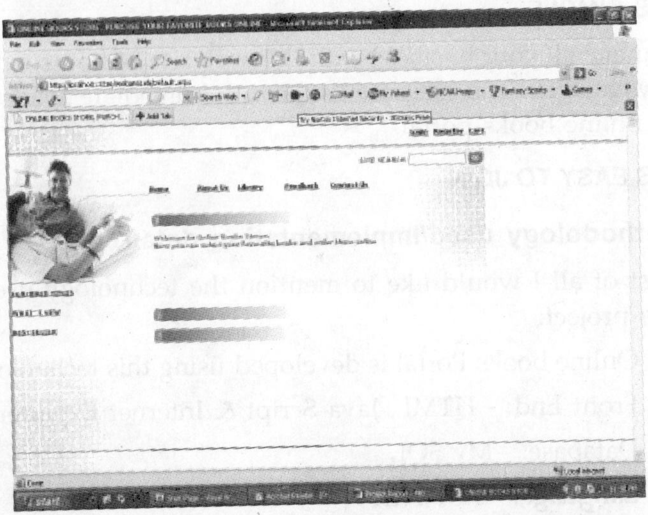

The visitor can use any of the options or links as per his requirement.

ABOUT US.HTM

The second page gives the details about the company, such as the Foundation, Company's Mission, Vision, Guiding Values, about company's Management, Infrastructure.

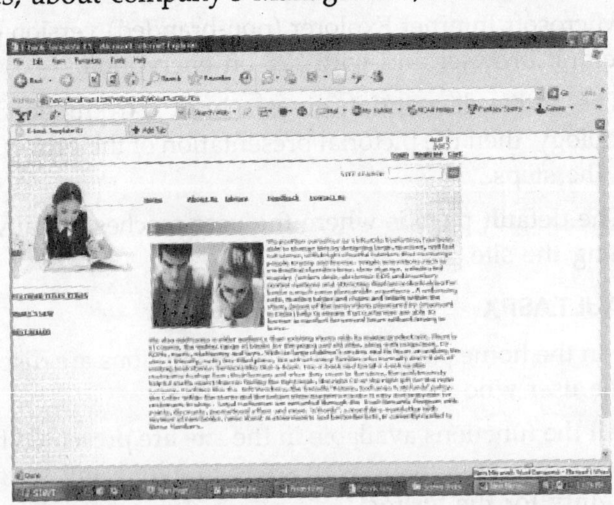

The visitor can get to know about the company through this page.

LIBRARY.HTM

This page contains the main data for the B2C Portal; here all kinds of books are arranged under appropriate categories such as Computers, Biographies, Travel, Health, Children & Arts, and Entertainment etc.

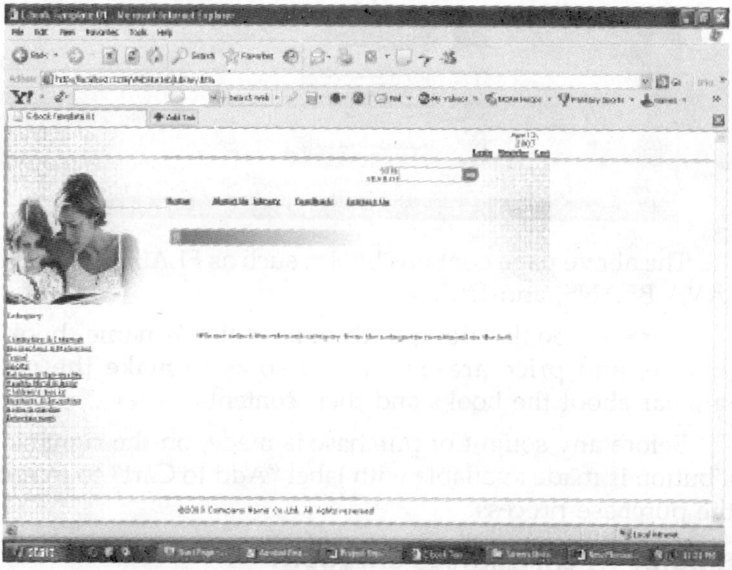

The visitor can select from the appropriate category the book of his/her own choice, through the links, and the books available under that category would be displayed along with their picture, brief description, price, author and an option is made available for adding the book to the cart.

For example, certain categories are mentioned below:

COMPUTERS & INTERNET CATEGORY

CI.htm

This page displays the books which are placed under the category of Computers & Internet.

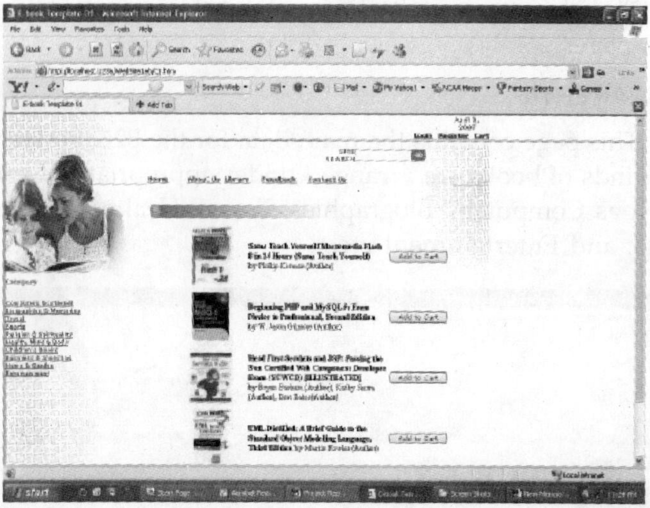

The above page contains books; such as FLASH, MY SQL, JAVA BEANS, and UML etc.

Here the books along with their author's name, book's picture, and price are mentioned so as to make the user familiar about the books and their contents.

Before any sought of purchase is made, on the right side a button is made available with label "Add to Cart" to initiate the purchase process.

BIOGRAPHY & MEMORIES CATEGORY

BM.htm

The second category contain books about the Biographies & Memories.

This page, for example, contains books about great personalities such as Abraham Lincoln, Nelson Mandela, John Marshall, Madona etc.

Any person interested in this category would click the link of Biographies.

And all the books would be displayed under this category; the options available are the same for the user to make the purchase.

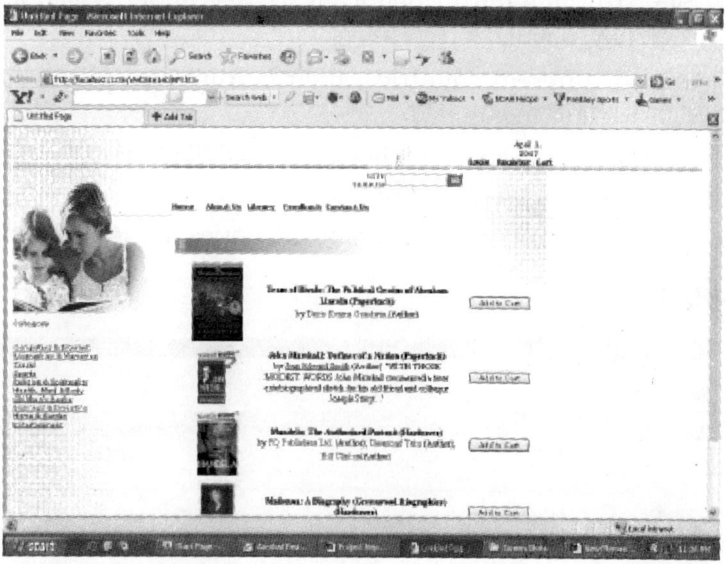

TRAVEL CATEGORY

Travel.htm

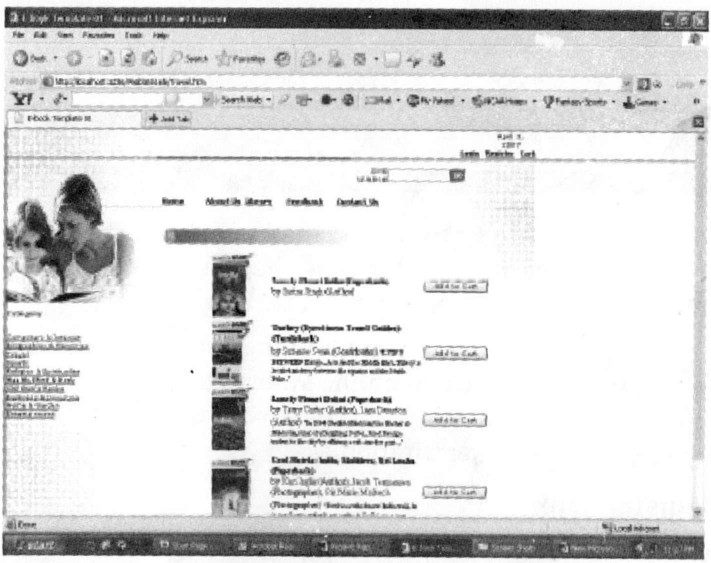

Similarly, the third category is Travel, under which are books citing details.

About different countries, their culture etc., places for tourism etc are mentioned.

The above page contains books about INDIA, MALDIVES, NEPAL, SRI LANKA, DUBAI etc.

So, in the same way different categories are mentioned.

Login.aspx

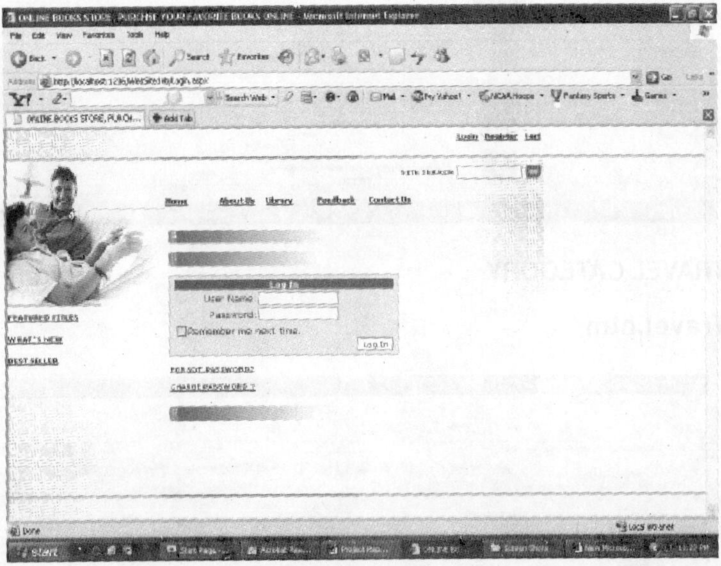

When the user has selected the book of his/her choice, then to continue for the shopping, he/she has to first login with a unique username & password.

This page is made to recognise the user, i.e., whether or not he/she is registered with the system, the user is asked to enter the unique username and password which was entered during the time of registration.

Register.aspx

Any visitor, before making any purchasing has to register

with the system, for the system to recognise him/her for the current & future purchases.

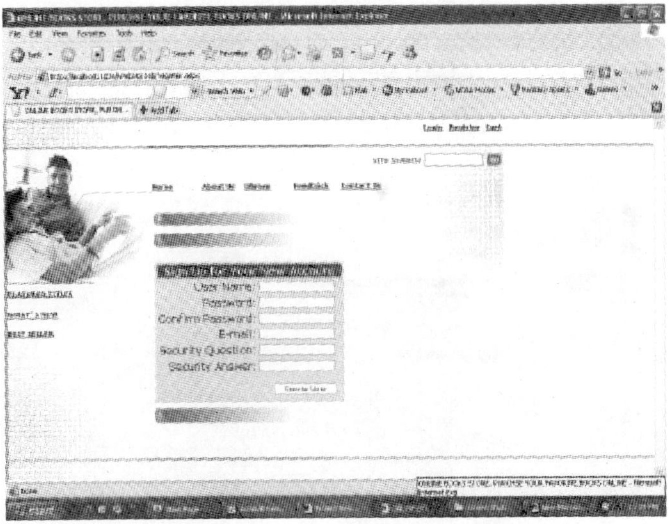

The following details are asked to be filled:

- Usename
- Password
- E-mail
- Security Question
- Security Answer

After the registration, for the current and future purchases the user can log in with the unique username & password provided by him/her during the time of registration.

Forgotpassword.aspx

What happens when a user who is already registered with the same, tries to log in but forgets the password?

This page gives the solution to this particular problem. The user is asked to enter the username which was provided during the registration, after which if the username is verified by the system, the security question which was provided during the time of registration is displayed in front of the user, and he/she is asked to fill in with the answer for that question.

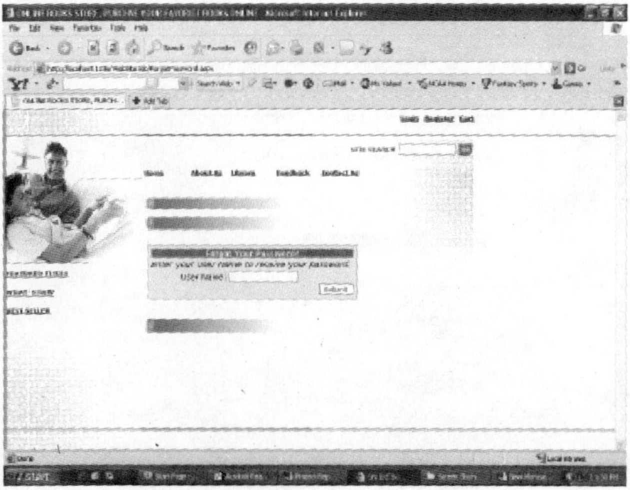

If everything is provided in order, then the new password is sent to the e-mail address of the user.

CHANGEPASSWORD.ASPX

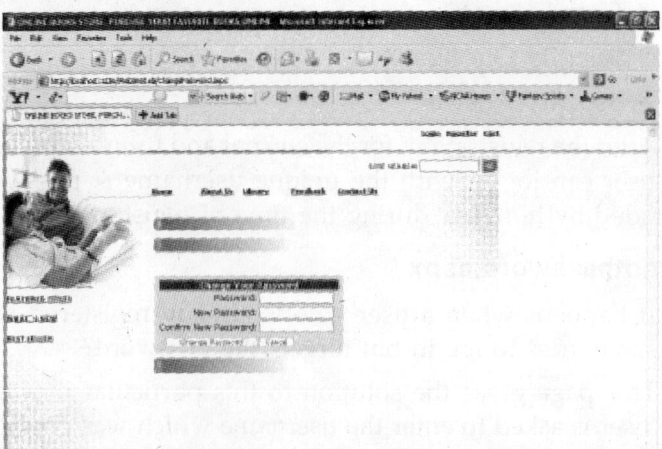

If the user wants to change the existing password for any reason (too easy for anyone to crack, to long etc.), this feature for the system provides the user with this option.

The existing user is asked to enter the existing password, and the new password which he/she wants, for which a confirmation is asked by asking the user to re-type the new password, and then if everything is in order, then the password is changed.

CART.ASPX

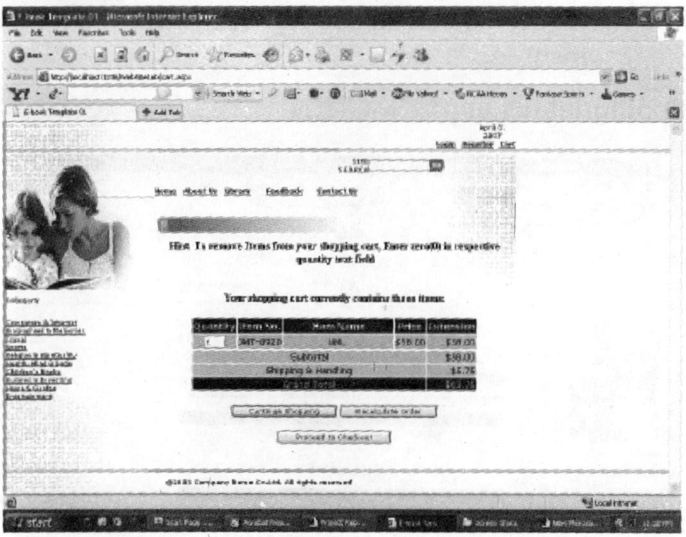

After the user has selected the book which he/she wants to purchase and has successfully logged into the system by providing the appropriate username and password, the cart for the user having the details of the purchases made is presented in front of the user.

The user is provided with the following three options:

- Continue Shopping: If the user wants to make more purchase, then by selecting this option , the user is directed to the library from where the selection for books has to be made, any purchase is added to the existing cart, which keeps the details of the shopping made by the user for that session.

- Recalculate Order: With this feature , if the user wants to alter the quantity for the books purchased, then by entering the new quantity in the text field provided, and clicking on the button named "Recalculate Order", the new price and shipping cost is displayed.
- Proceed to Checkout: When the user has completed the shopping, then by clicking on this button, the procedure for the completion of the shopping starts, where he/she is asked for the shipping details, payment mode etc.

Shippingdetails.aspx

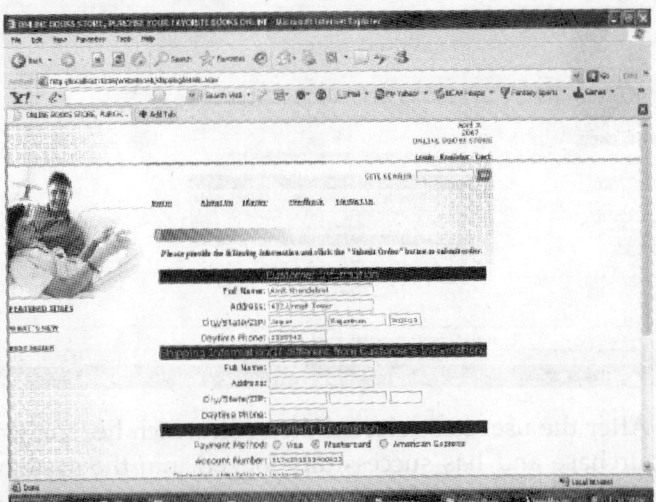

After clicking on the button "proceed to checkout", the user is directed to this page for the completion of the order where the following details are asked by the user:

- Customer Information (Name, Address, City, State, Telephone etc.)
- Shipping Information (If other than the customer information)

- Payment Information: The payment can be made using credit card of type Visa, MasterCard, American Express. The user is asked to enter the card number and the expiry date for the card.

Here, a particular algorithm is used for the validation of the credit card.

After this, if everything is validated and is in order, then the system asked for the confirmation and then the Invoice is presented to the user for the purchase made, and the order is complete.

Feedback, htm

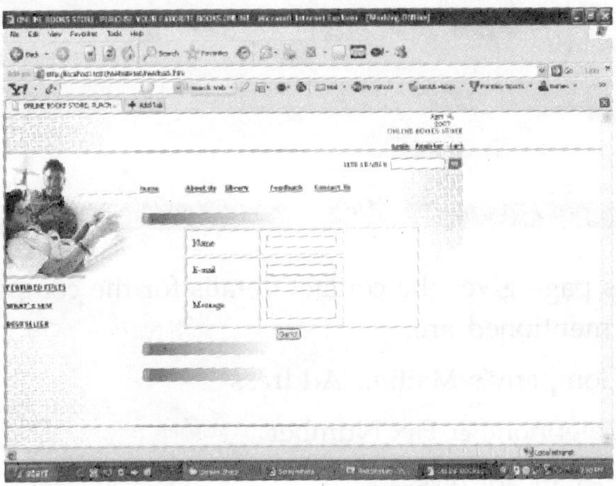

Through this functionality, any person can contact online books store.

Give his/her feedback and ask any query. The user is asked to enter his/her name, the e-mail address, and the message, this information is sent to the company's e-mail address, and depending upon the message content, its authenticity and other parameters internal to the system , reply is being made to the e-mail address which the user had mentioned while sending the feedback.

The user need not be a registered user for sending the message.

CONTACT US.ASPX

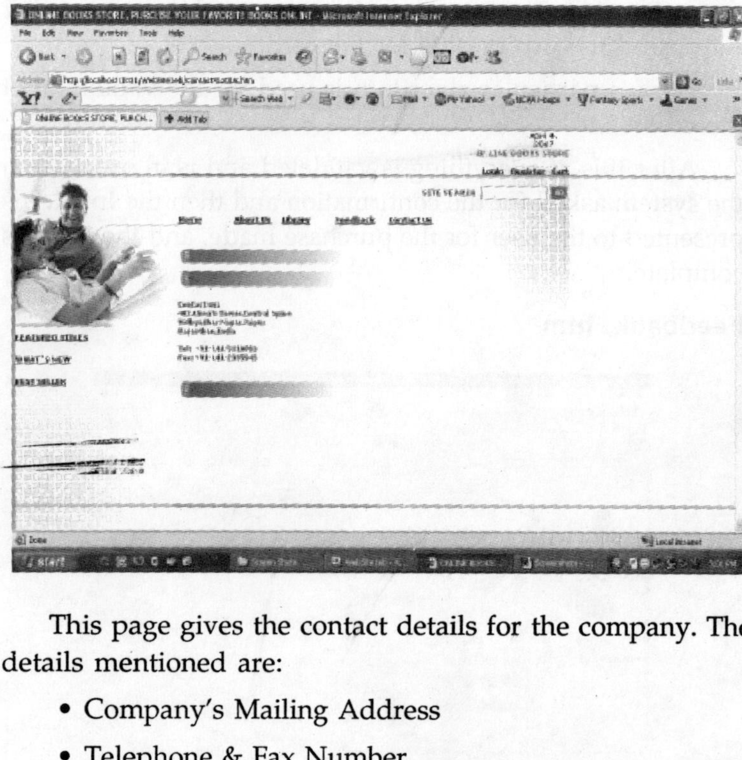

This page gives the contact details for the company. The details mentioned are:

- Company's Mailing Address
- Telephone & Fax Number
- E-mail address

So any customer can contact the company for any query using the details mentioned in this page.

FEATURED TITLES

Featured.htm

This link which is presented on the left side displays the most featured titles, and by clicking on this link the books kept under the featured titles are displayed in front of the user, so that for such books the user doesn't have to go to the library and search for the books under the category's mentioned.

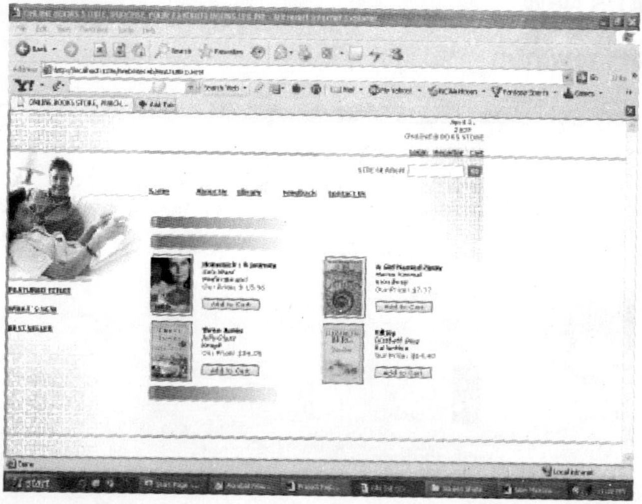

BEST SELLERS

Bestseller.htm

This link contains the books which falls under the category of Best Seller as per the purchasing pattern, i.e., those books which are purchased more are put under this category.

WHAT'S NEW

Whatsnew.htm

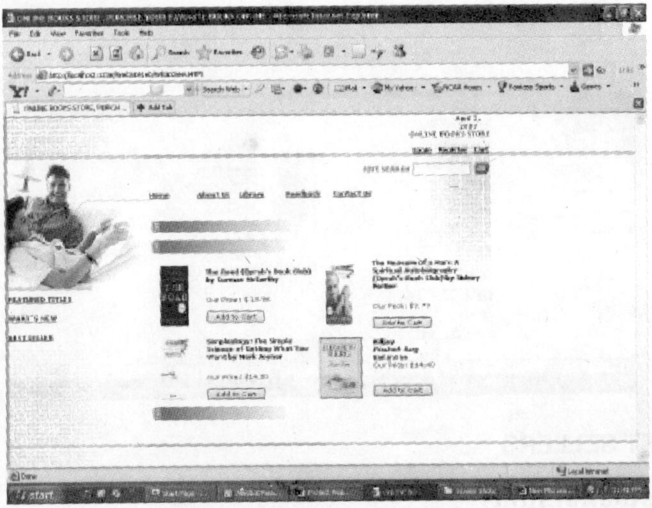

As the name suggests, this page contains the books which have recently hit the stores. The user can scroll down to see the latest releases and if wants to make the purchase, then can log in to the system and add the books to the cart.

FUTURE ENHANCEMENT

Unlike other projects Online Book Portal Project is a continual enhancement project. Different features are to be added for future prospective. Generally, most of the requirements come from the customer for improvement and for enhancing the current project. Some of the upcoming features in modules are:

Personalisation and Auto-Merchandising

Most people think the days are long gone when you could walk into a bookstore and have the owner remember your name and recommend new titles to you based on your personal tastes. This new feature would enable every time a customer walking into a store, the merchandise, sales items, end caps, and point of sale display all changed to reflect each person's individual taste, demography, and previous buying history.

Online Downloading

Some customers would not like to wait for the new releases and carry the books physically; instead they would like to download the latest books of their own choice, for this a new feature would be added which would enable the customers download the books either in the Word Format or the PDF Format

Discussion Board

Here all the customers would be able to share their views and comments with other's for a particular release

Connecting Unique Books with Unique Customers

The portal would look at ways to better serve the customers, and to provide them with new ways to discover products they wouldn't have necessarily found otherwise. It would have two basic types of book customers: people who already know what they want, and people who are browsing our site to discover something new and interesting to read. The people who know what they want simply type the name of the book into our search engine to quickly find and buy it. People who are browsing tend to look at our category pages, recommendation features, or bestseller lists. They would use the unique ability to proactively put undiscovered books in front of the most qualified and receptive potential buyers. Automated Merchandising can't distinguish between a top seller and a book from the back of the catalog – it works for every one of our millions of items.

COMMENTS

(1) For any student field work is always helpful. My field work gives me a vision about industry work culture. This project gave me a good knowledge of how the several B2C online business models work and what

is required to be competitive in implementing such models.

(2) This concept of online selling can be easily extended to other products as per customer requirements and their feedback giving the customers all the possible products they want thus enhancing customer retention.

21

Indian Agricultural Doctoral Dissertations Repository Krishiprabha Database

— *Anoop Kumar Bajpayi*

ABSTRACT

In this paper we are discussing the meaning, objective, and how to search Krishiprabha database. In this project the data providers are–46 State Agricultural Universities and Deemed Agricultural Universities [SAUs and DAUs]. These universities have free access to the Full Text of this Digital Library database. The access requires password as well as IP-address. Here we have been providing some screen shoot for how to search this database while using internet. In this project 46 State Agricultural Universities' and Deemed Universities' e-thesis /doctoral dissertation record is available.

Keyword: *Krishipraba project, Electronic thesis, Doctoral Dissertation, HAU, ICAR.*

INTRODUCTION

The title "KrishiPrabha" has its own significance. "Prabha" means "morning", in other words "beginning of the day". Since, this project is first of its kind in agricultural discipline in India, hence the title "KrishiPrabha". It was sanctioned by ICAR under its National Agricultural Innovation Project [NAIP] in November 2007. The objectives of the Project had been achieved at a cost of Rs. 127 lakhs.

The data providers – 46 State Agricultural Universities and Deemed Agricultural Universities [SAUs and DAUs] – have free access to the Full Text of this Digital Library database. Besides the ICAR institutes, Directorates of Research and other constituents will also enjoy the same privileges as the SAUs/DAUs. While on the other hand ***the Non-member users may have the access of Meta-data and Abstract only directly by-login www.hau.ernet.in.***

National Agricultural Innovative Project (NAIP)

The NAIP—the world's second biggest World Bank assisted the agriculture project being executed by the National Agricultural Research System (NARS) with lifespan of six years (July 24, 2006 to 2012). The signing ceremony of the project was held on July 24, 2006 at the Ministry of Finance, Govt. of India in the presence of Mr. Prafull C. Patel, Vice-President, and the World Bank. The credit agreements were signed by Dr. Michael Carter, Country Director, World Bank Office, New Delhi and Mr. Madhusudan Prasad, Joint Secretary, Ministry of Finance, Govt of India. The project Agreement was signed by Dr. Michael Carter and Dr. Mruthyunjaya, National Director, NAIP, ICAR-DARE, Govt. of India. The NAIP was launched successfully on July 26, 2006 by Shri Sharad Pawar, Union Minister for Agriculture in the presence of Dr. Montek Singh Ahluwalia, Deputy Chairman, Planning Commission, Govt. of India and Dr. Mangala Rai, Secretary, DARE & DG, ICAR.

RATIONALE

In India there are 45 Agricultural Universities/Deemed Agricultural Universities which award Doctoral Degrees in agriculture and allied disciplines. These doctoral dissertations are one of the very important and valuable original sources of information. There is a need to unveil this resource to the scientists across the world. This objective can be achieved only if:

- Indian Agricultural Dissertations Repository (IADR) is set up for the preservation of information enshrined in these dissertations for the posterity and used by the current generation;
- the Repository so established, is used for evaluation of research findings, and the evaluation reports are used for further pursuit and for the generation of agricultural knowledge;
- the same Repository is utilised for the creation of electronic Database of Doctoral Dissertations;
- the Database, so created, is made accessible online to national and international users; and
- the same Database is further utilised for the publication of an e-journal reporting abstracts of the dissertations in order to disseminate information.

SCOPE OF KRISHIPRABHA

Access to doctoral dissertation is severely restricted due to absence of appropriate policy and infrastructure. A systematic effort to develop and maintain a national repository of these resources, digitise them and make them accessible online would facilitate their potential use for extracting maximum value from them. Use of modern technologies for effective data capturing, organisation and storage, and information retrieval will enhance the value of these resources further. This project was envisioned in this backdrop to establish, develop and maintain a repository of Indian agricultural doctoral dissertations. This Project envisages:

- The digitisation of about 10,500 agricultural doctoral dissertations produced in India during 2000-06;
- The maintenance of the Digital Library thus created;
- Collection of hard copies of the old dissertations; spare copies are available with the respective universities; and

- Collection of soft copies of dissertations to be produced in future for updating of the database of the Digital Library.

OBJECTIVES OF KRISHIPRABHA

Initially the project was approved with the following objectives:

1. To develop, organise and sustain knowledge based Indian Agricultural Dissertations in digital form and make it accessible online.
2. To develop a standard format for submission of e-theses to the SAUs/DUs.
3. To upgrade skills of human resources of SAUs/DUs.
4. To publish a journal in electronic form/ hard copy form the Database.

The objectives of this Project do not terminate with the establishment of the Digital Library and the Repository. It has to be perennially updated by the addition of dissertations that have come up during 2008 and 2009 and will be produced in future. In fact, the coverage should go back to at least 1995, if not prior to it.

E - ELECTRONIC THESIS AND DISSERTATION (ETD)

Now a days, thesis is presented in an electronic medium which is called an e-thesis or e-dissertation. An ETD is an electronic document that explains the intellectual works or research of a researcher. It is expressed in a form simultaneously suitable for machine archives and world-wide retrieval as well as similar to its paper predecessor. ETD is different, however, it provides a technologically advanced medium by word processor for expressing ideas with less expensive, small space, easy handling, high longevity and never collect dust. At user's choice, they can be available to any one that can browse the following World Wide Web.

MANUAL FOR SEARCHING KRISHIPRABHA DATABASE

Krishiprabha is a full-text electronic database of Indian

Agricultural Doctoral Dissertations submitted by research scholars to the 45 States' Deemed Agricultural Universities during the period from 1.1.2000 to 31.12.2006. This database, listing about 10500 Dissertations, has been created by Nehru Library, Chaudhary Charan Singh Haryana Agricultural University, Hisar (Haryana) with financial support from Indian Council of Agricultural Research, New Delhi under its National Agricultural Innovation Project (NAIP).

1. Open CCS HAU Website (URL: http://www.hau.ernet.in).

Click on Nehru Library

2. Screen as shown above follows:

On Campus User—This option is meant for access by CCSHAU Intranet users. Click on this Option to go to the next screen.

Off Campus User—This option is meant for access by users from the rest of the world. Click on this Option to go to the next screen.

Click on Off Campus User

3. **Screen as shown below will follow.**

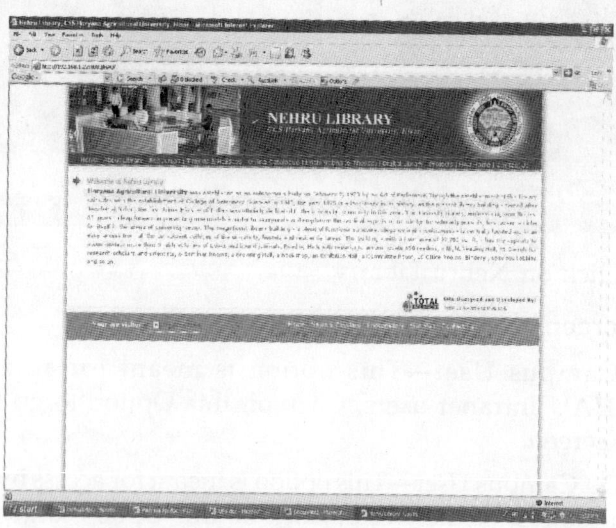

Click on KrishiPrabha (e-Theses)

4. Screen as shown below will follow.

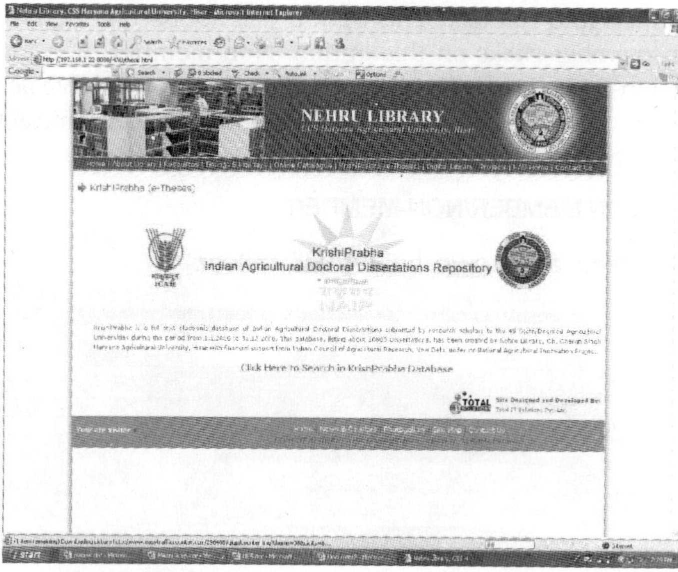

Click on: Click Here to Search in KrishiPrabha Database.

5. Screen as shown below will follow.

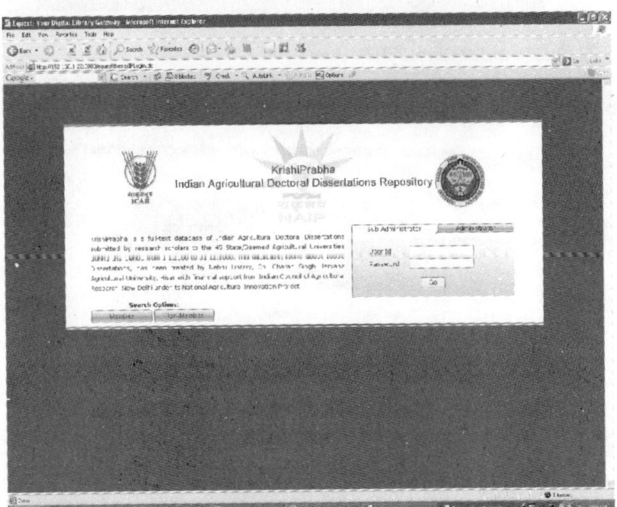

Member – It is meant for SAU/DAU/ICAR users. All these users will have web-based access to the Metadata, abstracts and full text. This option will not become active if a non-member clicks on this option. **Non-member**- It is meant for non-SAU/DAU/ICAR users. These users will have access to metadata and abstracts only. This option will become active irrespective of the category of users.

CLICK ON MEMBER/NON-MEMBER

6. Screen as shown below will follow.

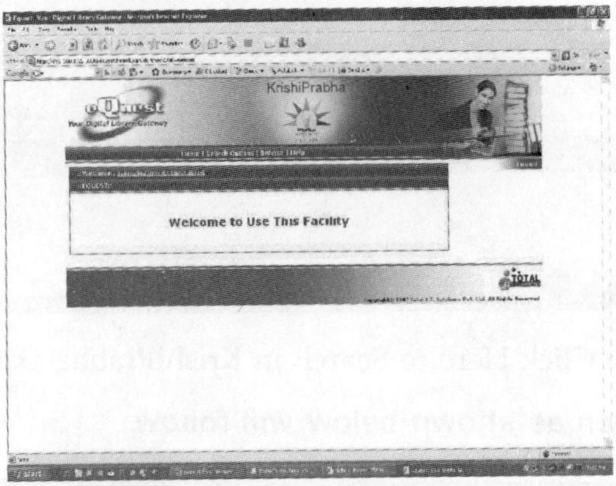

Click on Search Options.

7. Screen as shown below will follow.

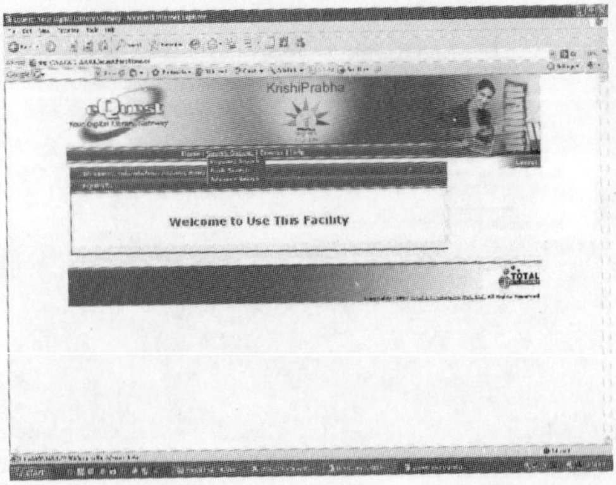

Search Options comprises of Keyword Search, Basic Search and Advance Search Browse—these display all records authorwise/titlewise in alphabetical order.

Click on Keyword Search

8. Screen as shown below will follow.

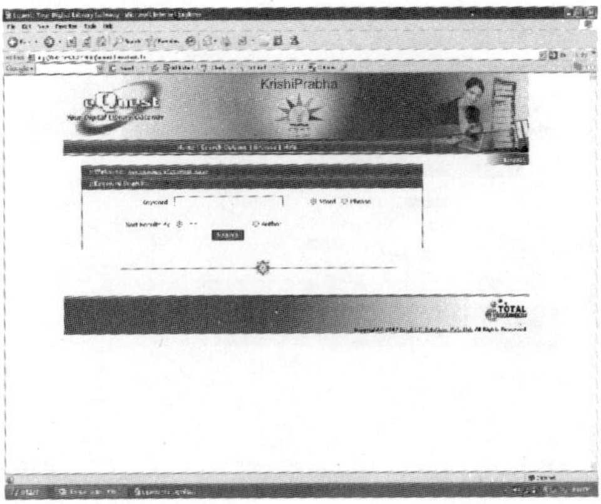

Type Keyword in Text Box, followed by click on Search Box. Click on title/author Check Boxes to get titlewise/ authorwise alphabetical list of records. If neither title nor author is selected, titlewise list of records will be displayed by default.

9. Screen as shown below will follow.

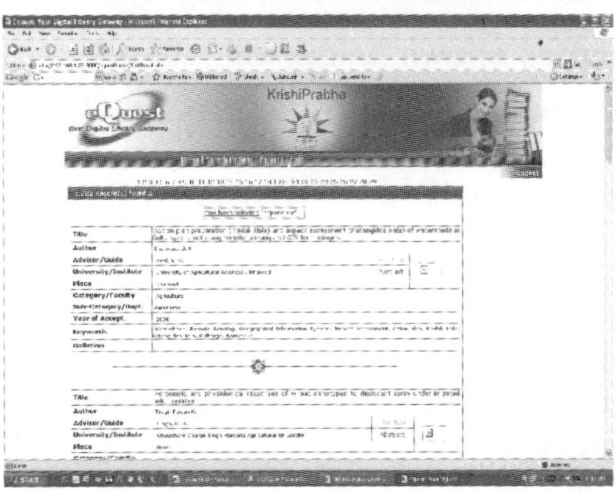

Click on Abstract to view and to print abstract. Click on Full Text to view full text.

Click on Basic Search in Search Options

10. Screen as shown below will follow.

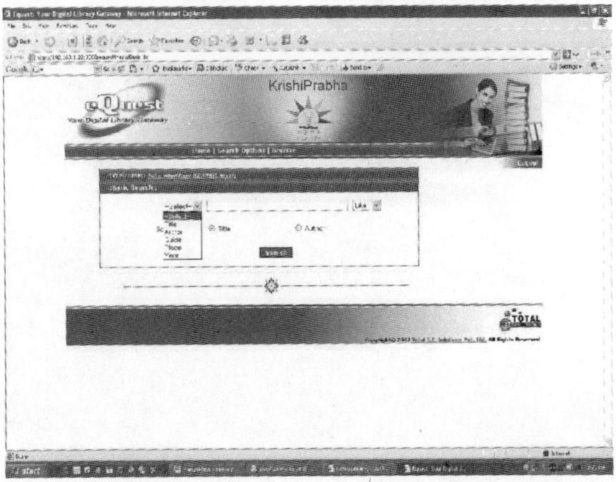

Select Title/Author/Guide/Place/Year from the drop down menu and type appropriate word, followed by click on Search Box. Click on title/author Check Boxes to get titlewise/authorwise alphabetical list of records. If neither title nor author is selected, titlewise list of records will be displayed by default.

Click on Advance Search in Search Options

11. Screen as shown below will follow.

It is a combination search. Select one option or a group of options and click on Search button to get a listing of selected records. For example, select University, Category and Sub-Category from University/Institute, Category/Faculty and Sub-Category/Dept drop down menus, respectively, and go on narrowing the search, follow to click on Search button. Alphabetical titlewise list of selected records will be displayed by default. Select Author or Publication Date to get Alphabetical authorwise or datewise list of selected records. Click on Browse menu

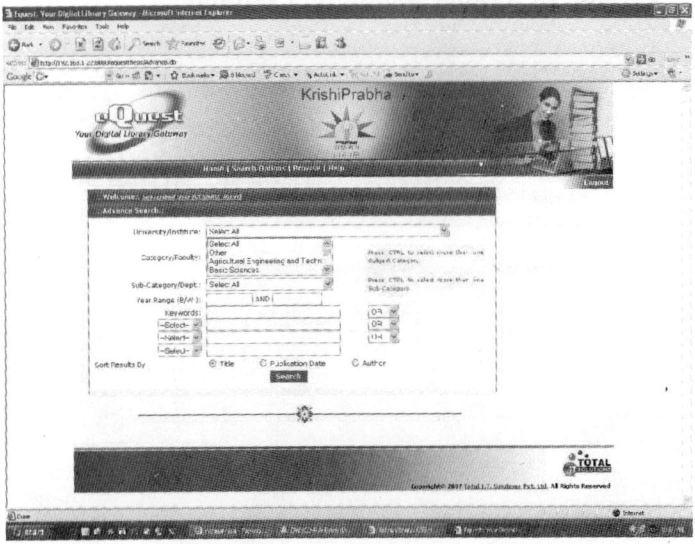

12. Screen as shown below will follow.

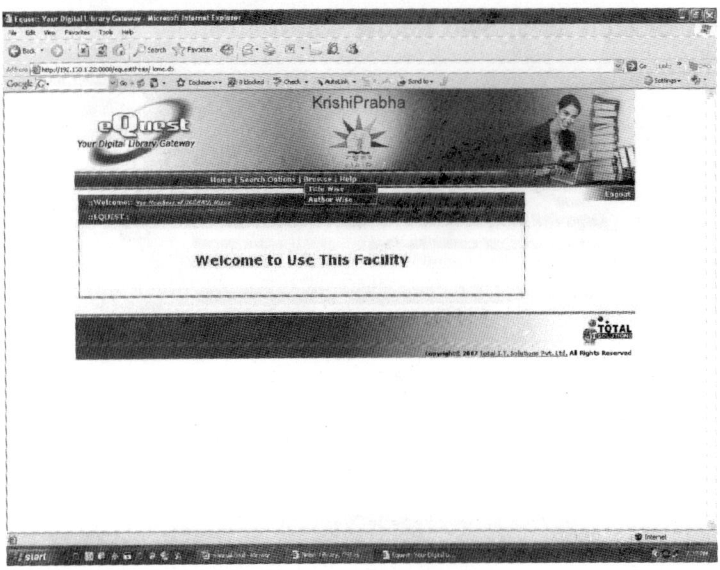

Click on Title Wise in Browse menu.

13. Screen as shown below will follow:

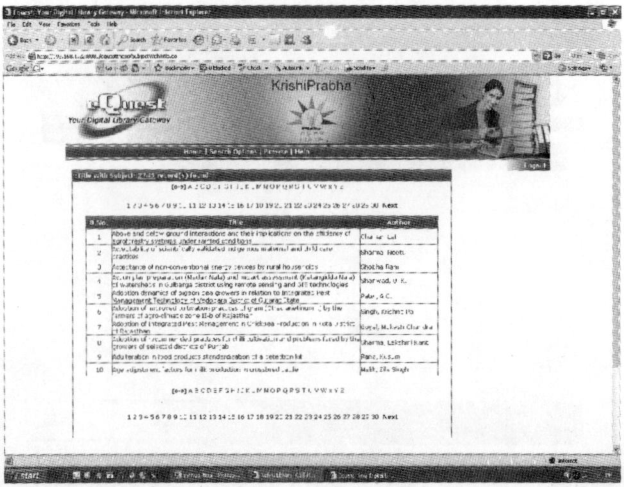

Alphabetical titlewise list of records as shown above will be displayed. Click on Author-wise in Browse menu.

14. Screen as shown below will follow.

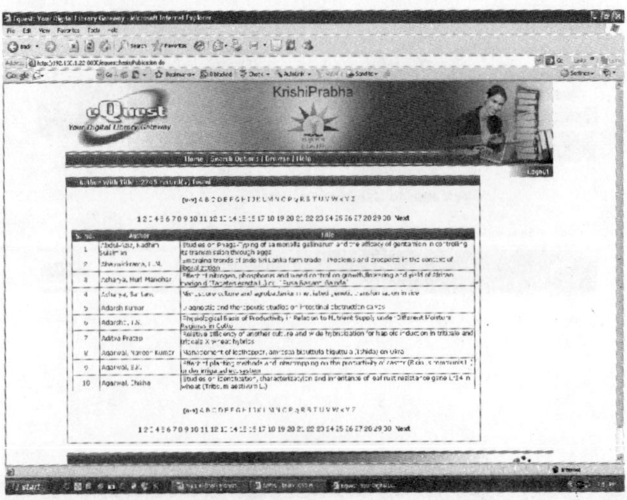

Alphabetical author-wise list of records as shown above will be displayed.

CONCLUSION

In this paper we are giving useful information and some screen shot about Krishiprabha database. In this paper user and researcher get details of Krishiprabha database and will know how to access of this database. Krishiprabha database provides e-theses/ online theses searching facilities for the students in the fields of agricultural and related subject, animal husbandry, home science, basic science.

REFERENCES

KrishiPrabha: Indian Agricultural Doctoral Dissertation Repository. Project Document. Nehru Library, CCSHAU, Hisar.2007.

www.hau.ernet .in

www.google.com

www.cera.jccc.in

www.wikkipedi.com

Annual report Nehru Library CCS HAU, Hisar.

Bajpayi (Anoop Kumar) and Sharma (Hemant). Electronic Publishing: An Overview – National Conference on Knowledge Management in the Globalised Era held at IARI, AALDI- New Delhi: 21-23 April 2010. pp.422-29.

Bajpayi (Anoop Kumar), Balwan Singh and Sharma (Hemant), Collection Development of Nehru Library, Ccshau, Hisar With Special Reference To Digital Resources – Library Conference 2010 held at Accman Institute of Management, Noida 14 September 2010.

Dr. R.G. Garg and Rajive Kr. Pateria : Electronic Resources for National Agricultural Research System (NARS) – India: ILA Conference 2010 held at Noida.

Sharma (Hemant) and Bajpayi (Anoop Kumar). Electronic Publishing ; Types Sources and Problem in Academic Libraries in Modern Era – National Seminar cum Workshop On Building Digital Libraries Using Open Source Software held at Bhopal – 1st to 5th Feb. 2010. pp. 93-98.

www.naip.icar.org.in/

Visakhi (P), Resource Sharing of Agricultural Libraries in Electronic Era : An overview- India Journal of Agricultural Library and Information Service. Vol. 24, 2008. pp. 31-38.

22

Use of SMS and E-mail in Current Awareness Services: A Practical Approach

— *Fayaz Ahmad Loan*

ABSTRACT

The landscape of knowledge is rapidly changing. In order to keep the academic community well-informed and up-to-date promptly, current awareness service is provided to the users. Traditional methods include routing print journals, distributing photocopies of journal contents, displaying notifications on bulletin board, preparing a documentation list, publishing a newsletters and the like. In new methods, the use of modern communication gadgets like Phone and Internet is highly used. The present study shows that how Short Message Service (SMS) and E-mail can be used to alert users about new developments in their subject areas. The results reveal that the SMS is highly suitable for informing users about recent developments whereas E-mail is mostly fit for delivering the online information.

INTRODUCTION

Information is the soul of research and research is the prominent factor for sustainable development. Therefore, every country gives special preference to research in order to generate new information and knowledge. The researchers need current information to keep them updated regularly. Hence, it becomes the primary duty of library managers to keep them abreast with the new developments in their fields of interest. The traditional librarianship, library and information professionals continuously provide current awareness services to achieve this goal. Current awareness service (CAS) alerts users about the new publications, developments, issues and trends in their circle of knowledge. Current awareness Service means "the dissemination of information that keeps users well-informed and up-to-date in their basic fields of interest as well as in the related subjects" **(Kumar 1980)**. In current awareness services, library and information professionals are supposed to provide information regarding tables of contents (TOC) of new issues of serials, new publications, new arrivals, new articles, news clippings and other relevant publications. It also incorporates reporting of new developments, programmes, forthcoming seminars, conferences, workshops, events, training programmes, etc. Library and information professionals use various methods to provide these alerting services. Traditional methods include routing print journals, distributing photocopies of tables of contents, displaying notifications on bulletin board, preparing a documentation list, publishing a newsletters etc. Each of these methods has some disadvantages: routing of print material moves slowly, distributing photocopies is labour intensive, preparing documentation list or publishing a newsletter requires extra time and effort. Now to overcome these problems, the library and information professionals apply Information Communication Technology (ICT) to provide these services. ICT is a broad term that covers wide range of technologies. It is the convergence of computers, communication and microelectronic-based techniques. The technologies and devices like Radio, Telephone, Telegraph, Fax, TV, Telephone, Mobile phone, Internet and World Wide Web (WWW) are major components of the ICT. The Internet has changed the way people communicate, interact, acquire, share knowledge, search, investigate and participate in the creation and re-use of content **(Arora, 2008).** The electronic communication has brought revolution in the library and information services. It has affected the way libraries operate and provide services. With the emergence of Internet in libraries, the modern communication technology has become the primary mode of communication in electronic reference services in general and current awareness service in particular. The current awareness service through electronic means is the only service that disseminates the current information to researchers in no time to keep them update in their respective fields. These electronic services include Short Message Service (SMS), Electronic Mail (e-mail), Instant Messaging (IM), Social Networking Sites (SNS), Blogs, Wikis, and Really Simple Syndication (RSS). These electronic communication services have many advantages like:

- Availability (24X7)
- Time saving (It is fast)
- Less expensive (It is cheap)
- Accessibility (Anywhere access)
- Prompt feedback (Quick Response)
- Group Communication (One message for all)
- Viability (Everyone makes use of one or the other service)

The library managers in the developed world have already started to provide current awareness services to user community through electronic means. The libraries in developing and third world countries are lacking behind due to various reasons like lack of Internet facilities, lack of infrastructure, lack of awareness, lack of training and lack of skilled man power. However, most of the libraries in these countries also use one or the other communication services as per their feasibility to alert users. In my study, I have selected SMS and E-mail to provide alerting services to the user community due to the fact that all the members of the academic community use one or the other form of communication service. SMS stands for Short Message Service. It is a technology that enables the sending and receiving of messages between electronic gadgets especially mobile phones. SMS first appeared in Europe in 1992 **(Kumar & Chitra, 2008)** and since then its use is increasing rapidly in communication for personal, business and other informative purposes. Libraries have also used SMS for providing various alerting services regarding new publications, new arrivals, new issues of journals, overdue of documents, notifications, etc. Electronic mail, commonly known as E-mail, was invented by Ray Tomlinson in 1972 **(Peter 2007).** It is the only Internet service widely used by netizens in general and academic community in particular. E-mail offers speedy and economical transfer of messages irrespective of geographical boundaries and time barriers. Library and information professionals widely apply this medium for various services like reference, referral, alerting, and circulation. For the collection of Information, I initially use E-mail alerts and Google alerts and later introduce RSS feeds as well.

GOALS OF THE STUDY

The goals of the present study are:

- To test the applicability of the SMS and E-mail in the current awareness services, and
- To observe the impact of these services on user attitude and behaviour.

RESEARCH DESIGN

The study was conducted in the Centre of Central Asian studies, University of Kashmir, Srinagar. The Centre of Central Asian Studies is the biggest interdisciplinary centre in India consisting of 19 faculty members having expertise in 12 subject fields. The Centre has presently more than fifty (50) research scholars conducting research on different aspects of Central Asian Republics. The process was started with collecting information about the academic community (i.e. scholars and faculty) regarding their interests and fields of specialisation. Later, different groups were made on the basis of subject interests. The information was saved in e-mail, way2sms accounts and mobile phone. The current awareness service was started in January 2010 using new modes of communication. Whenever, the information was received, it was evaluated, matched with the interest groups and communicated immediately using the suitable communication service. The record of the whole process was maintained. Besides, the users' attitude and behaviour was observed for future strategies.

PRACTICAL ANALYSIS

The data reveals that more than 1500 alerting services were received and most of the items were received through Google alerts followed by RSS feeds and E-mail alerts respectively. The received items were evaluated and almost 37% were found either irrelevant or less informative and was deleted to avoid E-mail overload on users. The hits received from E-mail alert and RSS feeds proved to be more relevant than Google alert. The Google provide maximum hits from a wide range of sources from newspapers to theses but all of them not relevant to the research community. However, these can be more useful for teaching and learning purposes. The majority of the hits received (63.23%) were delivered to user groups (Table 1).

Table 1 : Items received and delivered in 2010

Name of Service	Received	Delivered	Deleted
E-mail Alert	217	153 (70.51)	64 (29.49)
Google Alert	1023	554 (54.15)	469 (45.85)
RSS Feeds	443	294 (63.33)	149 (33.63)
Total	1583	1001 (63.23)	582 (36.77)

The maximum number of information items was delivered to research community through E-mail. However, due to portability of the cell phones, the information regarding the item was also communicated through SMS (Table 2).

Table 2 : Mode of information delivered in 2010

Mode	Delivered	Feedback
E-mail	806	363
SMS (Mobile)	271	43
SMS (Online)	630	62

The category-wise data shows that research community was alerted about various sources like books, journals, articles, news items, conferences and seminars etc. The information was mostly based on new arrivals, new publications, new issues of journals/magazines, table of contents, call for papers, conference/ seminar schedules, links to full text, online lectures, etc. The research papers/articles got the most attention followed by books, journals and news items perhaps because the researchers mostly rely on primary information sources (Table 3).

Table 3: Category-wise information delivered in 2010

Category	No. of items
Books	201
Journals/Magazines	179
Research papers/Articles	272
News items	166
Projects/Working papers	51
Thesis/Dissertations	12
Conferences/Seminars	67
Workshops/Tutorials	19
Others	34

DISCUSSION

The new way of current awareness service proved to be very effective. The combination of SMS and E-mail supports in informing and delivering the nascent information promptly. SMS was highly used for informing whereas E-mail was used as a delivering tool. The response of the users was enthusiastic. The feedback messages mostly read as "Thanks", "Thank you", "Thank you very much", "Thank you very much, Sir", "Thank you very much, Dear", "Thanks, keep it up", "Very relevant", "Precious information", "Please inform about coming issues", etc. The research community also appreciates the new ways of providing information verbally and demands to continue it in future as well. The outcomes of the study reveal that SMS is a mobile service, and is used to serve the user outside the four walls of libraries but the problem with the SMS is that data cannot be attached with the message. However, E-mail overcomes this barrier. Undoubtedly, E-mail makes it easier to take the information on the door steps of users and helps to serve research community promptly and quickly. The problem with the e-mail is time lag in checking the mail. The SMS helps to eradicate this problem as SMS reaches out to the users promptly and informs the user about the current information waiting in the inbox of E-mail. In this way, the time lag due to delay in checking mails is eliminated. Moreover, the SMS like E-mail is cost effective and efficient communication service as it can be sent from online SMS service providers like WAY2SMS free of cost.

LIMITATIONS

The service proved to be very useful for research community but to keep the service intact, I personally face some problems. The SMS service was banned in the Kashmir due to political reasons and thus later only E-mail was used to inform and deliver. The other limitation with the WAY2SMS service was that only up to 70 words can be sent at a time and not beyond that. So, I was sometimes handicapped to provide complete information in one SMS.

REFERENCES

Arora, Jagdish, "Library 2.0: Innovative Technologies for Building Libraries of Tomorrow." Paper presented at the ETTLIS Conference, JIIT University, Noida, December 18-20, 2008.

Kumar, Krishan, "Changing paradigm in journals based on current awareness services in libraries." *Information Services and Use* 28 (2008): pp. 59-65.

Kumar, Vimal & Chitra, S, "Innovative use of SMS technology for the excellence in library services in Kerala." Paper presented at the IASLIC 23rd National Seminar On "Library Profession in Search of a New Paradigm", Bose Institute, Kolkata, December 10-13, 2008.

23

Data Curation in Digital Library: A Reference to Invenio Digital Library

— *Naresh Kumar*

ABSTRACT

This chapter talks about digital library, its meaning, need and purpose etc. This article will take through the various features of the digital libraries. A special reference to Invenio digital library is also included in this paper. A brief coverage of various formats on which documents are recorded in a digital library are given in this chapter. The article highlights how we can catalogue, upload and update a document on digital library by providing suitable examples of Invenio digital library's European Organisation for Nuclear Research (CERN) document server.

Keywords: *Digital library, CERN, Invenio, MARC format, Dublin Core*

INTRODUCTION

Digital library is the solutions of many emerging problems of the information acquired, storaged, retrieved and disseminated. Virtual libraries are covering all files of audio, video and images. Digital libraries are developed in different ways depending on need. Digital libraries like D-Space, Greenstone, Invenio Digital Library and e-prints at IISc are used by most of the librarians around the world for meeting information needs of the users. Digital libraries provide current awareness, learning and teaching facilitation, acquisition, cataloguing, user training, reference query fulfillment, and information seeking and retrieval search. So every librarian must know its technical processing to satisfy the users' need.[1]

Meaning and Definition

Digital library is a set of electronic resources and associated technical capabilities for creating, searching, information storage and retrieval systems to manipulate digital data in many mediums. It exists in distributed networks. It combines all the benefits of the multimedia, digital coding and Internet. It acts as a set of tools to locate, search, and retrieve information. It is regarded as the digital face of traditional libraries.[2]

CERN Document Server (CDS)

CERN has its own library management system, Invenio Digital Library, whose application is the CERN document server. The CDS has a broad collection of materials. ALEPH is an integrated library system, version- 18.01of Ex libris which provides so many features like acquisitions, serials, cataloging, circulation, inter library loan. Aleph is library automation software, used to manage all scientific information on the CDS.[3]

Purpose of Digital Library

The main purposes of digital library are given below:

- To provide latest information.
- To save the time of users and staff.
- To solve the space problem in library.
- To use and disseminate.
- To improve cost effectiveness of library operations.

Need of Digital Library

We need digital library because of the following reasons:

- Usable any where any time.
- Interactive.
- To access national and international journals in different formats.
- Helpful for physically disabled users as they can hear audible e-resources.
- Provide background music and animations.
- Save human efforts for shelving, rectification, binding and repair.
- User can not misplace e-books.
- In buying e-resources, the overhead charges like shipping, postal, handling are totally ruled out.

Features of Digital Library

There are many features of digital library. They are given below one by one:

- Search options: Title, Subject, Author, and Keyword.
- Browse options: Title, Subject, Author, Language, and Year.
- Languages: English, French, Italian, Spanish, German ...depend on database to database of Digital Library.
- Registration: To access some Digital libraries' content, registration is required.
- Presentation of Content in Digital Library:
  (a) Listing of E-resources: Alphabetically, Year-wise, Topic-wise, and Subject-wise.
  (b) Availability of abstract and full text in Html, PDF, and Document etc.
  (c) Availability of Audio and video files.
  (d) To add feature: Option to post selected articles on any one's social networking sites like Face book, twitter etc.
  (e) Bookmarks.

Different Formats of the Digital Library

There are various formats on which documents are recorded in a digital library are given below:

MARC Format - a Machine Readable Catalogue for the purpose of communicating bibliographic information to large number of libraries. A MARC record involves three elements, such as the record structure, the content designation, and the data content of the record.

CCF Record Format—Common communication format is UNESCO Sponsored project. It consists of record label of 24 characters and directory of 14 characters. Data field consists of indicators, subfields and field separator.

Dublin Core—It is a small set of metadata elements for describing information resources. The bibliographic data is expressed by Meta and Link tags of hypertext markup language (HTML) in digital library. There are 15 primary elements of the Dublin core. They are Title, Creator, Subject, Description, Publisher, Contributor, Date, Type, Format, Identifier, Source, Language, Relation, Coverage, and Rights. The title of the document can be written like this in Dublin core format.

<meta name = "DC.Title" content = "introduction to philosophy">

In the same way the link to any resource or webpage can be recorded in this way.

<link rel = "schema.DC" href ="http://DRDO.org/>

For example, CERN Document Server has different output formats of all its documents like HTML MARC, Dublin Core (DC), extendable markup language (XML) MARC, HTML. Brief, and Bibliography text (BibTex) for displaying any file. In the same way INSPIRE-â database has file output formats like: HTML MARC, Dublin Core (DC), National Library of Medicine (NLM), XML MARC and Endnote etc.

Updating any Document on Digital Library

To update any document placed on digital library one must know in which format and where the document is kept. The place of document is identified by the system number or identity number (ID No.) of particular record in a database of digital library. Now once you know the location of the document second is to know its format like HTML MARC format. In this format some extracted fields are given below with their codes:

773 – Imprint (Place, Publisher, Year) (773 $$p)

100 – Author (100 $$a),

245 – Title (245 $$a),

260 - Year (260 $$c),

690C - Indicators (690C $$a),

037 – Record source,

LKR – link to source,

BAS - Base number (BAS $$a).

If your digital library is having many preprints uploaded before five years then now, those preprints may be get published; so we can now update our digital library by finding the publication references from any reputed database like Web of Science and placing that on our database. For example, *to update the preprint records of CERN Document Server by finding the full publication reference on Web of Science database.*

The full publication references of Journal like title, volume, year of publication and pages can be found in Web of Science (WoS) by searching with the title or keywords. So, given below is a preprint record in HTML MARC format which is being updated as it is found published in WOS.

002891730 100 L $$a Abdallah, J$$u Paris U., VI-VII

002891730 245 L $$a Study of the Dependence of Direct Soft Photon Production on the Jet Characteristics in Hadronic Z^0 Decays.

002891730 260 L $$c2009

002891730 690C L $$a ARTICLE

002891730 690C L $$a CERN

002891730 773 L $$p Eur. Phys. J. C

002891730 BAS L $$a13

If the preprint gets published in any journal, then the publication details is updated in the field 773 in this way:

000000000 773 L $$p Journal Title $$V Volume $$Y Year $$C Page From- Page To $$N Issue.

Here is an example of full publication:

001265170 773 L $$p Phys. Lett. B $$v 678 $$y 2009 $$c 465-469 $$n 1

In case of the year of publication field 260 $$c, there shouldn't be a large gap in preprint and publication year e.g. Preprint of 1995 should not be published in 2005! The papers would be different in that case.

Uploading Documents on Digital Library

In digital libraries the new reports, conference proceedings, articles, books can be uploaded by using the submission option of the digital library. This process involves these steps. Firstly, save the documents you want to upload on your desktop. Then convert them in Portable Document Format (PDF) after this —> "Proceed to file uploading" —> "Add new file" —> Browse file —> put "Published version from source from where you have taken that document to upload" as link name —> "Upload" —> Then "Finish submission". In this way many records can be uploaded on the server. The process may be slightly different for different digital libraries. This process is used to upload the articles on CERN document server (CDS).

Cataloguing of Documents on Digital Library

This information available on every digital library is being catalogued for easy retrieval and dissemination of information. The information can be browsed and searched very quickly if that is categorised, indexed and catalogued properly. It is very simple to do cataloguing of different records. Cataloguers have to fill all fields given in digital library like author, title, imprint (publisher, place, and year), abstract, subject, affiliation, pages. Then automatically a record will be created in various formats like Machine Readable Catalogued (MARC) format, Dublin Core format, CCF format etc.

For example: *Cataloguing of EPS-HEP 2009 conference proceedings by ALEPH cataloguing*. Proceedings of science (POS) publish the conference papers. To catalogue this on Invenio Digital Library, first of all, from the list of articles of conference papers the availability of the particular article in CDS record was checked with title, author or by page no. In ALEPH cataloguing, a new record have been created by filling all the information of the article like author, title, Imprint, abstract, subject, affiliation, pages etc. and record was saved and the control no. was copied down for further use. F6 was used to create new sub-fields.

CONCLUSION

Today everybody wants information on his/her own desk without taking any pain. To fulfill this preference, a new technology, digital library is invented with keeping Internet as base. I was CERN Summer Student in 2010, so I did lot of data curation there in CERN library on CDS. The Invenio digital library with its database CERN document server provides many million documents of particle physics. It is regarded as best digital library based on panther and HTML languages. Now librarians have to be tech savy and should know the creating, cataloguing, uploading and updating of various electronic documents on digital libraries.

REFERENCES

Kontratchi, Yalda. "The role of Ontologies in the development of digital libraries." ETTLIS 2010. Shimla: KBD publishers, 2010. pp. 430-34.

Borgman, C. 2000. From Gutenburg to the Global Information Infrastructure: Access to information in the networked world. Cambridge, MA: MIT press.

Kumar, Naresh. *European Organisation for Nuclear Research (CERN) Indian Summer students*. Rep. Geneva: European Organisation for Nuclear Research (CERN) Indian Summer, 2010. *CERN Document Server*. Web. <http://http://indico.cern.ch/getFile.py/access?contribId=23&resId=1&materialId=1&confId=99464>.

24

Digital Libraries and Services in India

— *Dr. Sham Kant Deshmukh*

— *Mr. Kuldeep Pawar*

ABSTRACT

This is the era of globalisation. In this era, Human resource development and management is crucial. Today's life is very fast. So everyone is busy with his duties and responsibilities. If we want total human resource development then there is only one way, i.e. read more and more books.

When human mind is empty, he /she can't do anything; his growth stops because his thought process gets stopped. If we want development, it is necessary that more books reaches to the people.

If we want to provide books on internet, it is necessary that digitalisation takes place. Digitalisation means Automation. Books are available on Compact disks and in electronic form. So it is easy to maintain ancient and valuable books as well as for managing big libraries. These resources must be whole works, with which humans can have a complete cognitive or affective engagement. A digital library may allow either online or offline access to the elements it organises and houses, and may include multimedia as well as multilingual data.

There are several advantages of a digital library over a conventional library. These include minimising storage space and cutting down costs of library maintenance and resource distribution. A digital library is also not merely an automated conventional library, where the resources are electronically catalogued and are available only for browsing purposes.

Although conventional libraries do preserve socio-cultural ambiences within their spaces, a digital library can provide more equitable and widely distributed access at lower costs. Moreover, it may be most appropriate means of organising intellectual artifacts that cannot be represented or distributed in printed formats, such as audio/video multimedia content. Thus a digital library may evolve into a complex system that makes information available in hard copy, on magnetic tape and discs, CD-ROMs and videodiscs, including those from online sources.

In this paper I give information of all digital libraries and automation process in India. I also give brief account why new technologies are necessary and how we can adopt these technologies easily.

INTRODUCTION

A **digital library** is a library in which collections are stored in digital formats and accessible by computers. The digital content may be stored locally, or accessed remotely via computer networks. A digital library is a type of information retrieval system.

The work needed to ensure that digital content is maintained and accessible into the future is beginning to be addressed.

A digital library is a collection of documents in organised electronic form, available on the Internet or on CD-ROM (compact-disk read-only memory) disks. Depending on the specific library, a user may be able to access magazine articles, books, papers, images, sound files, and videos.

On the Internet, the use of a digital library is enhanced by a broadband connection such as cable modem or DSL. Dial-up connections can be used to access plain-text documents and some documents containing images, but for complex files and those with animated video content, a downstream data speed of at least several hundred kilobits per second (Kbps) can make the user's experience less tedious, as well as more informative. Internet-based digital libraries can be updated on a daily basis. This is one of the greatest assets of this emerging technology.

On CD-ROM, the amount of data is limited to several hundred megabytes (MB) per disk, but access is generally much faster than on an Internet connection. Several CD-ROMs can be combined in a set, and because the disks are small, a large library can be accommodated in a reasonable physical space. The main limitation of CD-ROM is the fact that updating cannot be done as frequently as on the Internet. In addition, producing and distributing CD-ROMs involves overhead costs that are largely nonexistent in Internet-based libraries.

Some institutions have begun the task of converting classic books to electronic format for distribution on the Internet. Some files can be viewed directly in HTML format; others can be downloaded in PDF format and printed. Some publishers keep electronic files of books and produce them one unit at a time in printed and bound form on demand.

SOME DIGITAL LIBRARIES IN INDIA

- Indian Parliament library
- Indira Gandhi Memorial library , University of Hydrabad
- Indian Institute of Technology, New Delhi
- Indian Institute of Technology, Kharagpur
- Indian Institute of Technology, Mumbai
- Indian Institute of Science, Bengaluru
- National Institute of Technology, Calicut
- National Institute of Technology, Rourkela
- Indian Institute of Management, Kozikode
- Punjab University, Chandigarh

GOVERNMENT POLICY FOR DIGITAL LIBRARY

National Centre for Science Information (NCSI) is the information centre of Indian Institute of Science, Bangalore that provides electronic information services to the Institute of Academic Community. The Centre also undertakes sponsored R&D projects and conducts a training programme on Library and Information Management.

Indian Institute of Science, Bangalore decided for implementation of Digital libraries in India and with the help of other 21 participants they established Digital Library of India. For this project government of India gave special attention and also provided budget for it.

VISION

To bring world class electronic information services to the academic community and all.

MISSION

The mission is to create a portal for the Digital Library of India which will foster creativity and free access to all human knowledge. As a first step in realising this mission, it is proposed to create the Digital Library with a free-to-read, searchable collection of one million books, predominantly in Indian languages, available to everyone over the Internet. This portal will also become an aggregator of all the knowledge and digital contents created by other digital library initiatives in India. Very soon this portal would provide a gateway to Indian Digital Libraries in science, arts, culture, music, movies, traditional medicine, palm leaves and many more. The result will be a unique resource accessible to anyone in the world 24x7, without regard to socioeconomic background or nationality.

Typical large high-school libraries house fewer than 30,000 volumes. Most libraries in the world have less than a million volumes. One million books, therefore, is more than the holdings of most high-schools, and is equivalent to the libraries at many universities and represents a useful fraction of all available books.

OBJECTIVES

- Provide network access worldwide, scholarly information resources of relevance to the academic community, facilitating improved learning, teaching, research, collaboration and information sharing.
- Provide orientation and training to the academic community in making effective use of electronic information sources, tools and services.
- Participate in the e-publishing and e-dissemination of Institute's intellectual contributions.
- Conduct teaching, research and training in Library and Information Management, with focus on set-up, operation and management of digital information facilities and services.

DIGITAL LIBRARY SETUP

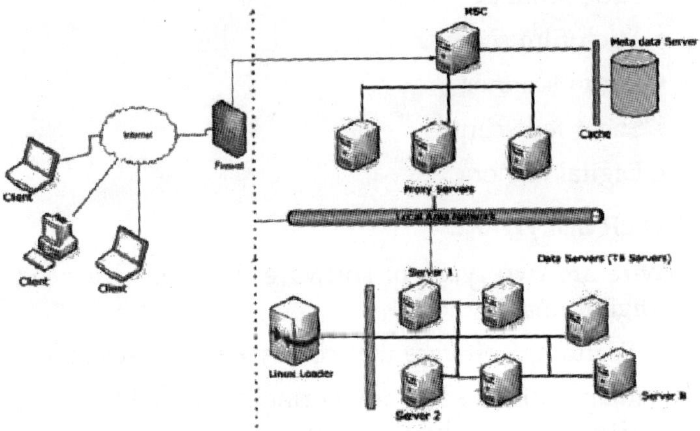

SOFTWARES AND SCANNERS USED IN IMPLEMENTATION OF DIGITAL LIBRARIES

Open source digital library software derives its strength from several enabling technology and metadata based inter operability protocols, which have become available recently. Examples of some of these are as follows:

1. Green stone digital library software (GSDL)
2. E-prints
3. DSpace from MIT
4. Site search (OCLC): www.sitesearch.oclc.org
5. PEARS (OCLC): www. oclc. org/ research/ software/ pears
6. Open source software for online journals and conference publishing (e.g. OJS system from the public Knowledge Project, University of British Columbia, Canada)
7. Fedora – Developed by Cornell University & University of Virginia

TYPE OF SCANNERS

- Flatbed scanner
- Slide scanner
- Microfilm scanner
- Drum scanner
- Sheet fed scanner
- Digital camera

SCANNER SOFTWARE

There are two types of software that you will need for most digital imaging jobs.

- Scanning software that comes with the scanner.
- Image editing software, normally applied to the image after it has been scanned. Optical Character Recognition (OCR) Software. Once the text has been scanned it needs to be run through the OCR program to convert it to a machine-readable encoded form. It allows to scan printed, typewritten or hand written text (numeral, letters or symbols) and/or convert

scanned image to a computer readable format, either in the form of a plain text or a word document or an excel spread sheet, which can be used or reused in other documents. (Tip: See tips on indexing also to decide what and what not to OCR).

ADVANTAGES OF DIGITAL LIBRARY

The advantages of digital libraries as a means of easily and rapidly accessing books, archives and images of various types are now widely recognised by commercial interests and public bodies.

1. No Physical Boundary

The user of a digital library need not to go to the library physically; people from all over the world can gain access to the same information, as long as an Internet connection is available.

2. Multiple Accesses

The same resources can be used simultaneously by a number of institutions and patrons. This may not be the case for copyrighted material: a library may have a license for "lending out" only one copy at a time; this is achieved with a system of digital rights management where a resource can become inaccessible after expiration of the lending period or after the lender chooses to make it inaccessible.

3. Information Retrieval

The user is able to use any search term (word, phrase, title, name, and subject) to search the entire collection. Digital libraries can provide very user-friendly interfaces, giving clickable access to its resources.

4. Preservation and Conservation

Digitisation is not a long-term preservation solution for physical collections, but does succeed in providing access copies for materials that would otherwise fall to degradation from repeated use. Digitised collections and born-digital objects pose many preservation and conservation concerns that analog materials do not. Please see the following "Problems" section of this page for examples.

5. Space

Whereas traditional libraries are limited by storage space, digital libraries have the potential to store much more information, simply because digital information requires very little physical space to contain them and media storage technologies are more affordable than ever before.

6. Added value

Certain characteristics of objects, primarily the quality of images, may be improved. Digitisation can enhance legibility and remove visible flaws such as stains and discoloration.

PROBLEMS IN IMPLEMENTATION OF DIGITAL LIBRARIES IN INDIA

1. Lack of proper Information & Communication Technology (ICT) infrastructure

- Powerful Servers , Intranet facilities, ideally optical fiber based Gigabyte networks.
- Required number of Workstations capable of providing online information services, computing and multimedia applications
- Internet connectivity with sufficient bandwidth, capable of meeting the informational and computational requirement of the user community.

2. Lack of Proper Planning and Integration of Information

Presently the library acquisitions in India are either paper based and electronic. In most of the libraries, paper based documents outnumber the electronic subscriptions and acquisitions. Some of the libraries need retro-conversion and digitisation of library holdings too. Literature on related studies show that there is a severe lapse on the libraries with regard to proper planning of their information resources which are conducive for developing digital libraries.

3. Improper data formats and Rigidity in the publishers' policies

Having successfully installed and configured a digital library does not qualify a library to automatically populate all its digital collection into the digital library. One has to obtain publisher's consent and copyright permissions for the same. Digital library softwares usually accept and process all popular and standard digital formats such as HTML, Word, RTF, PPT, or PDF. Most of the publishers put their materials in their own proprietary e-book reader formats, from which the text extraction becomes almost impossible. A vast majority of the scholarly content rests in journal literature and due to copyright issues they cannot be easily (almost impossible) find its way into the local repositories of digital library.

4. Lack of Technical Skills

The Human Resources available in the libraries need time-to-time professional enrichment inputs and rigorous training on the latest technologies which are playing around in the new information environment. The kind of training programmes being imparted in India at the moment is not able to meet the demand in terms of quantity as well as quality.

5. Management Support

For the provision of world class information systems, resources and services, the libraries need wholehearted support from respective management. Institutional support in terms of proper funding, human resources and IT skills enrichment are prerequisites for the development and maintenance of state-of-art digital library systems and services.

6. Copyright / IPR Issues

Issues of copyright, intellectual property and fair use concerns are posing unprecedented array of problems to the libraries and librarians are struggling to cope with all these related issues in the new digital information environment.

SOLUTIONS OF THE PROBLEMS

India is a large country. People here are intelligent. India is a country which export maximum software or give technical support to other countries for their development in Information technology. We can take the help of IT experts in the implementation of Digital libraries.

1. For private libraries, there is no problems to take the support from other companies which are in the field of digitalisation. If government wants to start digital libraries in India they can take the help of IIT's and IIMs. We can see it as National Centre for **Science** Information (NCSI) is the information centre of **Indian Institute** of **Science**, Bangaluru—is an example of it.
2. With the proper consent of people, we can decide a proper format of storing books which are more convenient and suitable for use.
3. If we discuss with the publishers of the books and authors, and show them the digital libraries are more safe and no one make copies of books and there is no obligation of IPRS(Intellectual property Rights) then they also agree for digitalisation of books.
4. With the proper paper planning and distribution of work, no duplication of data will occur in the digitalisation process.
5. If we discuss with the management and show them how the digital libraries save money and time and convenient to all, then we will get the sufficient budget and moral support from top management.
6. In India there is a problem of skilled technicians. If we arrange workshops and seminars for the technicians and give proper training then this problems also get eliminated.

CONCLUSION

Digital library development in India has been started well. Even among these libraries, focus has been on developing digital libraries without focus on issues such as education and training, copyright, management and promotion. There is a need to amend copyright legislation to suit the electronic environment. Few institutions have taken initiatives to hold workshops on digital libraries and digital technologies. Other important areas on which Indian studies have been few or totally missing are digital rights management, digital library security, content management, business and pricing model and policy studies. With several digital library initiatives reported, it will be useful to have a survey of the digital libraries in India to understand the present status of the digital library initiatives. With advanced technologies we can setup digital libraries in India and everyone can access it for innovation, research, studies, etc.

REFERENCES

Marchionini, G., and Maurer, H. 1995. The roles of digital libraries in teaching and learning. Communications of the ACM, Volume 38(4): pp. 67–75.

McCray, A. T., and Gallagher, M. E. 2001. Principles for digital library development. Communications of the ACM, Volume 44(5): pp. 48–54.

Vamshi Ambati1, N.Balakrishnan2, Raj Reddy1, Lakshmi Pratha, and C.V. Jawahar. The Digital Library of India Project:Process, Policies and Architecture.

25

Impact of IT in Modern Libraries of India: A Study

— *Anjali Sharma*

ABSTRACT

This paper is interested in a new phenomenon of libraries with the influence of IT in this field. Information Technology is changing the nature of libraries and librarians, and it continues to exert a major influence on the strategic direction of libraries in society. Today, the library services are transitioning from local traditional collections to global resources provided on demand via the most advanced networking technologies. It is now possible to retrieve information independently of time zones and geographical location, and to obtain the most up-to-date information from the form of the library without walls, or the virtual library. Libraries need to evaluate, measure the impact of information technology on them.

Keywords: *Information Technology, Library, Computer, Internet, Networking etc.*

INTRODUCTION

Libraries of all types are challenged to provide greater information access and improved levels of service, while coping with the pace of technological change. Information technology has influenced the very nature of business and management libraries. The conventional set up of brick and mortar libraries that store information within a constrained physical space have given way to data centers that integrate data sources around the globe by means of networking. (Gupta & Jain (1996).

With the advancement in technology and its direct application to libraries, management libraries are becoming lean and agile libraries that streamline information supply. The pervasive nature of Internet, coupled with platform independent database connectivity, is making library portals more and more effective.

Today people use internet as a primary source of information, often relying on books as a last resort due to the issues of time and money. In terms of infrastructure, libraries now devote space to public computer facilities and librarians undergo additional training in order to be well-equipped to deal with queries related to modern research techniques and online resources as well as the traditional questions related to finding and borrowing books. In terms of administration, running a library is now much simpler than before, thanks to the aid of computerised systems. Modern systems are also beneficial to customers who are able to reserve and renew items online as well as being able to explore the extensive library catalogue. No one cares about the Dewey Decimal System nor how to look up stories from individual magazines. Knowing facts and figures is not so important today when one can click and find everything he/she needs on the information technology highway.

NEED FOR THE STUDY

In the present everchanging information environment, libraries are encountering both opportunities and challenges. Information technology has introduced many changes in the way information is identified, procured, processed and disseminated to library clientele. Management libraries and information centers are witnessing new paradigm shifts. These shifts include:

- Transition of information sources and systems from paper to electronic media.

- Complexity in information needs of highly demanding clientele.
- Increase in the cost and quality of information.

It is an accepted fact that the information technology has influenced all the components of a library system: information sources, services, human resources and users *(Ramesha and Kumbar, 2004)*. It is more so in case of management libraries where the emphasis is more on the currency of information.

OBJECTIVES OF THE STUDY

The primary objective of the present study is to examine the impact of information technology innovations on resources and services of management institute libraries affiliated to University of Mumbai, Mumbai. The specific objectives are to:

- Survey the existing information technology infrastructure.
- Study the impact of IT on library services.

METHODOLOGY, ANALYSIS AND INTERPRETATION OF DATA

The present study utilised a combination of historical analysis, literature review, questionnaires and personal interviews for data collection. Historical analysis and literature review were useful in collecting textual data from published and unpublished sources. The questionnaire method was quite useful in soliciting information from the librarians of management institutes. Interviews were also held with the librarians to interpret the questions to them and to collect the data.

IT BASED CONVENTIONAL SERVICES IN LIBRARIES

IT has tremendously changed the Management of Resources or House Keeping Operations as well as the way services are delivered. While general IT application tools and Integrated Library Management Systems are largely used in house- keeping operations, like acquisition, cataloguing, circulation control, serials control etc. Internet has been used extensively as a resource as well as a tool to deliver the Library and Information Services (LIS).

We will now briefly discuss a few types of information services.

REFERENCE SERVICE

Asynchronous tools such as email, subject gateways, FAQs, and electronic libraries and interactive tools like chat rooms, virtual reference desk, and ask-me are replacing the conventional means of post, phone or in-person reference enquiries.

BIBLIOGRAPHIC SERVICE

Electronic databases also provide unique search features such as searching on multiple criteria (key-word, subject, author, source, classification code, year of publication, language etc.), and a variety of display formats & styles. *STN* and *Silver Platter* are some of the popular database companies that offer bibliographic and reference databases on CDROM and Online platforms.

CURRENT AWARENESS SERVICE

A current awareness service may be as simple as copy of table of contents or a bulletin containing bibliographic records, of articles selected from the current issues of journals and other material, and usually organised by subjects. Some publishers even offer free email update of table of contents.

DOCUMENT DELIVERY SERVICES

IT has made the document delivery services very simple and reliable. From searching the holdings to ordering and delivery have been benefited by the use of IT. Many library networks such as *INFLIBNET* and *DELNET* maintain union catalogue of their member's journal holdings.

INTER-LIBRARY LOAN SERVICE

Access to the catalogue of partner libraries is crucial to inter-library lending. Union catalogues, standardisation and machine readable catalogues are aimed at promoting resource sharing. Printed union catalogues and Computer Output on Microfiche (COM) catalogues and CDROM are now being replaced by web OPAC and web based union catalogues.

AUDIOVISUAL SERVICES

Many libraries particularly media libraries and large academic and public libraries hold audio visual material such as music, films, pictures and photographs etc. Multimedia documents can now be played on standard PCs, stand-alone or networked.

CUSTOMER RELATION & USER EDUCATION

Use of new means of communications such as email, web forms, bulletins boards, discussion forums and listserv are fast replacing these. Not only these tools provide a fast, convenient and transparent and cost effective medium, but also offer scope for innovations and greater peer participation. (Lancaster & Sandore (2001).

IT BASED NEW SERVICES

Apart from the IT enabled conventional services, libraries are making use of potential of internet and computing power to provide new and innovative services. In a web enabled environment the new LIS services can be grouped into the following three categories:

INTERNET ACCESS

Internet is not only a medium for digital communication but also the world's largest repository of information. However, underdeveloped internet infrastructure in a country like India, poses a serious challenge to the growth of IT enabled services. Libraries, therefore, provide free or controlled access to internet and email.

ACCESS TO WEB BASED RESOURCES

As already discussed, many types of library materials such as journals, books, patents, newspapers, standards, photographs, pictures, motion pictures or music are now available in electronic or digital form which is timeless and convenient.

DIGITAL LIBRARY & ARCHIVES

Archives or record management is also part of LIS function. Libraries are developing digital repositories of such resources, and providing Internet or intranet access to these. Digital libraries are a natural progression from electronic document sharing. The main benefit of digital library is the ability to provide 24-hour, remote access to high-demand or restricted materials for multiple concurrent users.

IT'S INFRASTRUCTURE AT LIBRARIES

In the recent decades, a lot of information has been made available in a wide variety of formats like CD-ROM, online databases and e-journals. It becomes necessary for a library to have adequate computer facilities to serve users better. In order to ascertain the availability of computer infrastructure, certain questions on status of automation, hardware and software availability were asked of librarians. Their responses are recorded in Table 1.

STATUS OF LIBRARY AUTOMATION

The first step towards taking advantage of the benefits of IT is the automation of library activities. The majority of the libraries, 13 (59.09%), have indicated that their automation is complete. However, a considerable number of management libraries, 9 (40.91%), are still only partially automated.

HARDWARE AND SOFTWARE AVAILABILITY

Table 1 indicates the availability of computer hardware and software at different management libraries. The availability of information technology related infrastructure is good in the majority of libraries.

Concerning hardware, the majority of libraries, 20 (90.91%), have Pentium computers; 11 (50.00%) have servers to maintain library databases; 10 (45.45%) have workstations to access the library OPAC and other electronic resources. Fourteen (63.64%) libraries have their own printers, 17 (77.27%) have CD-ROM readers, 8 (36.36%) have CD-ROM writers. In addition, 8 (36.36%) of libraries have scanners and one (4.55%) library possesses a CD tower for accessing several CD-ROMS simultaneously.

Table 1 : Hardware and Software Availability

Hardware and Software Availability	Number of Libraries
HARDWARE	
PC AT 286/386/486	7 (31.82%)
Pentium I/II/III/IV	20 (90.91%)
Servers	11 (50.00%)
Terminals/Workstations	10 (45.45%)
Apple Macs	0 (0.00%)
Printers	14 (63.64%)
Modems	4 (18.18%)
CD-ROM (Read)	17 (77.27%)
CD-ROM (Write)	8 (36.36%)
CD Towers	1 (4.55%)
Scanners	8 (36.36%)
SOFTWARE	
DOS/UNIX/LINUX/Windows	22 (100.00%)
Library Management Software	20 (90.91%)
Word Processing Software	22 (100.00%)
Networking Software	15 (68.18%)

Concerning software, the majority of libraries, 20 (90.91%), are using Library Management Software; all the libraries, 22 (100%), are using word processing software and they also use different operating systems like DOS, UNIX, LINUX and Windows. Fifteen (68.18%) libraries have indicated that they have networking software as well.

FINDINGS AND SUGGESTIONS

The present study has evaluated the availability of information technology infrastructure in management libraries affiliated with the University of Mumbai. It also studied the impact of IT innovations on library resources and services.

Findings of the Study:

- It is revealed from the survey that the majority of the libraries have automated their functions and the remaining libraries are partially automated. The availability of software and hardware in these libraries is also encouraging, with most libraries having Pentium IV machines, servers to maintain databases, workstations to access Web resources and all the required software.
- Information sources are available in various formats like CD-ROM, DVD and Web versions. The study indicates that libraries can save much storage space by acquiring journal back volumes, dissertations and books in digital form. It also finds that libraries can greatly decrease the amount being spent on binding, shelving, cleaning and maintenance of bound volumes by migrating to digital sources.
- However, the survey also indicates two things about which librarians are very cautious. E-resources require expensive infrastructure and, though user friendly, they demand a certain degree of efficiency to access them.

CONCLUSION

Libraries have had to adapt to the growth of information and technology in recent years. Today people use the internet as a primary source of information, often relying on books as a last resort due to the issues of time and money. In terms of infrastructure, libraries now devote space to public computer facilities and librarians undergo additional training in order to be well-equipped to deal with queries related to modern research techniques and online resources as well as the traditional questions related to finding and borrowing books. Library archives and records are also now computerised meaning a more efficient and effective borrowing and returns system and a faster method of locating resources and assessing availability of items. In terms of administration, running a library is now much simpler than before, thanks to the aid of computerised systems.

REFERENCES

Ramesha and Kumbar, B. D. (2004). Performance evaluation of Karnataka State University Library resources and services: A librarian's approach. *Journal of Educational Media & Library Sciences, 41*(3), pp. 299-314.

Khode, S. & Dhar, U. (2002). Library services and functions in changing environment - An overview". *Indian Journal of Information, Library and Society, 15*(1&2), pp. 24-29.

Gupta, D. K. & Jain, S. L. (1996). Library and information centers in new economic era: An overview. *Herald of Library Science, 35* (1, 2), pp. 42-47.

Lancaster, E W and Sandore, Beth. (2001). Technology and management in library and information services. London, Library Association.

Index

A

Academic Libraries, 150
  Knowledge Management role in, 157
Academic setting, 84
Advanced Process of Knowledge Management, 193
AIRTEL
  managerial guidelines, 211
AJAX
  application model, 249
Application Programming Interface(API), 249
Attribute searching, 82
AudioVisual services,337

B

Bestseller.htm, 287
Bibliographic Services, 336
Biographies and Memories
  online portal, 278
Blogging, 251
BM.htm, 278
Brainstorming tools, 185
Bureaucratic structure
  and Knowledge Management,30
Business/Corporate libraries, 134

C

CCF Record Format, 316
CD- ROM, 107, 109 323
  features, 109
Centre of Central Asian Studies , Srinagar, 308
  use of Electronic Technology study, 309
CERN Document Server (CDS), 314
Change Management, 68
Chief Knowledge Officer (CKO) system, 54
Cl.htm, 277-78
Collection Development, 265
Combination stage mechanisms, 216
Commitment Building, 69
Consortia, 230
Contactus.ASPX, 286
Content Push, 185
Content searching, 82
Copyright/ IPR issues, 329
Cultural knowledge, 23, 44, 143
Cultural Roadblocks
  to Knowledge Management, 65
Cultural role
  in Knowledge Management, 65

Current Awareness Service, 306, 336
Customer Relation
  and User Education, 337
Customers of Library
  importance, 95 expectation, 95

D

Data mining, 185
Data Warehouse, 79, 185
Delhi University libraries
  IT application in, 238
DELNET, 336
Digital Environment
  and Knowledge Management, 55
Digital Libraries, 37-38, 259, 313
Digital Library management, 131
  organising, 133
  staffing, 133
  Knowledge Management in, 147
Digital library
  and archives, 338
  definition, meaning, 314, 322
  features, 315
  purpose, 314 need, 315
  implementation problems, 328
  solution, 330
  in India-list, 323
  cataloguing documents, 318
  formats, 316
  updating documents, 317
  uploading documents, 318
  set up, 325
  advantages, 327
  implementation problems, 328
Digital media Preservation, 266
Digital Public Libraries
  advantages, 136
  disadvantages, 137
Digital Video Discs (DVDs), 109
Digitalisation, 321
Digitised Knowledge services, 52
Distributors of Information, 100
Doctoral dissertation, 291
Document Delivery Services, 336
Document Management Systems, 183
Documentation and Information Centers, 101
Documents change in formats, 230
Dublin Core, 316

E

E Books, 108
E- Database, 109
E-Electronic Thesis and Dissertation, (ETD), 294
E- Journals, 107
E Resources, 33, 105
  features, 105
  advantages, 106
  types, 106
Education expansion
  and libraries, 23

Electronic Communication Services
advantages, 307
Electronic Information Services (EIS), 36
Electronic Publishing Systems, 184
Electronic Thesis, 291
E-mail, 305
Explicit Knowledge, 23, 44, 62, 79, 207
Externalisation Stage, 214 actions, 214
Externalised knowledge, 79

F

Featured.htm, 287
Feedback.htm, 285
Fission, 225
Forgotpassword.aspx, 283
Formalisation of Knowledge, 212
Full - Text - E - Resources, 112

G

Gartner Group
Knowledge Management definition, 192
Genetic Knowledge, 22
Government Policy
Digital Libraries, 324
Groupware, 184
Growth of knowledge, 224
pattern, 226
implications, 27
..for information centers, 228

H

Hardware and Software
in Libraries, 339
HAU, 291
Help- desk applications, 185
Hierarchical searching, 81
Human Resource
perspective, 48
Human Resource Management, 48
Hybrid library, 259
concept, 260
technologies, 263
definition 261

I

ICAR, 291
Implicit knowledge, 44
INDEST - AICTE
Consortium, 111
Indian National Digital Library in Engineering Science & Technology (INDEST), 110
Industrial revolution, 223
INFLIBNET, 237, 336
Information Analysis Centre, 101
Information and Communication Technology(ICT), 96, 155, 306
impact on Knowledge Management, 53
technologies used, 306
Information Management, 159
Information Networks, 230
Information Processing Paradigm, 38-39
Information retrieval engines, 184
Information Services, 89
in Electronic database, 336

Information Technologies, 233-34
in libraries, 237
application in Universities, 238
impact on Knowledge Management, 52
impact on libraries, 335
in application of Knowledge, 30
adoption factors, 240
limitations, 239
benefits, 234-35
Intellectual Capital, 159, 161
Intellectual Property Rights, 329
Inter-library Loan services, 336
Internalisation stage, 215
actions, 217
Internet, 35, 337, 110, 321
Intranet, 155, 183
advantages, 156
IT development aspects, 243

J

Joint Information Systems Committee (JISC), 260
on hybrid libraries, 262

K

K Agent, 71
K Mail, 71
K Search, 73
K- Seek/ Submit, 197
K Speak, 72
K summariser, 72
Knowledge - Creation process, 219
Knowledge meaning, 77, 125
categories, 78 types, 79
role, 19 meaning, 21 types, 20
and modern society, 25
creation, 61 innovation, 49 management, 50
Knowledge Agents, 61
Knowledge Application Management, 51
Knowledge Dissemination Management, 51
Knowledge enablers, 204-205
Knowledge Engineering, 80
Knowledge Engineers quality, 81
Knowledge Explosion, 159
Knowledge Framework, 70, 197
Knowledge Management solution, 83 people aspect, 83
process aspect, 84
and results, 68
Knowledge Management Architecture, 62-63
Process, 38
Education And Research, 38
searching strategies, 81 need in digital environment, 82
trends and surveys, 59 activity, 64
challenges, 196 elements, 193 benefits, 195
Cycle, 65
definition, 33, 60,141, 151 types, 151 components, 152 need, 152
features, 161 process, 163

creation and management, 172

functions, 174 challenges, 175 issues, 165 in libraries, 164 concept, 33 behaviors, 30

Knowledge Management, 143 Implementation, 134 ... obstacles, 176

in Digital Era, 164 ... benefits, 172

in E- Resources, 33

Information Network in India, 83

Infrastructure, 155

meaning, 123, 125 term, 10, 45,124 aim, 124 System, 125

Models, 170 modules, 145 meaning, 160

problems, 56 characteristics, 25, 145 objectives, 145 need for in LIS, 143-44 application, 33 value of, 39 myths, 39 division, 44 getting started, 45 process, 45-47 tools, 47 modern society, 25 ....benefits, 26

Knowledge Management System (KMS) and Data Warehouse, 79

Knowledge Management System Development, 150

Knowledge Management system support, 198

Knowledge Management systematic approaches, 84

Knowledge Management systems, 186 rotational process, 194

Knowledge Management Systems, 186

Knowledge Management in libraries, 27, 29

Knowledge Mobilisation, 199

Knowledge Sharing, 195 barriers affecting, 66

mechanisms, 215

Krishiprabha Project, 291 scope, 293 Database ..manual searching screen solution, 295-303

L

Leadership, 62

Learning, 63

Librarian 2.0, 254-55

Librarian role, 85-87

important points for, 221

challenges of, 186-87, 334

role in Knowledge Management, **135-36**

paradigm shift, 334

Libraries

Knowledge Management in, 27, 48

TQM in, 117 function, 119 people, 119

Library primary functions, 233

Library and Information Centers(LICs) success, 150

Library and Information professionals, 85

Library and Information Services, 89 managers role, 97

Library Blogs. 100, 252

Library efficiency ways, 135 Knowledge Management need, 152

Library Flickr, 253

Library Knowledge Management theorey in, 55

Library management, 90

Library Networks, 336

Library staff educating, 48

Library.HTM, 277

Login.aspx, 280

M

Machine vs Human Perspective, 229

Management Libraries Paradigm shift, 335

Management, 43

Manuscripts, 222

MARC Format, 316

Marketing of libraries and information services, 89

Marketing

meaning, 91 concept, 92 philosophy, 93 approach, 93 definition, 94

Marketing and Value Added Services, 98

Marketing Mix, 89

Marketing of Libraries requirements, 98

Media Sharing, 253

Meta searching, 81

Metadata, 37

Migratory knowledge, 79

Modern Society Knowledge Management, 25

Multi locational knowledge, 79

N

National Agriculture Innovative Project (NAIP), 292

National Centre for Science Information(NCSI), 324

Networked e- journals, 107

Nonaka's four step model (SECI), 206 Knowledge and Quality theoretical framework, 207

O

Online Book Portal, 269 Project, 288

benefits, 274 technologies in , 270 registering, 270 logging in, 271 examples, 276

payment options, 271 modules, 270 credit card use method, 272

Online Catalogues, 99

Online Downloading, 289

Online Journals, 107

Online Public Access Platform (OPAC), 99, 229 , 260 services, 100 in libraries, 35

module of Integrated Lbrary Management System, 264

Ontology, 38

Open Access Resource, 112

Open Database Connectivity(ODBC), 186

Organisation, 62

Organisational Culture, 66

Organizational Knowledge, 188 creation Process, 206

P

Personalization and Auto Merchandising, 289

Printing, 223

Project Management, 87

Psychological factors, 66

Public Library, 127 librarians role in Knowledge Management, 135

services, 28 ...use of technology, 20

Knowledge Management in, 128-29 ..benefits, 135 operation, 129

Q

Quality Management, 115

Quality Services, 97

R

Recorded knowledge, 225

Referral Centers, 101

Regional Centre for Strategic Studies, 40

Register.aspx, 280-81

Rennaisance period, 223

Resource Sharing Networks, 239

Result Driven Knowledge Management model, 70

Return on Investment Analysis, 200

Return on Investment(ROI) parametres, 73

S

Scanners types, 326

SECI Model, 217 of Knowledge Management, 206-207

Semantic Web, 37

Shippingdetails.aspx, 284

Short Message service use, 305

Social factors role in Knowledge Management, 67

Socialisation process of Knowledge Management, 210 ...actions to foster, 213

Software Technology in Knowledge Management, 199

Softwares and Scanners used, 325

Staffing implications, 179

Storage of knowledge, 226

Structured Query Language(SQL), 186

T

Tacit knowledge, 23, 62, 142, 207 vs Explicit knowledge, 79

Teamwork, 211

Technology advance, 233

Technology, 62 and Knowledge Management, 130

for Knowledge Management, 183 role, 186

Technology Preservation, 260

Tools and techniques for Knowledge Management, 47, 162

Total Quality Management(TQM), 97 challenges, 120 barriers, 117 objective, 116-17

evolution, 115 – 17 need, 116-17 in libraries, 117

role, 203

Travel category online portal, 279

Travel.htm, 279

Twentieth Century knowledge growth, 24

U

UGC - Infonet, 111 Digital Library Consortium, 111-12

US.HTM, 277

V

Virtual Libraries, 313

Vocational Training, 165

W

WEB 2.0, 248 Technologies, 131, 248

Web based resources, 337

WebOPAC, 100

Whatsnews.htm, 288

What-You-See-Is What-You-Get, 251

Wikis, 251Workflow systems, 185

World Wide Web (WWW), 36, 110, 137

X

XML and RSS, 250

Z

Z39.50 server, 264, 266